Dreams of Small Countries

THE DAVID J. WEBER SERIES IN
THE NEW BORDERLANDS HISTORY

Andrew R. Graybill and Benjamin H. Johnson, editors

The study of borderlands—places where different peoples meet and no one polity reigns supreme—is undergoing a renaissance. The David J. Weber Series in the New Borderlands History publishes works from both established and emerging scholars that examine borderlands from the precontact era to the present. The series explores contested boundaries and the intercultural dynamics surrounding them and includes projects covering a wide range of time and space within North America and beyond, including both Atlantic and Pacific worlds.

Published with support provided by the William P. Clements Center for Southwest Studies at Southern Methodist University in Dallas, Texas.

Dreams of Small Countries

How Californios, Land Conflicts, and Race Shaped the Golden State

Camille Suárez

The University of North Carolina Press CHAPEL HILL

This book was published with the assistance of the William P. Clements Center for Southwest Studies.

Set in Merope Basic by Westchester Publishing Services

Library of Congress Cataloging-in-Publication Data
Names: Suárez, Camille author
Title: Dreams of small countries : how Californios, land conflicts, and race shaped the Golden State / Camille Suárez.
Other titles: David J. Weber series in the new borderlands history
Description: Chapel Hill : The University of North Carolina Press, 2026. | Series: David J. Weber series in the new borderlands history | Includes bibliographical references and index.
Identifiers: LCCN 2026018186 | ISBN 9781469698014 cloth | ISBN 9781469698021 paperback | ISBN 9781469691978 epub | ISBN 9781469698038 pdf
Subjects: LCSH: Mexicans—California—History—19th century | Settler colonialism—California—History—19th century | Land tenure—California—History | Elite (Social sciences)—California—History | California—Ethnic relations—History | California—History, Local | California—History—1850-1950 | California—Race relations—History | BISAC: History / United States / State & Local / West (AK, CA, CO, HI, ID, MT, NV, UT, WY) | Social Science / Ethnic Studies / American / Hispanic American Studies
Classification: LCC F870.M5 S824 2026 | DDC 305.8009794/09034—dc23/eng/20260416
LC record available at https://lccn.loc.gov/2026018186

Cover art: *Mine Wash Trail, Anza Borrego State Park, Dec. 31, 2022,* by Camille Suárez.

For my mother and my daughter.

Contents

Acknowledgments

This book took years and the support of numerous people and institutions to complete. I would not have been able to write this book without the generous feedback and support of friends, colleagues, and family, and I take great pleasure in thanking them all now.

Throughout my life, I've had the blessing of wonderful mentors, advisors, and teachers. I had the great fortune of working with Mary Frances Berry. Due to our robust discussions and her unwavering support, I pursued the research that led to this book. Other advisors would have discouraged me, but Dr. Berry trusted my instincts and intellectual curiosity. I was also lucky to work with Stephanie McCurry. She took a special interest in my writing and ideas, and as a result, I have become a much better scholar. I am also fortunate to have worked with Eiichiro Azuma; his generosity, guidance, and criticism steered me in the right direction.

I had numerous conversations—some lasting just minutes, others lasting for hours—with scholars who generously listened to my ideas and asked the right questions. Kathy Peiss, Cheikh Babou, Heather Williams, Barbara Savage, Amy Offner, and Kathy Brown, thank you for your time and suggestions. A special thank you is extended to Eve Troutt Powell, who mentored me when her plate was already too full. And thank you to Karl Jacoby and Andrés Reséndes for asking questions that helped broaden my research and sharpen my analysis.

I had the opportunity to work with fantastic scholars before I knew that I wanted to pursue a PhD. A very special thank you to Richard Pierce. Our long office hour discussions put me on the path that led me to this book. Karen Richman, thank you for your steadfast mentorship. Without the guidance and mentorship of John Deak, Gail Bederman, Dan Graff, and Rebecca McKenna, I would have never been ready to pursue a PhD. Lastly, thank you to Martin Mullarkey for teaching me about the pitfalls of the passive voice and for believing in my writing before I did.

As any scholar knows, we are indebted to those who read and comment on our work. Thank you to Reader #1 for sharing your knowledge of the sources and sharp criticism. Your comments have helped me make a better book. All errors are, of course, my own. A very special thank you to David

Torres-Rouff. Your support and questions have helped me write the stories I wanted to tell. Thank you to Beth Lew-Williams and Rosina Lozano for your engagement with early versions of the manuscript. Thank you to Greg Downs and Kate Masur for your guidance on the material that would become chapter 2. I was fortunate to share my work with the Newberry Library Borderlands and Latino/a Studies Seminar and received comments that helped me refine the arguments I was making in chapter 4. A special thank you is afforded to Emiliano Aguilar. Thank you to Ben Johnson for reading and commenting on the entire manuscript. Thank you to the staff at UNC Press, especially Cate Hodorowicz, Andrew R. Graybill, Tara Jordan, and Debbie Gershenowitz.

Thank you to the archivists and librarians who helped me conduct the research that made this book. The staff at Huntington Library, UCLA Special Collections, the Autry, the Bancroft Library, and the California State Library were particularly helpful. A very special thank you to John Cahoon of the Seaver Center for all of his help over the years.

Many friends supported me as I researched and wrote this book. Marlen Rosas and Nimrod Ben Zeev, our transnational text thread got me through the ups and downs of the last decade. Thank you to Liz Ellis for your support and friendship. Anthony Pratcher II, I am grateful for your brotherly guidance. Thanks to Kristian Taketomo, Alexis Neumann-Broderick, Kevin Waite, Julia Lewandoski, and Caitlin Collis. A special thank you to Joan Plonski and Octavia Carr for their invaluable assistance over the years. Marissa, Chelsea, Liza, Rivka, Chia (Mingo), Alex, Ali, Beeta, Dani, Kristen, Cindy, and Michelle, thank you for your friendship.

This book has travelled with me across the United States and led to new, yet lasting, friendships. My thanks go to Bagel, Roxanne, Nina, and Ivón—somehow, we always meet in LA. Teaching at Cal State LA was a transformative experience—a big thank you to the students. As I edited this book, I thought back to the many conversations I had with you all about California history. While I have only been at Cornell University for a short period, the history department has generously supported me as I finished this book, especially Maria Cristina Garcia, Tamika Nunley, Ed Baptist, Derek Chang, Aaron Sachs, and Larry Glickman. Thank you to the participants of the Collaborative History Colloquium and the Assistant Professors Working Group for taking the time to offer generous comments on multiple chapter drafts. Ruth Lawlor, Jonny Lawrence, Emma Teitelman, Aaron Swindles-Bartels, Rachel Sandwell, Cristina Florea, Kristen Roebuck, Justine Modica, Nick

Mulder, Mayer Yuni, Michell Chresfield, and Casey Schmitt, your friendship and collegiality have made Ithaca a home.

My final and biggest thanks are personal. Thank you to my mom, Gloria Ramirez, for all the support you have given me over the years. Since I was a young child, my mother encouraged me to quench my thirst for knowledge; she spent endless hours taking me to libraries, museums, and punk concerts. She also taught me how to love books, and now I get to dedicate one to her. To my sister, Hailey, thank you for your unwavering support. Thank you to all of my family in California. To my in-laws, John, Michelle, Marie, Tianyu, and my niece, Lilou, thank you for your love and encouragement, even as I worked on this book during visits. Quetzali, while I began this book long before you were born, you were there as I finished. You are a true joy, and I am grateful to be your mom. Thank you for being so good at taking naps and allowing me to complete the final edits. This book is also dedicated to you. And to Paraska, my life and intellectual partner, thank you for reading the entire manuscript, taking care of dinner when I was in the middle of a chapter, and for reminding me to have fun. Your love and support sustain me. Without you, I would have never finished this book.

Cast of Historical Actors

In order of appearance in the text:

Andrés Pico (1810–1876): Californio politician, rancho owner, and member of the prominent Pico family; general of the Californio Militia during the US-Mexico War (1846–1848) and signer of the Treaty of Cahuenga (1847); served as a California state assemblymember (1851–1860) and California senator (1860–1876); in 1859 presented a state division petition to the California Assembly; younger brother to Pío Pico.

John C. Frémont (1813–1890): Anglo-American military officer and politician, known as the "Pathfinder" due to the four US Army expeditions he lead in the West; served in the US–Mexico War and the US Civil War; signer of the Treaty of Cahuenga; served as US senator from California from 1850–1851; ran as the first Republican candidate for US president in 1856; served as territorial governor of Arizona from 1878–1881; married to Jessie Benton Frémont, daughter of Missouri senator Thomas Benton.

José Antonio Carrillo (1796–1862): Californio politician and rancho owner; captain of the Californio Militia during the US-Mexico War (1846–1848); signer of the Treaty of Cahuenga; 1849 California constitutional delegate and 1849 Constitution signer; served as Los Angeles Alcalde in 1826, 1828, and 1833; member of the prominent Carrillo family and married to María Estéfana Pico, the sister of Pío and Andrés Pico.

Pablo de la Guerra (1819–1874): Californio politician, rancho owner, patriarch of the de la Guerra family; served as a delegate during the 1849 California Constitutional Convention; elected as California state senator from 1851–1861; acting California lieutenant governor 1861–1862; elected as a California district judge from 1863–1873.

Antonio Coronel (1817–1894): Californio politician and rancho owner; immigrated to Los Angeles as part of the Híjar-Padrés colony; served as the Los Angeles mayor (1853–1854), Los Angeles County Accessor (1850–1856), and the California state treasurer (1867–1871); provided details on Californio culture to Helen Hunt Jackson for her book *Ramona*.

Pío Pico (1801–1894): Californio politician, rancho owner, the Pico family patriarch, and brother to Andrés Pico; the last governor of Alta California; refused to assume a political office under the American regime but publicly supported the Republican Party.

(María de la) Angustias de la Guerra (1815–1890): Californio and rancho owner; held social balls during the 1849 Constitutional Convention where she used her role as a social broker to ensure that women's property rights were protected under the California constitution; sister to Pablo and Antonio María de la Guerra.

Mariano G. Vallejo (1807–1980): Californio, rancho owner, and the Vallejo patriarch; known as the *reyezeulo* (little king) because of his vast land holdings—namely, Rancho Petaluma—and political influence; commander of military forces in Alta California during the 1830s; served in the US Army as an Indian agent; elected as California state senator in 1850; codrafted the 1850 Guardianship Act; brother to Salvador Vallejo.

Abel Stearns (1798–1871): Anglo-American who assimilated into Californio culture and became a rancho owner after immigrating to Alta California in 1829; owned a trade post at San Pedro Bay; delegate at the 1849 California Constitutional Convention; served in various political offices in Los Angeles; married to Arcadia Bandini of the prominent Bandini family.

José Castro (1808–1860): Californio and rancho owner; general of Alta California military; sometimes considered the unofficial governor of northern Alta California.

William B. Ide (1796–1852): Anglo-American settler born in Massachusetts; migrated to Alta California in 1854; leader of the Bear Flag Revolt and author of William B. Ide Proclamation.

José María Flores (1818–1866): Mexican national who migrated to Alta California for military service; comandante to José Castro; led the Californio militia during the US–Mexico War; fled to Sonora, Mexico, during the US–Mexico War and unable to reunite with his family after the fighting concluded.

Manuelito Cota (1820–1861): Chief of the Luiseño Pauma band; led a company of Luiseño men that attacked and killed Californio forces, an event now referred to as the Pauma Massacre in December 1846.

Juan Antonio (1783–1863): Chief of the Mountain Cahuilla band; collaborated with Californio forces to attack the Luiseño, their traditional enemy during the US-Mexico War; cooperated with Californio and Anglo-American settlers to suppress the revolt led by Antonio Garra.

José del Carmen Lugo (1813–1870): Californio, rancho owner, and patriarch of the Lugo family; attempted to colonize the current-day San Bernadino Valley with his brothers and a cousin from the Sepúlveda family; to facilitate the colonization of the valley, Lugo maintained an alliance with Juan Antionio, chief of the Mountain Cahuilla band; abandoned his San Bernadino land grants in 1852 to Indigenous resistance.

Antonio Garra (?—January 17, 1852): Chief of the Cupeño; attempted to organize a pan-Native revolt in which the Indigenous tribes of southern California expelled Anglo and Californio settlers from their traditional homelands; the revolt failed and the US government executed Garra on January 17, 1852.

Henry Halleck (1815–1872): US military officer and lawyer; briefly served as military governor of California during US Army occupation and authored a land report, which set the tone on Mexican land claims; served as a delegate in the 1849 California Constitutional Convention; founding partner of Halleck, Peachy, and Billings law firm, which specialized in land claims cases; served as a Union general during the US Civil War and wrote an influential treatise on war conduct.

William Gwin (1805–1885): Born in Tennessee; served as the US representative from Missouri (1841–1843); migrated to California in 1849; served as a delegate in the 1849 California Constitutional Convention; selected as the US senator from California (1850–1855, 1857–1861); as senator, he introduced the bill that would become the 1851 US Land Act, which required claimants of Mexican land grants to prove the legitimacy of their claims in front of the US Land Commission; leader of the Chivalry brand of Democrats in California.

Manuel Domínguez (1803–1882): Californio, rancho owner, and Domínguez family patriarch; held multiple political offices under Mexican and US regimes; served as a delegate in the 1849 California Constitutional Convention.

José Covarrubias (1809–1870): Californio and rancho owner; served as a delegate in the 1849 California Constitutional Convention; held multiple political offices under Mexican and US regimes, and served as the assemblyman from Santa Barbara from 1849–1862; married to (María) Concepción Pico Carrillo, niece of Andrés and Pío Pico and sister of José Antonio Carrillo.

Ignacio (Ygnacio) del Valle (1808–1880): Californio, rancho owner, and del Valle family patriarch; held multiple political offices under Mexican and US regimes, such as LA County judge.

Enrique Ávila (1818–1876): Californio and member of the Ávila family; served as the second alcalde of Los Angeles in 1847 and on the Los Angeles Board of County Supervisors from 1868–1872.

Juan (John) José Warner (1807–1890): Anglo-American who assimilated into Californio culture and became a rancho owner after immigrating to Alta California in 1831; developer of Warner's Ranch, which was located on Cupeño land and served as an important stop and trading post for emigrants traversing the Southern California desert.

José Antonio Estudillo (1803–1852): Californio and rancho owner; held multiple political offices under Mexican and US regimes; married María Victoria Domínguez, sister to Manuel Domínguez.

Antonio María de la Guerra (1825–1881): Californio, rancho owner, and Pablo de la Guerra's younger brother; held multiple political offices under Mexican and US regimes; captain of Company C, 1st Battalion of the Native California Cavalry.

José Cristóbal Aguilar (1816–1886): Californio and rancho owner; held multiple political offices under Mexican and US regimes, and served as the last Latine Los Angeles mayor until the city elected Antonio Villaraigosa in 2005.

Mifflin Gibbs (1823–1915): Black activist who migrated to California during the Gold Rush; founder of the *Mirror of the Times*, the first African American newspaper in California; organizer and leader of the California Colored Convention Movement; after the *Dred Scott* ruling, Gibbs led hundreds of Black Americans from California to British Vancouver in an effort to claim citizenship rights; became a British citizen in 1861; returned to the United States in 1870, where he practiced law and continued to participate in the Colored Convention Movement.

Peter Lester (1814–1897): Black activist who migrated to California during the Gold Rush; organizer and leader of the California Colored

Convention Movement; helped secure legal counsel for Archy Lee during his freedom case; migrated to British Vancouver after the *Dred Scott* case; returned to San Francisco during the 1890s.

Romualdo Pacheco (1831–1899): Californio and rancho owner; held multiple political offices under Mexican and US regimes; the first Latine person to represent California in the US Congress and the only Latine person to serve as governor of California (at the time of writing).

José Ramon Pico (1832–1905): Californio and rancho owner; captain of Company A, 1st Battalion of the Native California Cavalry; nephew to Andrés and Pío Pico.

Philip Bell (1808–1889): Black American born in New York; an abolitionist and participant of the Colored Conventions movement; migrated to San Francisco in 1860; a journalist for the *Mirror of the Times* and the *Elevator*, which Bell founded.

Henry Haight (1825–1878): Anglo-American lawyer and politician; born in New York and migrated to California during the Gold Rush; elected governor in 1867 election on an anti-Reconstruction platform.

Manuel Olegario (?–1877): An elected leader of the San Luis Rey band of Luiseño; led the Luiseño in their fight against white encroachment until his sudden death in 1877.

John (Juan) Forster (1814–1882): Born in England and migrated to Alta California as a teen; married Maria Ysidora Pico and became a member of the prominent Pico family; owned many ranchos; became the owner of Rancho Santa Margarita after a prolonged land dispute with Pío Pico, his brother-in-law.

Denis Kearney (1847–1907): Born in Cork County, Ireland, and migrated to San Francisco in 1868; founder of the Workingmen's Party of California, which espoused anti-Chinese and antimonopoly politics.

Dreams of Small Countries

Introduction

Hiding in Plain Sight

Sitting in the shadow of Universal Studios Hollywood theme park, at the intersection of Lankershim Boulevard and the iconic 101 freeway, is a replica adobe known as Campo de Cahuenga. The adobe memorializes the spot where Californio militia leader Andrés Pico and US Lt.-Col. John C. Frémont signed the Treaty of Cahuenga on January 13, 1847, ending the US-Mexico War in Alta California. On any given day, tens of thousands of people make their way to and from the park, where rides like the Studio Tour remind attendees of Western movies replete with their frontier myth and cowboy heroes. In the shadow of this theme park dedicated to Hollywood film history, the historical significance of Campo de Cahuenga goes unnoticed.

Yet, approximately fifty feet underground, an LA Metro station features pillars covered with mosaics that memorialize the signing of the Treaty of Cahuenga. One pillar includes portraits of Pico and Frémont accompanied by English and Spanish text that reads, "The Capitulation of Cahuenga was signed January 13, 1847, at this site, the Campo de Cahuenga. This Treaty ended the Mexican American War in California."[1] Likely as a result of its subterranean, mass-transit location, passersby ignore the artwork and its text. This site, rather than being recognized as crucial to the outcome of the US-Mexico War, functions as a gateway to a storied movie production company that helped make the cowboy and the frontier the leading figures of Western history.

The theme park's overshadowing of Campo de Cahuenga is emblematic of how the movie industry contributed to the misrepresentation of the region's history and buried the impact of historical actors. *Dreams of Small Countries* unearths the role prominent Californios—Mexican nationals with mixed Spanish, Indigenous, and African ancestry who settled Alta California—performed in the imagining and making of California as a US state. In doing so, this book is a retelling of California history. Prior to the US-Mexico War (1846–1848), an elite class of settler families, headed by Californio patriarchs, colonized Alta California by establishing presidios and pueblos along the coast. The colonization of the region began when Spanish soldiers and priests established the San Diego Mission on Kumeyaay land in 1769. Within a couple of decades, the Mexican and Spanish settler families

One of the mosaic pillars located at the Universal Studios/Campo de Cahuenga station platform. The text under Don Andrés Pico and John C Frémont states that both agreed to important terms, such as "primarily securing property" for Californios to end the war and establish "friendly terms of compromise." As colorful as the public art is, the mosaic and the history it tells goes largely unnoticed. Photo by author.

of Alta California referred to themselves as Californios to denote their regional identity and their status as *gente de razón*. Gente de razón directly translates into "people of reason" and is best understood by looking to its opposite, *gente sin razón,* meaning people "people without reason." A person of sin razón status was an Indigenous person who did not speak Spanish, was unbaptized, and did not assimilate into the Mexican settler society.

By the 1830s, elite Californios had become a landed gentry class that controlled the political and social world of Alta California. As a settler class, Californios attempted to impose their political imaginary, which I describe as "patria chica," on a borderlands landscape also shaped by Indigenous powers. While patria chica translates to "small motherland" or "fatherland," the phrase can also refer to an attachment to a hometown or region. Scholars of

New Spain describe patria chica as a regionalism shaped by common cultural practices and a sense of responsibility to an idea and ideals, rather than a place. In the Hispanophone Americas, one identified oneself in accordance with their patria chica.[2]

As Californios forged their patria chica, a diversity of Indigenous communities imposed their Indigenous world imaginaries on the same landscape. Crucially, Indigenous identities, motivations, and actions influenced Californio imaginaries of power, land, and belonging. During the Mexican Era (1821–47), Californio settlement and Indigenous power shaped this borderlands landscape.

When the US-Mexico War came to Alta California in July 1846, a handful of prominent Californio families claimed fourteen million acres of land and controlled settler politics through a patronage system. Californio power, however, was tenuous. Indigenous nations had continuously challenged Californio claims to the land. The war brought another challenge: Anglo soldiers and settlers who also contested Californios' claims to the land.[3] Out of anxiety that Indigenous raiding and an Anglo settler invasion imperiled their ranchos, Californio Militia Gen. Andrés Pico and Captain José Antonio Carrillo met with Frémont at Campo de Cahuenga to end the fighting while the war continued elsewhere in Mexico. Pico and Carrillo agreed to cooperate with the US Army to protect Californio property with their signing of the Treaty of Cahuenga on January 13, 1847. A year before the US-Mexico War ended, Anglo and Californio elites made a strategic alliance at Cahuenga. They imagined that by allying with elite Anglos—members of the US Army, rather than squatters—they would work with counterparts to preserve their patria chica. However, Anglo settlers did not intend to assimilate into Californio settler society; rather, they imagined this alliance as a means to craft their own white settler state. Due to the Black Legend and previous conflicts in Texas, Anglo-American settlers already viewed Californios as unassimilable into whiteness because of their Hispanophone culture and mixed ancestry.[4]

In January 1848, just before the Treaty of Guadalupe Hidalgo ended the war, the Californio-Anglo alliance began to fracture, with the discovery of gold in the Sacramento River. The discovery generated a transnational rush to Northern California, ultimately leading to an Anglo-American majority in the region. Due to their numbers in the north, Anglo settlers demanded US statehood and the removal of local Californios from positions of power on the basis that their mixed ancestry and Hispanic culture rendered them inferior and incompetent. As a result of Anglo settler maneuvering, California became the thirty-first state in just two years.

After statehood, however, Californios retained their land and political power in Southern California, shaping the state's politics for three decades. Far from the center of federal power, the US government required a loyal governing class to assert its sovereignty and to economically and politically incorporate the far-western territory into the nation. In the northern mining districts, the significant Anglo-American settler population provided the US government with the political connections and authority to quickly integrate the region into the nation. The existence of Californio rancho culture and Indigenous power in the south stymied the integration of Southern California and limited the US government's authority, especially its ability to control Indigenous polities. Thus, the US government required and accepted Californio participation in state making until the 1870s. Patriarchs of esteemed Californio families, like Pablo de la Guerra, Antonio Coronel, and Andrés and Pío Pico, allied with elite Anglo settlers to facilitate the integration of Southern California into the United States as elected politicians, land claimants, and soldiers. Without prominent Californio participation, California would not have been integrated into the United States as quickly as it was or with its current borders.

The alliance held for three decades because Californios imagined that by collaborating with Anglo-American settlers, they would fashion a settler state organized around whiteness *and* gente de razón. While they tolerated elite Californios' role in governing southern California, Anglo-American settlers simultaneously construed the trademarks of the gente de razón status—mixed ancestry, rancho landholding, Spanish language, and Catholicism—as markers of racial inferiority. By collaborating with Anglo-Americans, Californios helped facilitate a colonial process that displaced gente de razón settlers and Indigenous inhabitants with white settlers.

As a result of this process, I consider Californios to be colonized colonizers, meaning they were colonized and colonizer participants in a settler colonial process that shaped California.[5] Californios lost their claim to property and sociolegal privileges as they became colonized colonizers.[6] Without land and marked as inferior, elite Californios became a racialized group, often referred to as Mexicans. The resulting racialized construct marked people of Mexican ancestry as nonwhite and as perpetual foreigners unfit for citizenship. As other scholars have pointed out, this racialized Mexican identity is rooted in the US–Mexico War and immigration patterns.[7] In *Dreams of Small Countries*, I demonstrate that this construct is also a product of the settler colonial process that made Californio and Indigenous land holding and nonwhite citizenship a legal impossibility in nineteenth-century

California. Ultimately, Californios, motivated by their desire to protect their patria chica, helped lay the foundation of a white settler state.

Myth Making, History Making

Campo de Cahuenga hides in plain sight due to the persistence of myths that begin California history with the Spanish Catholic Missions or the Gold Rush. Odds are, if you were to ask a person to recount the history of California, they would begin with the California Gold Rush. They are likely to mention how Anglo settlers forged a democratic and free state on a wild and uninhabited frontier as the North and South fought over slavery. In my experience, one rarely mentions the Treaty of Guadalupe Hidalgo as a starting point for California history. Even rarer is the mention of the numerous self-governing Indigenous communities that engaged in international politics and tended the natural landscapes of the current-day state.[8] Most of our impressions of California's past come from myth making that centers Anglo actors. One just has to think of any Western film to grasp the prevalence of this myth.

Likewise, historical scholarship has yet to interpret the capitulation of Mexican statesmen to the US military as a pivotal moment of the region's past. In 1888, Hubert Howe Bancroft, who wrote the first history of California, helped cement the idea that the state's history begins with the Gold Rush.[9] In the *History of California*, Bancroft wrote that the year of the Gold Rush was "as different from every other California year before or since" because of the "just and ingenious [Anglo] settlers of California."[10] According to Bancroft, Anglo settlers set California on a path of civilization.

Just two years later, in 1890, historian Frederick Jackson Turner published his famous "frontier thesis" essay, which argued that American democracy in the West was formed by the Anglo-American conquest of the frontier.[11] Shrouded in Manifest Destiny presuppositions, Turner's thesis set the analytical tone for studies of the US West for a majority of the twentieth century. This changed in 1987, when historian Patricia Limerick published the *Legacy of Conquest: The Unbroken Past of the American West,* which argued that conquest, like slavery in the US South, shaped the history of the West and called for historical scholarship that analyzed the structure of conquest while considering race, class, gender, and the environment. A body of work, known as New Western History, emerged and asserts that US power in the West was premised upon the exclusion and agency of nonwhite and colonized communities.[12] Rather than fall into narratives of inevitability, scholars also embraced the concept of borderlands, meaning a landscape with contested and overlapping boundaries within colonial, imperial, national, and regional domains that create political and border complexity.[13] In this book, I build on both bodies of scholarship to investigate how a diversity of actors shaped and reshaped the land.[14]

It is still rare, however, to find historical scholarship that considers the motivations behind and the consequences of Californios as state makers before, during, and after US conquest. In part, this has occurred because scholarship on Californios and Spanish-speaking persons remains siloed in the fields of Mexican American, Chicano, or Latine histories, rather than being integrated into the national histories of the nineteenth-century US West. This is by no means a critique of the important scholarship on Californios and Mexican Americans that this work is intellectually indebted to; rather, it is a commentary on the power of racial ideology on the production of "US history."[15] In fact, this study builds on the research, analysis, and questions other scholars of Californios and Mexican Americans have posed. In her influential work *Manifest Destinies*, Laura Gómez stated, "We cannot fully understand the *second* imperial moment of the 1890s without understanding what occurred in the *first* imperial moment in the 1840s, in what is today the American Southwest."[16] *Dreams of Small Countries* tries to do just that by integrating two major bodies of scholarship to understand how Californio actions shaped local and national politics. Given it is my goal to recover Californios' role as state makers, whose political imaginaries shaped local and national political landscapes, I have chosen to mention the happenings of US national politics only when they were on the minds of Californios. Thus, consequential events, such as the Compromise of 1850, are briefly mentioned in contrast to events like Reconstruction, which is a primary focus of chapter 4.

To write this history, I have brought together a variety of sources, in Spanish and English, to reconstruct the lives, motivations, and actions of prominent Californios. I relied on constitutions, treaties, statutes, and political literature written by Californio and Anglo settlers. Most important to my reconstruction of Californio political imaginaries are their words, in the forms of testimonios, letters, and speeches. I have read over personal and business accounting records, court cases, and political meeting notes to recover Californio as well as Indigenous, Black, and Chinese voices. While not the primary focus of this book, I interrogate Indigenous, Black, and Chinese political imaginaries when they come into conflict with Californio imaginings of power and racial identity and, in turn, shape their political strategies.

By political imaginaries, I mean a commonly held vision of power, political possibility, and government expressed through popular art, political language, and political and economic decisions. A political imaginary serves as the basis for what a community believes to be politically possible, necessary, and legitimate in the making and maintaining of a society and its government.[17] The concept of the political imaginary, I believe, allows one to make sense of the motivation behind the political actions of the Californios.

Reframing California

Beginning in the late eighteenth century, members of European and American societies attempted to colonize the region we now know as California and transform the landscape into their imagined society, their dreams of small countries. The nineteenth century is a particular moment in this chronicle. Between the 1820s and the 1840s, prominent Californios built a settler society with a culture and institutions centered around the rancho, a large land grant given by the Mexican government to encourage permanent family settlement and cattle ranching. Californios were motivated by their want of land—Indigenous land. They imagined the land as their patria chia, where they would be a privileged gente de razón class that would dominate the Indigenous and the sin de razón. Building upon the colonial institutions of the Spanish Franciscan colonists, on their ranchos, Californios sought to transform the *indio* into a subordinate labor force that answered to Californio patriarchal authority.

In the 1840s, as Anglo-Americans arrived in Alta California in increasing numbers, they brought their own settler imaginaries, their own dreams of small countries. The racial logic of American settler society depended upon whiteness, which, as this book will demonstrate, became incompatible, despite some similarities, with the gente de razón status. As they immigrated to California, Anglo-American settlers, much to their surprise, or perhaps dismay, encountered Californio patriarchs with claims to hundreds of thousands of acres, political power, and a subordinated workforce. Anglo-Americans viewed Californio society as an obstruction to their settler imaginaries and set to absorb, if not destroy, it.

This book explores how members of two settler classes—Californio and Anglo-American—worked together and against each other to realize their settler dreams after the Capitulation at Cahuenga and, in turn, made California. By examining the damned alliance between prominent Californios and Anglo-American settlers, this book explains how Anglo settlers wrestled power from the hands of elite Californios and constructed a white settler state. As part of this settler project, Anglo settlers worked to exclude all racialized others—people of Mexican, Indigenous, African, and Chinese descent—from formal politics, all the while allowing for the possibility of exploiting their labor.

I contend that Californios and Anglos worked together despite their different settler imaginaries because they shared one goal—to suppress Indigenous and nonwhite power. While Californios—continuing the work of the Spanish—wanted to control Indigenous labor, Anglo-American settlers wanted to exterminate the Indigenous.[18] Indigenous power was so consequential that an "Indigenous interior world" stretched from the San Bernardino Mountains in the west to Apacheria in the east, where a diversity of Indigenous nations shaped the region's political, cultural, and economic systems.[19] Motivated by their individual dreams of small countries, the Luiseño, Cahuilla, Cupeño, and Kumeyaay shaped this borderlands landscape. Historian Natale Zappia coined the term "Indigenous Interior World" to challenge readers to view this Southern California region as defined by Native raiding and trading, rather than settler territorial claims. I will use the term the "Indigenous world" to connote not just a geopolitical space but a landscape shaped by Indigenous political imaginaries and actions.[20] Given the centrality of the Indigenous world to the Southern California landscape, the region's politics cannot be understood without Native politics. By using Indigenous world, I consider the landscape shaped by Native political and economic aspirations, as much as Mexican and American actions and policies.

Spanish, Mexican, and American colonization caused the death of an estimated four hundred and fifty thousand California Indigenous peoples.[21] During the first twenty-four years of United States control of the region, the Indigenous population fell from one hundred and fifty thousand to thirty thousand due to state-sanctioned violence. To abet their settlement, Anglo settlers formed militias with the backing of the state government to kill and remove Indigenous Californians from the land. The several thousand Indigenous peoples who survived colonial extermination had to contend with violence, exploitative labor, family separation, and removal. As crucial as the genocidal actions of the state's government and Anglo settlers are to the state's history, the events do not feature prominently in this book. Their emission is not done in an effort to obscure this history, but rather as an effort to demonstrate the distinctions between Californio and Anglo-American settler colonialism and the eliminatory logic of the white settler state, and to center Indigenous political action.

Divided into three parts, this study is organized around the themes of politics and land to demonstrate how prominent Californios, as a settler class, were instrumental to the realization of Anglo-American settler imaginaries in California. The book focuses on Southern California because it was a Californio stronghold for decades after US conquest and as a result, we can see how colonization unraveled where Anglo settlers were the minority. Each chapter begins with an environmental vignette that demonstrates how nature influenced the choices of the book's leading actors—Andrés Pico, Pío Pico, Pablo de la Guerra, and Antonio Coronel.

Chapter 1 introduces three elite Californio families—the Picos, the de la Guerras, and the Coronels—and the settler society they made. In this chapter, I detail how Californio society emerged after the Mexican government passed the 1824 Colonization Law and began issuing land grants to encourage permanent family settlement in frontier territories. Due to state-supported colonization, a small class of elite Californio families, headed by patriarchs who viewed their ranchos and the territory as their patria chica, came to rule Alta California. These elites saw themselves as gente de razón and made Californio a privileged sociolegal category determined by racial identifiers such as skin color and *limpieza de sangre*, as well as the performance of the gente de razón status.[22] While gente de razón does not translate or mean white, Californios often equated the privileged status with the construct of whiteness and used blanco and gente de razón interchangeably.[23] Emblematic of this binary is that the Mexican Census of 1836 recorded people into one of two categories—gente de razón or Indian.[24]

In the 1840s, elite Californios struggled to maintain their settler society due to Indigenous politics and a lack of Mexican government support. As prominent Californios strategized how best to protect their landholdings from Indigenous raids, Anglo settler immigration to Alta California increased right before the US-Mexico War began in 1846. Neglected by the Mexican government, elite Californios, such as Andrés Pico, opted to ally with the Anglo-Americans at Campo de Cahuenga rather than outright lose their land claims and political power. A year later, in February 1848, the Treaty of Guadalupe Hidalgo ended the US-Mexico War, transforming Mexican nationals into US citizens with property and citizenship rights.

The second chapter turns to politics and begins with the 1849 California Constitutional Convention, where seven Californios, including Pablo de la Guerra, and forty-two Anglo delegates drafted a state constitution. Every delegate brought their settler imaginaries to the table, but ultimately they created a document that established settler institutions and belonging according

Pablo de la Guerra, Salvador Vallejo, and Andrés Pico in 1865. As elite Californio men, de le Guerra, Vallejo, and Pico performed their gente de razón status and dressed in the style of upper-class men. The composition of the portrait also portrays power, importance, and wealth. Photo courtesy of the Sonoma County Library.

to whiteness, not the status of gente de razón. After the convention, elite Californios embraced electoral politics to maintain their political power in the 1850s. I examine a large cast of elite Californios but focus on the actions of Andrés Pico, Pablo de la Guerra, and Antonio Coronel as elected officials. By holding public office, Pico, de la Guerra, and Coronel imparted legitimacy on an Anglo settler government that brought persons of Mexican and Chinese ancestry, alongside persons of African and Indigenous descent, into the state as racialized others unqualified for citizenship. Scholars have written about the role of Southern political actors in shaping these laws, but this history is incomplete without a consideration of Californio contributions.[25] During the 1850s, Anglo and Californio legislators worked together to deny citizenship to Indigenous, Black and Chinese inhabitants, especially around the right to give testimony. In turn, Black American and Chinese immigrants challenged these laws and attempted to realize their own political imaginaries, which Californios rejected because of their own racial and cultural prejudices. Elite Californios' attempt to establish their own dominance vis-à-vis Indigenous, Black, and Chinese peoples was an assertion of their superiority as gente de razón settlers and crucial to their political strategy. Because Californios demonstrated their willingness to uphold a racial hierarchy that designated people of African and Indigenous decent to the bottom, the leaders of the California Democratic Party embraced elite Californios as allies, despite their mixed ancestry. Without Californio participation, the Democrats would not have won as many elections in California and would have been unable to forge a white settler state.

Chapter 3 then moves to the second theme of the book: land. A three-way land conflict emerged between Californios, the Indigenous, and Anglo-Americans in 1850s Southern California. In the days following the US–Mexico war, the biggest threat to Californio territorial control was not squatters and the biggest threat to US authority was not Californio resistance; rather, bands of Luiseño, Cahuilla, Kumeyaay, and Cupeño threatened both Californio and American settlement. Understanding the significance of this threat to property and identity makes sense of why Californios continued to ally with Anglo settlers when the US Congress violated the citizenship and property provisions of the Treaty of Guadalupe Hidalgo. This chapter focuses on the resistance campaign led by Cupeño leader Antonio Garra and the subsequent Californio and Anglo attempts to squash it. This collaboration ultimately contributed to the imposition of a land system designed to replace Californios' patria chica with a white settler state, which transformed Californios into colonized colonizers.

As a result of Californio participation, California became integrated into the United States and, thus, intertwined in the sectional conflict that became the US Civil War. To understand how prominent Californios perceived and reacted to the US Civil War, chapter 4, once again, follows the actions of the Picos, the de la Guerras, and Coronels. When the US Civil War began, most Californios did not publicly support the Union because of their own conservatism and belief in the natural racial hierarchy that the Democratic

Party—the party of secession—espoused. Not until 1862, when Californios could no longer ignore their declining social position and diminishing political power, did they begin to publicly support the Union. In addition to running their political machine for the Union, they organized the Native Californian Cavalry, a Californio cavalry battalion in the Union Army. This calvary provided a legible way for Californios to perform their gente de razón status because the unit was designed to protect the Mojave Desert and the Colorado River Basin, or the Indigenous world, from Indigenous raids. Californios, as well as US Army officials, did not view the Cavalry as a means to prevent Confederate designs on the Southwest but as a means to stop the Indigenous from asserting their politics on a still-contested region. Californio political strategizing during the Civil War allowed them to maintain their grasp on political power for a moment longer.

The chapter then turns to Reconstruction politics in California. With the end of the US Civil War in 1865, prominent Californios once again recalibrated their strategies to protect their diminishing political power. Confronted with the revolutionary fervor of Radical Reconstruction, Californios, notably Antonio Coronel and the de la Guerras, renewed their alliances with the Democrats. Threatened by Black activism and Chinese immigration, Californios allied with the outspoken politicians of white supremacy to obstruct the possibilities of Reconstruction. Again, prominent Californios attempted to perform their gente de razón status by distancing themselves from Black Americans and Chinese immigrants. As a result, the state legislature refused to approve the Fourteenth and Fifteenth Amendments and passed anti-Chinese legislation. Ironically, Anglo-American and Californio efforts to obstruct federal policies designed to establish biracial democracy emboldened Anglo settler attempts to strip Californios of US citizenship on the basis that they were racially inferior. In response, Californios doubled down on their roles as patriarchal enforcers of a racial hierarchy, a position that only strengthened the foundation of the white settler state and cemented their status as colonized colonizers.

Chapter 5 returns to the land conflict. The challenges posed by a land system designed to dispossess nonwhite landholders, as well as environmental calamity, finally forced Californios to lose their claims, allowing Anglo-American settlers to seize long-sought-after lands in Southern California. In the 1870s, Anglo settlers finally established settler communities on ranchos, ending Californio dreams of patria chica. As ranchos were razed from the landscape, the US Army removed the Luiseño, Cahuilla, and Kumeyaay to reservations and no longer relied on prominent Californios to control the

Indigenous. Crucially, Californio and Anglo-American efforts to disempower Indigenous polities during the US Civil War had strengthened US authority in Southern California and undermined Californios' political position. Anglo control of the land meant Anglo control of politics. In 1879, Anglo-American settlers had actualized their vision of a white settler state with the rewriting of the state constitution, which excluded Californio and Chinese residents from participating in political society as full citizens. As written, the 1879 California Constitution excluded Chinese immigrants from California society, years before the US Congress passed the 1882 Chinese Exclusion Act, and ousted Californios from politics.

As this book demonstrates, a diversity of people made California. Despite this diversity, however, a cast of people made California into a white settler state that belies the state's liberal reputation. It is my hope that after reading *Dreams of Small Countries*, if you are lucky enough to be on your way to Universal Studios Hollywood, you will see Campo de Cahuenga as the place where Californio and Anglo settlers began an alliance that made California years before the first Western hit the movie screens.

PART I | Becoming Californio

CHAPTER ONE

Hijos del País and the Making of Settler Societies

Clear water rushed through a riverbed bordered by oaks, willows, and sycamores.[1] The river came from the southeast curving its way through a valley, and then hugged the southeastern edge of the mountain range now known as the Santa Monicas. Along this river, on August 2, 1769, thirty-four Spanish colonists set up camp. The thirty-four men were a part of the Portolá Expedition, which Las Californias governor Gaspar de Portolá had organized to establish settlements that would cement Spain's claim to Alta California. One of the first Europeans to see the river, Franciscan Fray Juan Crespí named the body of water El Río de Nuestra Señora La Reina de Los Ángeles de Porciúncula, or the Los Angeles River.[2] After the Spanish colonists set up camp, six to eight Tongva men approached the Spanish colonists with sage, a bowl of prepared grass seeds, and strings of beads. While the Tongva men had their bows, they were disassembled. The leader of the group spoke to the Spanish colonists, after which the men shared tobacco. After a night's rest, the expedition crossed the river and continued north.

For years, this river had sustained Yaanga, the largest village and political center of Tovaangar, the ancestral homelands of the Tongva.[3] Crespí was impressed by Yaanga. In his journal, he noted that the spot should become a large mission settlement due to its ecological resources and sizable Indigenous village.[4] As a direct result of Crespí's recommendations, in 1771, Spanish colonists, under the leadership of Franciscan Fray Junipero Serra, founded Mission San Gabriel at the Bosque del Rio Hondo, just miles from Yaanga, to convert Indigenous peoples to Catholicism.

This mission system would violently alter Indigenous ways of life, culture, and politics, but Indigenous Californians developed strategies for surviving and challenging Spanish colonization. As missions disrupted subsistence patterns, bands and individuals forged labor and economic relations with the Spanish, sometimes through reciprocal means and other times through violent and strategic raids for survival. Within the missions, Indigenous communities held onto vital cultural elements, like dance, body adornment, and architecture, despite Franciscan priests' attempts to Catholicize them.[5]

Ten years after the founding of Mission San Gabriel, in 1781, Spanish soldier and Californias governor Felipe de Neve and forty-four settlers, known as *Los Pobladores,* founded the Los Angeles pueblo at Yaanga, just a mile from the de Anza campsite. The pueblo, in contrast to the mission, would serve as a permanent civilian settlement. The Pobladores, originally from Sinaloa and Sonora, were nonland-owning families with varying casta statuses. Only three Pobladores possessed fully Spanish ancestry. Two Pobladores were *criollos,* meaning they were born in the Americas, and one was a *Peninsulare,* meaning they were born in Spain. The remaining Pobladores consisted of mestizos, who had Spanish and Native ancestry, mulattos, who had Spanish and African ancestry, Indios, who had only Native ancestry, and Negros, who had only African ancestry.

In New Spain, Spaniards had constructed the *Sistema de Castas* (casta system) to control the conquered and, increasingly, racially mixed colonized population of the Americas. The system was based on the fifteenth-century *limpieza de sangre* (purity of blood) legal system, which excluded Spaniards with Jewish and Muslim ancestry from powerful positions. In central Mexico, the casta system was a socioracial hierarchy that kept political power and socioeconomic privileges out of the hands of racially mixed people. On the sparsely populated northern frontier, however, people with mixed ancestry or lower casta positions could seize the power and socioeconomic privileges that were out of reach in the center of the empire. The Pobladores, like other civilian settlers in Tejas and Nuevo Mexico, made the arduous journey to Alta California because they imagined opportunities of social ascension and wealth in the frontier territory, regardless of their casta status.[6]

After the founding of the Los Angeles Pueblo and over the course of six decades, gente de razón settlers from Mexico transformed land grants into their small countries. This chapter examines the society Californios imagined and forged in Alta California, as well as their efforts to preserve their social structures up to the end of the US-Mexico War (1846–48). The chapter opens with the histories of the Pico, de la Guerra, and Coronel families to demonstrate how a diversity of settlers shaped the elite Californio identity and the land as their patria chica. The chapter then turns to the fighting that broke out between Californios, Indigenous Californians, and Anglo-Americans during the US-Mexico War. To end the war and preserve their settler society, elite Californios, in 1847, a year before the US-Mexico war ended with the Treaty of Guadalupe Hidalgo, capitulated to the US Army to protect their property and to suppress Indigenous uprisings. This capitulation marks the beginning of elite Californio attempts to hold on to power through strategic collaboration with the Anglo settler class rather than outright resistance.

Creating the Californio Identity

In the mid-nineteenth century, Alta California was a sparsely populated settler society on Mexico's remote northern frontier. Years after settlers first camped alongside the Los Angeles River in 1769, hundreds of Spanish soldiers, Franciscan priests, and settlers established military, religious, and civilian settlements all along the de Anza expedition path, which hugged the coast. In San Diego, Santa Barbara, Monterey, and Yerba Buena (current-day San Francisco), the Spanish Army established *presidios* (military forts) designed to ward off Russian, English, and, crucially, Indigenous threats to Spain's claim.[7] Franciscan padres founded twenty-one missions from San Diego to San Francisco to convert Indigenous Californians to Catholicism as part of Spanish, then Mexican, colonization efforts. When Mexico won its independence from Spain in 1821, there were four presidios and twenty missions in Alta California. The eastern edge of Californio settlements overlapped with the Indigenous world, which extended from the western mountain ranges to the deserts in the east, creating a borderlands. Just beyond Los Angeles and San Diego, the Cahuilla, Luiseño, and Kumeyaay controlled the land and linked Alta California trade with Apacheria and beyond.

During thirty years of Spanish colonization, the settler population grew to 3,270 while the Indigenous population declined from three hundred and forty thousand to two hundred thousand; of that two hundred thousand, about twenty thousand lived in the California missions.[8] Three years after independence, in 1824, the Mexican Constitutional Congress passed the General Colonization Act to strengthen its claims to the remote frontier territories with permanent family settlement.[9] Less than a decade later, the 1832 Secularization Act, which nationalized the missions and transferred property from the church to Mexican nationals, resulted in a large land transfer to Californios. Mexican officials distributed land according to personal relationships, and a small number of families claimed a majority of rancho land. Both acts accelerated the Mexican colonization of Alta California by facilitating the birth of the rancho system centered on permanent family settlement, the exploitation of Indigenous labor, and a sociopolitical culture defined by gente de razón.

In Alta California, a person of gente de razón status not only spoke fluent Spanish, upheld European gender norms, performed their class status with European-style clothing and home furnishings, and practiced Catholicism, they also had a sense of patria chica and upheld *compadrazgo*, a system of reciprocal and fictive kinship based on the godparent-godchild

Carta esférica de la costa de la Alta California was drawn in 1839 and depicts the Alta California coast with missions and presidios. The cartographer, rather than depict Indigenous power, has notably left the interior blank. Courtesy of the Library of Congress.

relationship within their family and with other elite families.[10] In family, as well as political life, patriarchal authority was paramount. Patriarchal authority, in great part, stemmed from the wealth created by the rancho and the hide-and-tallow trade. When describing the Californio society of the 1830s and '40s, elite Californian Angustias de la Guerra explained that social interactions were determined by "one's blood relationship or official position."[11] The concept of gente de razón undergirded the identities, power dynamics, and obligations between men and women, fathers and children, rancheros and laborers, and settlers and natives.[12] For Californios, many of whom were of mixed-race ancestry, becoming landowners, dominating the native, and successfully performing gente de razón while upholding compadrazgo allowed them to claim the top rungs of the social structure.[13]

The selective distribution of rancho land allowed a small class of families to pursue their settler imaginaries. The patriarchs of these landed families imagined themselves and their peers as masters of small countries. In the 1840s, members of Alta California society referred to Mariano G. Vallejo as the *reyezuelo* (little king) of the north and the de la Guerras as the royal family of the south. In southern Alta California, the elite patriarchs of the Pico, de la Guerra, and Coronel families exerted control over women and children, the nonelite, the Indigenous on their ranchos, as well as the politics of southern Alta California.[14] In the span of decades, Californios transformed Alta California from a remote *frontera* into a patria chica.

In southern Alta California, the ascendancy of the Pico family and, in particular, Andrés and Pío Pico exemplifies how settler families of Spanish, African, and Indigenous descent became members of the elite settler class through the successful performance of gente de razón. In 1775, Santiago de la Cruz Pico served as a soldier in the de Anza expedition. Soon after, Pico settled in Alta California with his wife, María Jacinta de la Bastida Pico, and their seven children. In choosing to relocate to Alta California, the Picos imagined that they could remake their identity and transcend their lower-casta status as settlers on the remote frontera. As a mission guard at San Gabriel and San Diego, Pico directly enforced colonial rule over Indigenous peoples who challenged Spanish settlement. After twenty years of service, in 1795, the Spanish government granted Pico the land grant, Rancho Simi, in the current-day Simi Valley. The small settler population in Alta California meant that Pico's mestizo status did not prevent him from becoming a landowner and entering the elite settler class.

Santiago Pico's son, José Dolores Pico, became a leading member of elite Californio society through his marriage to María Estaquia Gutiérrez, an *española*.[15] In the 1790 Census, Gutiérrez was categorized as an española even though she was born in New Spain, not in Spain, to two Spanish parents. Gutiérrez's categorization as española in the census meant she successfully claimed the identity and its privileges in Alta California. José Maria Pico's marriage to an española resulted in his own re-categorization as español in the 1790 census while his brothers were categorized as mulattos.[16] Pico's social ascension demonstrates how, in Alta California, women were social brokers who helped men attain the family ancestry and compadrazgo networks necessary to become elites.[17]

In 1801, Pío Pico was born to José María Pico and María Estaquia Gutiérrez at Mission San Gabriel. Andrés Pico was born nine years later. In total, José María Pico and María Estaquia Gutiérrez had nine children. Following in the footsteps of their family patriarchs, Pío and Andrés joined the military, with the hopes of obtaining land grants and political power. When their father died in 1819, Pío Pico assumed the role of the family patriarch.

The institution of marriage created opportunities for Pío Pico to perform the role of family patriarch. He facilitated the marriages of his six sisters. In 1823, his sister Estéfana Pico married Californio José Antonio Carrillo, which brought two prominent families of Los Angeles and Santa Barbara together. That same year Casimira Pico married Joaquin Ortega, which brought together two prominent families from Los Angeles and San Diego. Pico, himself, married María Ignacia Alvarado, the cousin of Juan Bautista Alvarado, who served as governor of Alta California from 1837 to 1842. Each marriage deepened the Picos' connection to the elite.[18] These marriages, like most unions between elite Californios, resulted in the reproduction of the Californio social hierarchy and the consolidation of land holdings because women could inherit and own land.[19] Women, despite their gendered positions, brought elite families together and, as social brokers, controlled membership in elite society. Californio women played a crucial role in the making and remaking of the settler society.

As a result of familial ties, Pico entered San Diego politics in 1826 and received the Rancho Jamul land grant in 1829.[20] Just six years after entering politics, Pío served as the governor of Alta California in 1832, just as the Mexican government embraced a policy of secularization. Under the 1832 Secularization Act, the Mexican government confiscated mission lands for the purported purpose of redistributing land to Indigenous Californians. The act charged Alta California governors with redistributing the land. Rather than redistribute the land to the Indigenous, governors selectively distributed land

This photo of Pío Pico was taken later in his life. The portrait, depicting Pico with a cane and a book, conveys his gente de razón status. Courtesy of the Bancroft Library.

grants to members of their compadrazgo networks. In this way, prominent Californio families amassed acres upon acres of land.[21] In the decade after secularization, governors granted 75 percent of all Mexican ranchos to 7 percent of the Californio population.[22]

As governor, Pico distributed large and favorable grants to men in his compadrazgo network. In fact, during his second term as Alta California governor, from 1845 to 1846, Pico distributed more land grants than any other governor. Among the many grants he issued, Pico granted his cousin Manuel Castro nine square leagues and his nephew Francisco Pico eight leagues in 1846. Most notably, he granted his brother, Andrés, and brother-in-law, Juan Bautista Alvarado, Rancho ex-Mission San José, which totaled thirty thousand acres.[23]

Crucial to Californio ideas of power was their control and exploitation of Indigenous land and labor, especially on their ranchos. The Picos held many land grants in the borderlands. Land grants in the Californio-Indigenous borderlands were essential to elite Californio imaginings of themselves as settlers. After receiving the Rancho Jamul grant, Pío and his brother, Andrés, brought cattle and unfree laborers to create wealth and weaken Indigenous claims to the surrounding landscape. Their undertaking was continuously challenged. Throughout the 1820s, Kumeyaays and Cahuillas attacked ranchos in San Diego, taking guns, livestock, and people, compromising the viability of trade routes and settlements.[24] In 1837, an Indigenous group, likely a Kumeyaay band, attacked and burned down Jamul. The attack on Rancho Jamul was one of many similar incidents.[25] After the attack, Andrés left the military and devoted his energies to rebuilding and defending Ranch Jamul. Together at Rancho Jamul, Andrés and Pío reasserted their Californio identity by grazing cattle and sheep and violently coercing Indigenous peoples to labor.[26]

In contrast to the Picos, the founding patriarch of the de la Guerra family of Santa Barbara, José de la Guerra y Noriega, migrated to Alta California with español status. Born in 1779 in Spain, José de la Guerra y Noriega migrated to Mexico City in 1792 to assist his uncle, Pedro Noriega, with his mercantile business. José de la Guerra y Noriega's español status ensured his access to privilege in a colonial city with extreme wealth disparity and a rigid casta system. About twenty years after the Picos' arrival, nineteen-year-old José de la Guerra, perhaps imagining the opportunities that settlement on the remote frontera promised, enlisted in the Spanish Royal Army and traveled to Alta California.[27] In 1801, de la Guerra was first assigned to the presidio of Santa Barbara. He quickly climbed the ranks and became the comandante of the Monterey presidio. As comandante, de la Guerra was in charge of supplying the presidio, which brought many lucrative business opportunities.

In 1804, José de la Guerra y Noriega and María Antonia Carrillo y Lugo brought the Lugo, Carrillo, and de la Guerra settler families together with their nuptials.[28] Once married, José de la Guerra and María Antonia Carrillo y Lugo cultivated a reputation as the town's *padrinos* (godparents) by upholding compadrazgo and claiming responsibility for unmarried women and Indigenous people, building a church, sponsoring outsider converts to Catholicism, and supporting the education and health care for their "children." In reality, these relationships were exploitative. According to the 1827 census, nearly every sin razón inhabitant was indebted to de la Guerra's retail store and lived on land claimed by the de la Guerra family.[29]

In addition to exerting familial authority over Santa Barbara, José de la Guerra and María Antonia Carrillo y Lugo had twelve children. Their son, Pablo de la Guerra, was born in 1819 and entered politics at the age of nineteen. Like his peers, he married strategically. He married Maria Josefa Moreno y Castro, a member of the prominent Moreno and Castro families. Additionally, Pablo's six sisters reproduced Californio society and facilitated beneficial political alliances for their family. Emblematic of Californio women's power as social brokers is Teresa de la Guerra's marriage to William Hartnell, originally from England, in 1852. Through his marriage to Teresa de la Guerra, Hartnell, despite being born in England, became a member of elite Californio society. She opened the door to ranchos and political positions, as long as he assimilated into Californio society and performed the attributes of gente de razón. Through marriage, the de la Guerras established compadrazgo links with other prominent families and immigrants to protect their patria chica.

As a young boy and teenager, Pablo de la Guerra received a formal education in Mexico City and at the short-lived Alisal Patrocinio school in Monterey.[30] De la Guerra learned English and French, and at the age of nineteen, de la Guerra was appointed an apprentice at the Monterey customs house, likely due to his language skills.[31] On the eve of the US-Mexico War, de la Guerra was a prominent figure in Alta California politics and Pacific world trade. In contrast to the Picos who used acts of violence against Indians to assert their gente de razón identity, the de la Guerras assumed the role of the sophisticated elite to distance themselves from the sin razón. The de la Guerras' Spanish ancestry made it all the easier for them to perform their gente de razon status in this manner.

The Coronels settled in Alta California after the Picos and the de la Guerras. Born in Mexico City in 1817, Antonio Coronel migrated to Los Angeles with his family as a part of the Híjar-Padrés Colony. In 1834, the Mexican government ordered the migration of families to Alta California, and 204 settlers migrated from Mexico City to the small pueblo. Coronel's father, Ygnacio Coronel, was recruited to the Híjar-Padrés Colony because he was a schoolteacher. Once in Alta California, he established the first Spanish-language school in Los Angeles.

The Coronels' Spanish ancestry—Antonio's paternal grandfather was born in Andalucía, Spain—provided the family with quick access to political and social power. Like the de la Guerras, they did not rely on violent acts to achieve the status of gente de razón. Without military service, the Coronels received political appointments and land grants. Six years after arriving in the pueblo, his father, Ygnacio Coronel, received a grant and built the Coronel Adobe on Calle de Los Negros, current-day Los Angeles Street. At the age of twenty, Antonio Coronel received his first political appointment as

An engraved portrait of Antonio Coronel, circa 1860. Coronel is wearing a three-piece suit, an assertion of his gente de razón status. In more candid photos taken later in his life, he can be seen wearing a sombrero-like hat and playing the guitar. Courtesy of the University of Southern California Library and California Historical Society.

assistant secretary of tribunals, just four years after arriving in the pueblo. In 1846, Alta California governor Pío Pico approved the Rancho La Cañada grant for Coronel, cementing his individual status as a landowner.

Indigenous laborers performed the labor that kept the rancho society running, such as cooking, caring for children, and serving as personal servants.[32] They also performed the rancho labor that generated Californio wealth. In one account, José Ramon Pico, member of the Pico family, described Christmas celebrations during the 1840s. According to Pico, over the course of six weeks in November and early December, "los Indios" drove, killed, and prepared the cattle that became the hides and tallow on which the Alta California economy relied upon. They worked day and night, "ladling out melted tallow with big wooden dippers into bags [which] held from one to five hundred pounds of tallow. When filled . . . they were stitched up [and] piled with the hides in the adobe sheds in the courtyard to await the time when Los Gringos should come in their ships from Boston, bringing groceries, dry goods and merchandise of every sort to trade for."[33] When they completed this task, "los Indios" then prepared the beef for the week-long Christmas fiesta. Pico's nostalgic account underplays the importance of Indigenous labor while asserting his family's role as gente de razón and benefactors of patria chica. Like benevolent kings, according to Pico, Californio patriarchs provided plenty of food and accommodations for "los Indios," as well as the "many of the whole families of our relatives and rancheros."[34]

Through their performances of patriarchal authority, gente de razón, and compadrazgo, the de la Guerras, Picos, Coronels, and other elite Californio families maintained a settler society that produced unequal relationships between family patriarchs and their family members, nonelites, and the Indigenous. By the beginning of the 1840s, elite Californio men had become *hijos del país* (sons of the land) and Alta California had become their patria chica.[35] By founding schools, taking in unattached people, cultivating the land, and controlling Indigenous labor, these elite families were neither grandstanding nor imagining themselves as powerful individuals; rather, they were working toward creating the connected familial, economic, and political world of patria chica.

Resistance, Collaboration, and Capitulation

During the 1840s, elite Californios demanded more local control from the central Mexican government just as Indigenous polities and American settler challenges mounted.[36] Throughout Alta California, Indigenous raiders jeopardized ranchos by stealing horses, livestock, and people. More than an attack on the Californio settler project, the raids led by Kumeyaay, Mojaves, and Utes, among others, were an attempt to forge an alternative economy and politics in the region. In 1840, Californios lost three thousand horses during one raiding operation, led by Ute chief Wákara, in Southern California.[37] These raids ruffled dreams of patria chica. In 1840s Santa Barbara, according to Pablo de la Guerra, Indigenous raids made ranchos uninhabitable.[38] As a result of raiding in Monterey, Californio families abandoned their ranchos because they "no longer fel[t] safe."[39]

These raids induced elite Californios to be all the more dissatisfied with the Mexico City-installed governor Manuel Micheltorena (1842–45), who had neither the knowledge nor the resources to directly address these raids. In 1845, a political crisis emerged, which resulted in discontented Californios sending Micheltorena back to Mexico City. After the crisis, Alta California was ruled by Governor Pío Pico in the south and General José Castro in the north. Indigenous raids had fractured the fragile Californio political system.

At the same time, Californios also had to contend with Anglo-American settlers. Since the Bidwell-Bartleson party migrated from Missouri to California by wagon in 1841, the Anglo-American population grew. Prior to the mid-1840s, the few hopeful Anglo settlers who arrived in Alta California took the long way by boarding ships that traveled around the tip of South America and often stopped in the Hawaiian archipelago. Given the small Anglo-American population, the handful of US-born men in Alta California assimilated into Californio culture by performing the attributes of gente de razón, including learning Spanish, practicing Catholicism, marrying into elite families, and upholding compadrazgo.

Massachusetts-born Abel Stearns, for instance, settled in Alta California in 1829.[40] When Stearns first arrived in Monterey, Alta California, he failed to acquire a land grant. With few prospects in the north, Stearns migrated south and established a coastal trading post, Casa de San Pedro, in 1832. After successfully connecting the Los Angeles Pueblo to the Pacific world, Stearns purchased Rancho Los Alamitos, current-day Long Beach. In 1841, at the age of forty-three, Stearns officially became a member of elite Californio society when he married the fourteen-year-old Arcadia Bandini, a member of the elite Bandini family of San Diego. Again, a marriage between an Anglo settler man and elite Californio woman forged intimate, political, and familial ties. Social broker Arcadia Bandini provided Stearns with a legitimate avenue into the elite Californio culture, and, as a result, they could both pursue their dreams of wealth and influence. Through marriage, Stearns became "Don Abel Stearns." Californios' use of "Don" demonstrates Stearns's position in and assimilation into elite society. When reflecting on the US invasion of Alta California in 1846, William Heath Davis, an Anglo merchant who married into the elite Estudillo family of San Diego, wrote that Stearns "had been in the country so long that he was rather considered as belonging to it."[41]

After the 1841 success of the Bidwell-Bartleson party, US citizens began migrating west in earnest. Unlike Stearns and Hartnell, the Anglo-American settlers who migrated to Alta California post-1841 had no intention of assimilating into Californio society; they intended to establish their own settler societies with their own property and political systems. John Bidwell, the Anglo-American leader of the thirty-four-member Bidwell-Bartleson settler party, claimed his intent for migrating to Alta California was "to take the country and annex it."[42]

By 1845, there were six hundred and eighty Anglo-American immigrants, concentrated in the north, and seventy-three hundred Californios in all of Alta California.[43] Unlike the previous Anglo-American immigrants who assimilated into Californio society, these newly arrived Anglo-American settlers intended to bring their own social norms and customs. Instead, these settlers characterized Californio rule as an "oppressive oligarchy" and Californios as corrupt to justify their settlement attempts and violation of Mexican laws and customs.[44] Just as tensions between non-Mexican-citizen settlers and northern Californios increased, the US government signaled its support for Anglo-American settlement in the region by ordering First Lieutenant John C. Frémont to map the region with the Corps of Topographical Engineers.[45] The US government ordered Frémont to provide accurate maps and information about Mexican territory coveted by the US government and its citizens.[46]

As Anglo-American immigration increased, Californios, such as Pablo de la Guerra and Mariano Guadalupe Vallejo, warned the general and de facto governor José Castro of the threat Anglo settlers posed in the current-day Sacramento Valley and San Francisco Bay. In response, in 1845, the Alta California government issued a decree that required all American immigrants to apply for a settlement license and take a loyalty oath in Sonoma. Only twenty Americans applied for settler licenses.[47]

Elite Californios called on the departmental government, not the Mexican government, which had continuously refused to send the weapons and money required for defense against Indigenous raids, to address the situation. In March 1846, José Castro convened a junta (a political meeting, council, or committee) to determine to whom and where the hijos del país should turn for assistance as illegal Anglo-American settlement increased. The junta met in Monterey on March 17 and debated whether or not Alta California should remain a part of Mexico, claim independence, or annex itself to Great Britain, France, or the United States. Already weakened by Indigenous raiding, most Californios thought that in order to hold onto their ranchos, they needed to collaborate with a wealthy empire or republic.[48] José Castro advocated for a French protectorate because both countries practiced Catholicism. Pablo de la Guerra, on the other hand, advocated most strongly for an independent Las Californias. Pío Pico, who did not attend because his nemesis Castro called the junta, had made known his support for making Alta California an English protectorate. Vallejo, as did others at the meeting, proposed annexation to the US because it was a republic, not a monarchy, which meant they would retain their "political autonomy."[49] Given the limited resources they had to protect their ranchos from growing threats, in March 1846, elite Californios were willing to ally with a nation that would allow them to maintain their patria chica.

Emblematic of the political disagreement that afflicted the elite Californio population, the junta disbanded without a consensus, and the men returned to their ranchos.[50] In turn, General Castro continued to issue proclamations. On April 17, 1846, he issued a proclamation that declared that foreigners could not work, rent, or purchase land in the territory and were subject to expulsion.[51] As news of this proclamation spread, so did the rumor that General José Castro was on his way north to extract tax payments and expel foreign settlers. Upon hearing this rumor, William B. Ide, an Anglo-American settler from Massachusetts, led thirty-three settlers in taking up arms against the Californios.

On June 5, 1845, the Bear Flag Revolt began when Ide and the armed men marched into Sonoma and declared the pueblo occupied.[52] As the leader of the Bear Flag Revolt, Ide penned a proclamation that explained why American settlers revolted against the local government. According to Ide, the Alta California government had "invited [the settlers] to this country [Alta California] by a promise of Lands on which to settle themselves." They arrived only to be "denied even the privilege of buying or renting Lands" and the protection of a "Republican Government."[53] Ide had imagined the region would be open to his settlement, only to discover that Californios controlled the territory with their own land practices and political institutions. Ide also accused elite Californios of "Military Despotism" and of "shamefully oppress[ing] the laboring people of California."[54] Ide described Californios as "indolent, ignorant, and backward."[55] According to Ide, Californios' incompetence rendered their land claims and political authority null. This was a righteous revolt.

As part of their occupation, the Bear Flag insurrectionists took over Mariano Guadalupe Vallejo's house, Casa Grande. Vallejo, the wealthiest Californio in the north, claimed over one hundred and seventy-five thousand acres of land, owned more than fifty thousand cattle, and controlled the labor of hundreds of Indigenous laborers. The Bear Flaggers targeted Vallejo because he obstructed their settler imaginaries. When the insurrectionists entered Casa Grande, Vallejo, who was already a proponent of US annexation, signed a pledge stating that he would "not take up arms against the founders of the state of California."[56] Perhaps he imagined this was the first step toward California entering the Union and protecting his family, political control, and property.

Unfortunately for Vallejo, the Bear Flaggers drank all of his alcohol and forgot the pledge. They arrested Vallejo and forced him to ride a horse to the Sacramento River. Before making this ride, Vallejo sent a message to US captain John Montgomery about the siege of Casa Grande.[57] The US had not yet declared war on Mexico, so out of obligation to Vallejo, Captain Montgomery offered protection for Casa Grande and Francisca de Vallejo, Mariano's wife, demonstrating that US Army men abided by a similar social code.

The Bear Flag Revolters took Vallejo to the New Helvetica rancho, John Sutter's land grant, on the Sacramento River. Sutter, a Swiss immigrant and naturalized Mexican citizen, agreed to imprison Vallejo. Although Sutter became a Mexican citizen in 1840 and had even solicited advice from Vallejo on how to start his own rancho, he did not want the region to remain under the Mexican flag. French-speaking Sutter had hoped Alta California would become a French protectorate and had even encouraged French immigration to the territory.[58] Although Sutter imprisoned him, he recognized Vallejo's gente de razón status and held him in the finest room and "treat[ed him] as well as possible" because he was a "man of property."[59]

The occupation of Sonoma ended with the beginning of war. On July 7, 1846, the US Pacific Squadron, under the command of US Navy commodore John D. Sloat, brought the war between the United States and Mexico to Alta California, nearly a month after the conflict began in Texas. After capturing Monterey, Commodore Sloat issued a "Proclamation to the Inhabitants of California," which justified the war. Sloat, like Ide, characterized the US Navy's conquest as a moral liberation from the "corrupt officers" of the oppressive Mexican government. Under US governance, Sloat claimed California would "rapidly advance and improve both in agriculture and commerce"; all inhabitants, "native or foreign," could own and sell property; and "a great increase in the value of real estate" was "anticipated."[60] Sloat's message proclaimed the righteousness of Anglo settler dreams and Californio society as inferior.

US forces quickly conquered the sparsely populated and poorly resourced northern Alta California. In the south, Californios took a stand against an American takeover. When Commodore Sloat arrived in Santa Barbara, Pablo de la Guerra, who at the time served as the alcalde, refused to give control of the customs house to the US Navy and fled. De la Guerra joined General José Castro, who was traveling south to recruit men and guns. Together, they continued to Los Angeles, where they hoped to combine forces with Governor Pío Pico. Despite their well-known dislike for each other, Pico and Castro—after a day of tense negotiations—agreed to cooperate in order to defeat the invading "Americanos."[61] In Los Angeles, Governor Pico called upon men to take up arms. The need for resources was so dire that General Castro wrote to Antonio Coronel asking him to seize any and all horses, arms, and ammunition for the war.[62]

Few elite Californios "offered their services when the hour came to defend the country," according to Angustias de la Guerra.[63] They did not want to leave their ranchos vulnerable to Indigenous raiding, which had increased in light of the conflicts between Anglos and Californios.[64] In turn, the US

Army exploited Indigenous desires to remove Californios from their lands. John Sutter, who went on to work with the US Army, and John Frémont enlisted Yokut, Miwok, Piupiumaksmaks, and Walla Walla men into Company H of the California Battalion. They ordered the company to raid Californio ranchos.[65] These Indigenous soldiers viewed the war as an opportunity to reconfigure the boundaries of their worlds and their alliances, especially since Frémont sent rations to the families of Walla Walla soldiers.[66] For Californios, defending their ranchos against Indigenous raiding was more important than ousting the US Army.

Just a month into fighting, the US Armed Forces outnumbered Californios willing to pick up arms. On August 9, 1846, Californio leaders held a territorial assembly in Los Angeles, which decided that Castro and Pico would flee to Sonora, where they would petition the Mexican government for adequate money, weapons, and soldiers. As the political and military leaders fled Los Angeles, Californios escaped to the hills and their ranchos to avoid the invading army.[67] Commodore Stockton and his troops entered the Pueblo de Los Angeles on August 13, 1846. The US Army met no organized military resistance, and Stockton quickly declared that Alta California belonged to the United States.

After establishing the rules of occupation, Stockton returned to Monterey and left Lieutenant Archibald Gillespie in charge of the pueblo. Gillespie encouraged his men to enforce martial law, a curfew, store closures, and a ban on social gatherings.[68] This was in stark contrast to John C. Frémont, who had also been in Los Angeles with soldiers, and "adopted the Californio way of life" by dressing like a ranchero and befriending elite families.[69] The contrast left pueblo residents outraged with Gillespie. Californios felt forced into a "position worse than that of slaves [by] the despotic and arbitrary laws" imposed by Gillespie and his men.[70]

As resentment brewed, nonelite Californios began to plan a counteroffensive.[71] Lieutenant Gillespie made an enemy out of Sérbulo Varela who, after receiving a fine, vowed to lead an offensive against the American troops.[72] After a month of occupation, in the early hours of September 23, 1846, ten to twenty men under the command of Varela fired at US troops stationed at the Government House in Los Angeles. The revolt of Los Angeles had begun. After this maneuver, Valera issued "Pronunciamiento de Varela y otras de California contra los americanos" (the Pronouncement of Valera and other Californios against the Americans), which declared that Californios did not want an American-ruled Alta California; they wanted a Californio-controlled California.[73]

Varela and his militia, which grew to one hundred men, trapped Gillespie's men on Fort Hill. Surrounded and without water, Gillespie surrendered the next day. Defeated, Gillespie and his men marched to the Pacific Coast and retreated to a US Navy ship anchored in the San Pedro Harbor on September 30, 1846.

Upon hearing of Varela's expulsion of Gillespie, elite Californios José María Flores, Andrés Pico, and José Antonio Carrillo rejoined the fight. The three men assumed control over Varela's militia, which now numbered in the hundreds. By seizing the leadership of the militia, Carrillo and Pico hoped to keep elite Californios in power. José Antonio Carrillo was also a member of the Los Angeles and Santa Barbara Californio elite. Married to Estéfana Pico, Andrés and Pío's sister, Carrillo claimed multiple land grants and previously served as the Los Angeles alcalde three times.

Over the course of three months, the Californio militia achieved Pyrrhic victories. Most notably, the Californio militia rid Chino and Santa Bárbara of American sympathizers. Despite successes in Los Angeles and the surrounding areas, the Californio militia was outnumbered by US forces due to the continued refusal of elite Californios to leave their lands vulnerable to Indigenous raiding. In southern Alta California, Indigenous actions upended Californio war efforts more than US war strategy.

Indigenous leaders in southern Alta California sought to shape the outcome of the war in their favor. In December 1846, the Luiseño of Temecula met with US General Stephen Kearny at the Warner Ranch, in current-day San Diego County, and allied with the Americans.[74] While serving as a captain in the Californio militia, Antonio Coronel was attempting to avoid capture by Kearny's Army when he learned from Chief Alejo that "all the tribes in the area were up in arms on the American side."[75] This stoked age-old Californio fears of a unified Indigenous attack. Once in Los Angeles, Coronel sent an Indigenous servant to Andrés Pico in San Pasqual, a Kumeyaay village and the base of Californio operations near San Diego, to warn him of Kearny's impending arrival and the coming Indian uprising.

On December 6th, US and Californio forces fought at San Pasqual. Californio troops under General Andrés Pico and American troops under General Stephen Kearny faced off in an undecisive victory.[76] After the Battle of San Pasqual, Californio soldiers broke up into smaller groups and stole horses as they made their way back to their ranchos. One group, consisting of eleven elite Californios, some of whom were related to the Picos, stole horses from a Luiseño village. After the theft, they headed to Rancho Pauma, owned by elite Californio Juan Antonio Serrano. In the evening,

Luiseño chief Manuelito Cota led a troop of men and captured the Californios who stole their horses. The Luiseño took the captive Californios to Warner's Ranch where tribal leaders decided to execute the eleven soldiers. This event is now known as the Pauma Massacre.[77] While the exact motivation for these executions is unknown, it is likely that Cota and the other leaders decided to communicate to elite Californios that they would not tolerate the raiding of their horses and food. Rather than interpret Indigenous actions as motivated by their own political objectives, Californios feared that this attack meant the Americans were inciting uprisings.

Upon hearing of the Luiseño attack, General José María Flores ordered José Maria Lugo to deal with the Luiseño. Lugo, along with his brothers, held land grants in current day San Bernardino Valley, and to protect his rancho from Indigenous raids, they had developed an alliance with the Mountain Band of Cahuilla, led by Juan Antonio.[78] Historically, the Cahuilla and the Luiseño were enemies, and Juan Antonio agreed to aid Lugo in the pursuit of their traditional enemy. Together, in December 1846, Cahuilla and Californio soldiers killed one hundred Luiseño men at Temecula.[79] This event is known as the Temecula Massacre. This was the deadliest conflict of the US-Mexico War in Alta California.

After the Temecula Massacre, a rumor circulated that Antonio Garra, a well-known Cupeño chief, had allied with the US Army in response to the killings.[80] Again, one can only assume the impression this made on prominent Californios who had spent their lives trying to destroy these bands. As the Indigenous threat grew, an additional six hundred men joined the US forces in Alta California.

Overwhelmed by Indigenous maneuvers, José Antonio Carrillo and Andrés Pico capitulated to John C. Frémont on January 13, 1847, at Campo de Cahuenga. In the days leading up to the capitulation, the Pico family and Californio Bernarda Ruiz convinced Frémont to include terms favorable to the elite Californios in exchange for their cooperation. According to Frémont's memoirs, José Pico, a cousin of Andrés Pico, set up a meeting with Ruiz. At the meeting, she convinced Frémont to agree to "just and friendly terms of compromise" to make an "acceptable and enduring" peace. Ruiz stressed that property terms would be of great concern to her people, elite Californios.[81] Although Pico and Carrillo were wary of Frémont's intentions, they welcomed peace if it meant the protection of their property, and the three men signed the treaty.[82]

Indeed, the Treaty of Cahuenga included terms that Californios found "acceptable" and "friendly." Article I required Californios to "assist and aid [the

US Army] in placing the country in a state of peace and tranquility" in exchange for the "guaranteed protection of [Californio] life and property," regardless of one's involvement in the war. Elite Californios would collaborate with the US Army due to the property protections outlined in Article II.[83] Pico and Carrilo assumed that the US military's need for their assistance in suppressing the Indigenous would safeguard their property and rights. The Capitulation of Cahuenga did not end the war; it merely halted the fighting, as the war continued further south. The treaty established the terms of US military occupation in Alta California and marked the beginning of elite Californios' official collaboration with Anglo-American settlers.

Once the fighting ended, elite Californios sought to reclaim and protect their ranchos. During the fighting, the US military had seized Californio property and imprisoned Californio men. Notably, Salvador Vallejo, the brother of Mariano Guadalupe Vallejo, had his rancho seized for "public service" while a prisoner of war. To uphold the Capitulation at Cahuenga, John Frémont established a commission to deal with property destroyed and seized by the US during the war. In Los Angeles, at least seven Californios requested restitution payments.[84] After serving in the Californio Militia, Antonio Coronel, rather than lose his property, pledged loyalty to the US government and promised to assist the US Army in placing the country in tranquility.[85]

While elite Californios collaborated with US settlers, they did not concede authority to the US military. They acted to maintain as many Mexican laws and privileges as possible. In Los Angeles, Coronel worked with the occupying government as a member of the Board of Magistrates for Water Regulation where he interpreted, but did not alter, the pueblo water rights system for Anglo-American settlers.[86] In 1847, Santa Barbara elected Pablo de la Guerra as an alcalde along with his cousin Luis Carrillo, brother to José Antonio Carrillo. The military governor at the time, Stephen Kearney, accepted the results but demanded that they pledge to uphold the US Constitution. De la Guerra and Carrillo refused. Rather than risk a revolt, Kearney conceded, and they held the office without taking oaths to the US Constitution.

While de la Guerra and Coronel held civil positions and maintained Mexican laws, US soldiers and Californios attempted to control and contain Indigenous Californians throughout Alta California. Due to the influx of Anglo-American settlers in the north, raids increased. Now that a treaty had been signed, the US Army tried to suppress the raids it once supported. Californios assisted American efforts. In one instance, a group of thirty Californios joined the US Army to end the activities of "the horse thief Indians."[87]

In April 1847, Mariano Guadalupe Vallejo accepted the position as a US Indian sub-agent to aid the army in controlling the Indigenous. As a US Indian sub-agent, Vallejo worked with John Sutter, who had imprisoned him during the Bear Flag Revolt, to end the Indigenous horse raiding in the region.[88] Later in 1848, after residents of San Diego County requested protection from raids, US colonel Jonathan Stevenson called on Andrés Pico to protect eastern Los Angeles from Indian raids organized by Antonio Garra. Pico not only pursued Garra, he fined able-bodied, California men who refused to join the efforts.[89] It is likely that Pico, like all elite Californios, envisioned a postwar society where Californio men and Anglo-American men worked together to subdue the Indigenous.

While Californio men were willing to work with Anglo-Americans, women did not feel the same. In her memoir, Angustias de la Guerra recounted her anger with the Americans for disrespecting her male family members and imprisoning them. She did not appreciate their disregard for Californio norms and patriarchal authority. She declared that "Californians did not like the taking of the country at all, least of all the women," but that "the Indians were out of hand," indicating that the alliance was worthwhile since it ended the Indigenous raids afflicting the Southern California ranchos.[90] The Treaty of Cahuenga established a workable peace.

The Road to the 1849 California Constitution

The Treaty of Guadalupe Hidalgo ended the war between the United States and Mexico on February 2, 1848.[91] Under the treaty terms, the United States government now claimed authority over five hundred and twenty-five thousand square miles in the North American Southwest and about one hundred thousand Mexican and one hundred and fifty thousand Indigenous inhabitants. The expansionist Polk administration sent Nicolas Trist to negotiate on behalf of the United States. Lawyers José Bernardo Couto, Luis Gonzaga Cuevas, and Miguel de Atristain represented the collapsed Mexican government. During negotiations, the Mexican delegates prioritized protecting the citizenship and property rights of Mexican nationals who would fall under US authority.[92] Their negotiations resulted in three articles: Article IX, which transformed Mexican nationals into citizens; Article VIII, which required the protection of Mexican property rights; and Article X, which explicitly required the US government to honor and guarantee Mexican land grants.[93]

The January 1848 discovery of gold at Sutter's Mill near Sacramento enticed hundreds of thousands of US-born settlers to California just as the war ended.[94] These Anglo-American settlers had imagined they would simply set their stakes in unsettled, gold-rich lands in California. However, they were frustrated by Indigenous peoples and by the less than two hundred Californio families that claimed fourteen million acres of the "best" land. Much like the Bear Flag insurgents, Anglo-Americans described Californio landholding as a corrupt land monopoly.[95]

With the war over and a treaty that transformed all Mexican nationals into US citizens with rights, frustrated Anglo-American settlers made public demands for a new civil government. In December 1848, the *California Star* editors published an article advocating for the establishment of a new government, a government that would allow Anglo-Americans to pursue their settler dreams. The article accused the Californio population and a hybrid US-Mexican legal system of creating "anarchical" conditions.[96] Settlers also demanded "able and *reliable* laws" so that they could govern the "Indian."[97] However, US Congress refused to organize California into a state. The body did not want to upend the free-state and slave-state balance and determine whether or not slavery would exist in newly acquired territory.[98]

In Northern California, Anglo-American settlers took matters into their own hands and held numerous meetings throughout the territory to establish a civil government with new laws. In response, on June 3, 1849, civil governor Brig. Gen. Bennett Riley called for a state constitutional convention to be held.[99] During the months of July and August, citizens selected delegates in county elections. Northern California county residents, who had Anglo-American majorities, elected Anglo-American men. For example, San Francisco County elected William Gwin, a proslavery Southern politician with slave empire ambitions, as a delegate.[100]

In Southern California, elite Californios elected their own delegates. In Los Angeles, a junta comprised of forty-eight powerful and wealthy men, one of whom was Andrés Pico, selected Californio and Anglo men to serve as delegates.[101] The junta chose Abel Stearns, who shared Californio concerns, and elite Californios Manuel Domínguez and José Antonio Carrillo. In Santa Barbara, a junta selected Pablo de la Guerra. San Diego elected Miguel de Pedrorena. The juntas directed the delegates to protect Californio ranchos by retaining territory status for the south. Once elected, elite Californios traveled to Monterey where they intended to work with Anglo-Americans to preserve their gente de razón settler society.

PART II | Imagining California

CHAPTER TWO

"A Los Votantes Californios"

Californio Politics in 1850s California

Introduction

For ten days, in November 1849, strong rains battered California. Los Angeles experienced "one of the severest rainstorms ever witnessed" in the pueblo.[1] Throughout the state, roads turned muddy and rivers flooded settlements. Newspapers blamed the storm for keeping seven-eighths of the voting population from casting ballots for the newly drafted state constitution on November 13.[2] The voting population only included Anglo and Californio men; Black American settlers, Indigenous Californians, and women could not vote.

More than inclement weather, however, kept would-be voters from the polls. At polling locations, election officials challenged Californios' right to vote on the charge that they were not US citizens. Just outside Sacramento at Scollan's Camp, election officials forced men with Spanish surnames to prove they had been born in Alta California in order to vote. At Mokelumne's Lower Bar, election officials only allowed Californios to vote once they cited the Treaty of Guadalupe Hidalgo. In Chino, which was located in Los Angeles County, only one out of sixty-eight Californio men voted.[3]

Despite these initial obstacles to voting, this chapter first argues that during the 1850s, Californios participated in electoral politics and allied with the Democratic Party to insulate their local power from outsider colonial authority and to protect their patria chica.[4] Anglo members of the Democratic Party imagined California as a white settler state with American institutions and welcomed Californio participation to achieve their exclusionary goals. Rather than challenge the other's settler imaginary, in Southern California, elite Californio and Anglo-American settlers worked together to achieve a similar goal—the exclusion of Indigenous Californians, Black American settlers, and, increasingly, Chinese immigrants from political and social citizenship. As a result of this partnership, Californio and Anglo legislators crafted a body of laws that disenfranchised nonwhite residents. Notably, the state legislature prohibited Indigenous, Black, and Chinese residents from giving testimony in court.

As Anglo and Californio elites crafted their state, thousands of Black Americans who willfully and unwillingly migrated to California during and after the Gold Rush, brought their dreams of California as a freedom frontier and imagined themselves as full-fledged participants in the settler project, only to be denied citizenship rights. In Sacramento, Black activists, Mifflin Gibbs and Peter Lester, began a civil rights movement to extend citizenship rights, specifically the right to give testimony in court, to Black settlers and impose their political imaginaries on the state.[5] Anglo and Californio elites worked in tandem to counter this challenge to the racial hierarchy they had propped up with the 1849 Constitution.

During the same decade, tens of thousands of Chinese men also immigrated to California in search of gold. Chinese immigrants, who were mostly young men, pursued their dreams of making fortunes that would deliver their families from poverty.[6] As Chinese men forged lives in California, they, too, imagined themselves as members of a settler society with mobility rights that allowed them to build transpacific lives.[7] Although they publicly distanced themselves from other racialized groups, the California Supreme Court categorized them as nonwhite and, therefore, unentitled to citizenship rights. Black and Chinese political imaginaries challenged Californio and Anglo state making efforts, which resolidified the alliance between the two parties.

The chapter closes by returning to elite Californios on the eve of the US Civil War. As a result of the laws they helped create, elite Californios, such as Manuel Domínguez and Pío Pico, were denied their right to testify in San Francisco courts in the late 1850s. Rather than reconfigure their political alliances, elite Californios continued to work with Democrats because the party espoused politics that aligned with Californio notions of gente de razón—the party advocated for the subjugation and exploitation of inferior peoples. During the first decade of US statehood, Anglo and Californio settlers interpreted Black and Chinese efforts to expand the contours of citizenship as a challenge to their political imaginaries, and this is a primary reason for Californios' willingness to continue collaborating with men who rejected gente de razón as a privileged political status.

Deliberating Statehood

Two months before the heavy rains fell, in September 1849, forty-eight men met in Monterey, California, to draft a state constitution. Forty-one Anglo-American men and seven Californio men—Mariano G. Vallejo (Sonoma),

Manuel Domínguez (Los Angeles), Antonio Pico (San Jose), Jacinto Rodriguez (Monterey), Miguel de Pedrorena (San Diego), Pablo de la Guerra (Santa Barbara), José Covarrubias (San Luis Obispo), and José Antonio Carrillo (Los Angeles)—served as delegates.[8] With the agreement at Cahuenga still fresh in their minds, Californios participated in the convention to protect their property rights and political power. At the convention, each delegate attempted to establish a legal system that coincided with their settler imaginaries.

Serving as one of the Los Angeles delegates, José Antonio Carrillo was one of the most vocal advocates for the Californio population despite requiring a translator.[9] On September 4, 1849, the first day of business, Carrillo requested an increase in Los Angeles and Santa Barbara delegates due to the large Californio population. San Francisco delegate William Gwin, an enslaver with imperialist aspirations, proclaimed that "it was not for the native Californians [they] were making this Constitution; it was for the great American population, comprising four-fifths of the population of the country."[10] At the time, the Californio population was about twenty-five thousand compared to one hundred thousand gold-seeking migrants, sixty thousand of whom were US citizens. The largest group at the time, however, was Indigenous Californians, with a population estimated at one hundred and fifty thousand. Indeed, the constitution was not for the "native Californians" but for Anglo settlers with US citizenship, which, despite Gwin's claims, comprised only 25 percent of the population. The Anglo delegates killed Carrillo's first motion.

Refusing to be obstructed, Carrillo spoke again the next day. He claimed that his constituents, Californios residing in Los Angeles, did not want an American government; they wanted to retain their territory status. Because Californios preferred "the current hybrid system [and] did not wish to live under another Constitution," Carrillo made a motion to maintain territory status.[11] Again, the delegates voted against Carrillo's motion.

Carrillo made his final motion—to divide California at San Luis Obispo, making the northern portion a state and keeping the southern part as a territory. He argued that division would ensure Americans and Californios had their own laws and their own government.[12] In addition to attempting to maintain Mexican laws, Carrillo's efforts signified that Californios were worried about what would happen to their land and political power under Anglo rule. In response to Carrillo's motion, San Jose delegate Kimball Dimmick alleged that Californios "were nearly unanimous in favor of a State Government."[13] Anglo-American delegates accused Carrillo of misunderstanding his constituents, indicating that they did not care to take Californio demands seriously. Once more, Anglo-American delegates voted down Carrillo's motion.

Since they would not have territory status, Californio delegates acted to protect their political power within a new state. All along the way, however, Anglo-American delegates obstructed Californio efforts. During the convention, Californios had limited time to talk and did not receive adequate translations. Repeatedly, Californio delegates had to request recesses so that reports, which were printed in English, could be hastily translated into Spanish.[14]

On the third day of the convention, Californio and Anglo-American delegates debated about the incorporation of Mexican nationals as citizens with equal citizenship rights. San Francisco delegate Edward Gilbert, originally from New York, made a motion to allow every male citizen, not just every white male citizen, the right to suffrage. In the 1850s United States, the right to vote was a proxy for full citizenship. To make his point, Delegate Gilbert read aloud Articles VIII and IX of the Treaty of Guadalupe Hidalgo, arguing that it did not confer the right to suffrage but required the delegates to take action to ensure this right to all male Mexican citizens, regardless of whiteness.[15] In his attempt to ensure Californio equality, Gilbert said what many Anglo-American delegates believed—Californios were not white.

Anglo-American delegates struggled with incorporating mixed-race Californios because they imagined California as a white, rather than a gente de razón, settler state. In US society, the racial hierarchy was divided by a color line whereas in Alta California the racial hierarchy was divided by the razón line. In American society, the color line was constructed to determine one's social position at birth.[16] In Californio society, the razón line was constructed to afford the transformation of mixed-race settlers into gente de razón settlers. As a result, the delegates debated whether or not gente de razón and whiteness were equal statuses. Charles Botts, originally from Virginia and serving as one of the Monterey delegates, declared that the two statuses were not the same and motioned to keep "white" in the constitution.[17] Delegate William Gwin, rather than completely alienate the Californios present, deflected, stating that he "did not think the descendants of Indians should be excluded, but the pure uncivilized Indians should not be permitted to vote."[18] Los Angeles Delegate Stephen C. Foster, originally from Maine, agreed and argued that "very few of the Indian race should be admitted to the right of suffrage."[19] Gwin and Foster were willing to acknowledge that some Californios possessed proper class traits, if not racial traits, that allowed them to participate in politics.

As Anglo-American delegates questioned whether or not Californios could have citizenship rights given their mixed ancestries, Pablo de la Guerra demanded an explanation of whiteness from the delegates who were insinuating that Californios were unqualified to vote. With his demand, he also clarified how the gente de razón status functioned in Californio society, stating: "Many citizens of California have received from nature a very dark skin; nevertheless, there are among them men who have heretofore been allowed to vote, and not only that, but to fill the highest public offices. It would be very unjust to deprive them of the privilege of citizens merely because nature had not made them white. But if, by the word 'white' it was intended to exclude the African race, then it was correct and satisfactory."[20] De la Guerra's comment demonstrated that while Californio and Anglo-American delegates both viewed themselves as fit to govern, they did so according to different standards—whiteness and gente de razón. While the Californio delegates considered the two statuses to be interchangeable, the Anglo delegates did not. Hoping to protect the gente de razón status, the Californio delegates also demanded that the law be written to allow for Indians and descendants of Indians to be given the right to vote at a future date if the legislature deemed fit because, as they argued, "some of the first men in the Republic were of the Indian race."[21] As the Californio delegates acted to safeguard the privileges of gente de razón, they demonstrated their willingness to uphold whiteness by excluding people of African descent from citizenship.

The next day, the convention approved Pablo de la Guerra's wording of "Article II," which stated: "Every white male citizen of the United States, and every white male citizen of Mexico who shall have elected to become a citizen of the United States." They also approved the provision that affirmed that nothing should prevent the legislature "from admitting to the right of suffrage, Indians or the descendants of Indians."[22] While the delegation voted unanimously for this change, their reasoning differed. For de la Guerra and the other Californio delegates, this wording reflected their understanding that whiteness and gente de razón were interchangeable. For the Anglo-American delegates, the wording meant that only white men could vote.

After deciding that only white men could vote, the delegates discussed the status of people of African descent. All agreed that California would be a Free State but they had to decide if the constitution would allow for free Black men and women to reside or work in the state. The delegates in favor of prohibiting free Black settlers in the state wished to ensure that expansion and settlement into the region was a white-only enterprise. Delegate Henry Teft, originally from Wisconsin, claimed he wanted a white-only California because "negro labor, whether slave or free when opposed to white labor, degrades it."[23] Delegate O. M. Wozencraft argued, "If we don't want slavery, then we cannot welcome Africans."[24] There is no record of a Californio speaking in favor or against the prohibition, but de la Guerra had already articulated the Californio desire to "exclude" people of African descent from the rights of citizenship during the voting debate.

This opposition to free Black settlers reveals that Anglo-American settlers imagined the colonization of California as a white-only enterprise. As a Free State, the delegates believed that an absence of slavery and the presence of free Black migrants in California would undermine white labor and US citizens' claims to the territory. Californio and Anglo-American settler imaginaries did not include free Black settlers. Ultimately, the delegates did not exclude free Black migrants because they worried that such a provision would impede statehood.[25]

About a week later, the delegates debated whether women should have property rights in California. In Alta California, gente de razón women could claim property independently of her husband, father, brothers, and sons once they were twenty-five years of age.[26] The right to property afforded elite Californio women economic independence and, while few women became landowners, it solidified their investment in gente de razón society and patria chica.

After a lengthy debate, the delegates decided that the state constitution would retain a woman's right to own property separate from her husband.[27] Rather than a reflection of progressive gender politics, this law extended the right of private property to women to ensure permanent family settlements.[28] While some Anglo-American delegates viewed this right as a violation of marriage, others supported the right for the potential it had to safeguard white settlement, as it was a crucial tool of Mexican settlement in the region. During the convention, Angustias de la Guerra, in her capacity as a social broker, hosted nightly soirées and likely convinced Anglo delegates that they needed to preserve women's property rights; perhaps she even made clear to Anglo men that they could access elite families' estates through marriage.[29] Henry Tefft, who had married Eliza Josefa Dana Carrillo in 1848, was a strong proponent of the law and argued that the delegates "must take into consideration the feelings of the native Californians who have always lived under this law" when casting their final votes.[30] Tefft made clear that this was a positive for not just native Californian families but "all classes in California."[31] Anglo-American delegates agreed to retain the Mexican law that they thought would help them achieve their settler imaginaries.

Following this vote, Pablo de la Guerra acted to ensure Californio participation in government beyond the convention. He introduced a resolution that required the state to publish all laws in English and Spanish.[32] Initially, de la Guerra was met with resistance because, as one delegate declared, "the day will arrive soon when every man in the State will understand the English language."[33] De la Guerra made the case that whether or not people would learn English, they needed to understand the laws now. As a harbinger of their alliance to come, delegate Gwin offered support of de la Guerra's resolution, stating that Louisiana had published laws in English, French, and Spanish since becoming a US state. After Gwin's comments, the delegation unanimously decided to publish laws in English and Spanish. The Anglo-American delegates were eager not to alienate the Californio delegates, whom they still needed to successfully establish authority in the state, especially in the south.[34] The protection of the right to Spanish translation assured Californios that they could still participate in politics.

After a month of debate, the delegates had written a constitution that established a foundation for a white settler society. Once California's inhabitants approved the constitution in an election, it was sent to the US Congress for approval.[35] Miles away, in Washington, DC, US congressmen debated for nine months over how to bring California into the Union. Since the war with Mexico had begun in 1846, Southerners had threatened to secede if land came into the US without the possibility of slavery. Thus, the admission of California presented a crisis. In September, congressmen finalized the terms of the Compromise of 1850, which admitted California as a Free State, banned the slave trade in DC, allowed for the possibility of slavery in the Utah and New Mexico Territories, and enacted a stronger federal fugitive slave law.[36]

News of this compromise arrived on the morning of Friday, October 18, 1850, when a large mail steamer, the ss *Oregon*, pulled into the San Francisco Bay announcing California statehood by firing its cannons thirty-one times and hoisting a banner that proclaimed: "California is Admitted."[37] In northern cities, like San Francisco, Anglo-American settlers celebrated upon learning about California's admittance into the Union as the thirty-first state.[38]

In southern cities with Californio-majority populations, elite Californios worried what statehood meant for them. As the US Congress debated over admitting California into the Union, in March 1850, a Santa Barbara junta led by elite Californio Ygnacio del Valle sent a letter to the body requesting, again, that Southern California retain its territory status because the 1849 constitution would bestow upon them the "humiliating character of a colony."[39] The letter urged the congressional members to vote "against the admission of California as a state [because] the people of South California have been opposed to the state formation."[40] The junta echoed José Carrillo's arguments during the 1849 Constitutional Convention and requested that the "honorable body divide California [and create] a territory with the name of Central California, governed and protected like the other territories of the Union."[41] If the will of the people was not enough, the junta argued that the 1849 constitution violated the Treaty of Guadalupe Hidalgo because it would force Californios to "deliver up their lands in payment of taxes."[42] The letter received no response. With the arrival of statehood, elite Californios would have to find a way to maintain their political power under the 1849 California Constitution.

Californio Legislators and Voters

Despite apprehension about what statehood would mean for them, a handful of Californio elites ran for state office and won.[43] Their electoral victories depended on the Californio population of Southern California, with one exception, Mariano Guadalupe Vallejo, who won a senate seat in Sonoma, a northern district.[44] In Santa Barbara, where Californios made up 80 percent of the population, and in Los Angeles, where Californios made up 90 percent of the population, voters elected the same men who had governed before the US-Mexico War.

Pablo de la Guerra and his brothers maintained their role as patriarchs by participating in US government institutions. The Santa Barbara electorate sent de la Guerra to the California Senate from 1849 to 1861. When he served as the US marshal from 1853 to 1854, his brother, Antonio Maria de la Guerra, held his senate seat.[45] Antonio Maria de la Guerra and the Carrillo brothers occupied the Santa Barbara mayorship throughout the 1850s and '60s. Despite his initial apprehension, Ygnacio del Valle served in the state assembly in 1852.

In Los Angeles, elite Californios also dominated local politics. Although he did not serve in the first legislative session, Andrés Pico was elected as a state assembly member from 1851 to 1860. Los Angeles voted Antonio Coronel into many positions, including the mayor's office in 1853.[46] During the 1850s, the seven-person Los Angeles Common Council, the lawmaking body of the city, always had Californio members, with Manuel Requena serving as the president for five of those ten years.

During one of their first acts of legislative business, Senator Pablo de la Guerra, along with Santa Barbara representative José Covarrubias, acted to protect Californios' right to translation.[47] The ability to use Spanish meant Californios could conduct business, testify in the courtroom, and participate in electoral politics. On February 15, 1850, de la Guerra and Covarrubias created a joint committee to ensure that the legislature employed a qualified translator—despite Anglo-American resistance—and successfully safeguarded their rights to translation.[48]

As elected officials, elite Californios acted to preserve gente de razón as a privileged status not just by protecting their rights but by demonstrating that they shared a settler identity and interests with Anglo-Americans. In California, as in all of the West, dominating the Indigenous remained a crucial aspect of the settler identity. In his only session as a state senator, Mariano Guadalupe Vallejo of Sonoma cowrote the 1850 Act for the Government and Protection of Indians with John Bidwell. This law maintained the Mexican system of Indian slavery in a Free State. Vallejo and other elite Californios had used this system to keep their ranchos filled with servants, farmworkers, and valets.[49] The only other Californio senator, Pablo de la Guerra, voted for the bill, as it retained a central institution of Californio society.[50]

The 1850 Act contained multiple mechanisms to transform an Indigenous woman, man, or child into an unfree, racialized laborer under the guise of guardianship. Under this law, Anglo and Californio men kidnapped and enslaved countless Indigenous men, women, and children.[51] They also manipulated the law to enslave people of African descent in the Free State.[52] Californio and Anglo legislators worked together to codify this unfree labor system that targeted Indigenous Californians and became a crucial tool of genocide in the state.[53]

California legislators also set to drafting and passing laws designed to create a settler state that excluded people of African, Indigenous, and Chinese descent from the rights of citizenship. While Californio legislators cocrafted these laws to maintain gente de razón settler society, Anglo-American legislators cocrafted these laws to create a white settler state. For example, in 1852, the assembly and senate passed a state fugitive slave law, which voided the antislavery provision of the California Constitution and empowered enslavers to legally hold people as slaves. Many slaveholding southerners migrated to California with enslaved men and forced them to mine for gold. Californio assembly members José Covarrubias and Ygnacio del Valle voted for the bill, indicating they did not imagine free people of African descent as part of the settler project.[54]

In addition to excluding people of African descent from California, the legislature worked to exclude noncitizens from the gold fields and the spoils of settlement with the 1850 Foreign Miners' Tax. While the law applied to all noncitizens, enforcers targeted Spanish-speaking and Chinese immigrants with the twenty-dollar tax. Confronted with the discriminatory tax, by 1851, thousands of Mexican and Chilean immigrants abandoned the gold fields.[55]

In his memoirs, Antonio Coronel, who travelled north during the Gold Rush and made a small fortune, recounted tensions between various nationalities. He described anglophone prospectors as unable "to bear others' good fortune" and left the diggings after a group of Anglo-American men violently declared that Coronel's claim was theirs.[56] In the legislature, however, elite Californios assembly members emboldened such miners' behavior by voting in favor of the Miners' Tax.

After the repeal of the 1850 tax, the state legislature instituted another Foreign Miners' Tax in 1852, which remained in effect until 1870. The second tax empowered tax collectors to target Chinese miners with the three-dollar tax. The Foreign Miners' Taxes was the first legislative step in excluding people of Chinese descent from citizenship rights in California.

State legislators also excluded people of African, Chinese, and Indigenous descent from performing citizenship in the courtroom. Again, during its first session, the California state legislature passed "An Act Concerning Crime and Punishment," which forbade any "black or mulatto person, or Indian" from giving testimony in favor of or against any white person in any criminal case.[57] A year later, in 1851, the California legislature prohibited Black and Indigenous testimony in civil cases involving white litigants.[58] In the mid-nineteenth-century US, the right to give testimony meant an individual was entitled to the right of due process, could exercise the right to vote, and could freely make contracts. The ability to give testimony meant that one had the ability to perform citizenship and claim rights.[59] By supporting laws that disenfranchised racialized others, Californio legislators demonstrated their role as settler counterparts to their Anglo allies.

In addition to supporting legislation that cemented socioracial privileges, elite Californios allied with the Democratic Party, the party of slavery.[60] Andrés Pico and José Covarrubias had run for the California Assembly as Democrats in 1851.[61] While Pablo de la Guerra and Antonio Coronel not only ran as Democrats, they offered their resources to the state party. During the decade, Pico, de la Guerra, and Coronel functioned as local party leaders by attending state conventions, campaigning for votes, and donating money. After securing plenty of votes in the 1851 election, state Democratic leadership rewarded José Covarrubias by sending him to the 1852 National Convention in Baltimore as Santa Barbara's representative.[62] Given their power and wealth, Californios were assets to the state party.

In the 1852 presidential election, Franklin Pierce ran on the Democratic ticket against Winfield Scott, a Whig, and John Hale, a Free Soiler. In California, Andrés Pico fiercely campaigned for Pierce and the Democratic ticket. Pico devoted so much energy to the campaign that one newspaper predicted that few would forget to cast their ballot for Pierce on Election Day.[63] In Santa Barbara, the de la Guerras also endorsed a straight Democratic ticket. The Californio-majority counties of Los Angeles, Monterey, and Santa Barbara contributed to a Democratic and Pierce win in the state.[64]

The outcome of this election cemented the alliance between elite Californios and members of the California Democratic Party, especially the proslavery Chivalry (Chiv) faction. Senator William Gwin, the head of the Chivs, was interested in establishing an Anglo-American propertied aristocratic class that had local rule and authority over a subjugated class of people in California.[65] For Gwin and the Chivs, this system was plantation slavery undergirded by white supremacy; for Californios, this system was the rancho justified by the ideology of gente de razón. Prominent Californios and proslavery Anglo-American politicians worked together because their settler imaginaries were marked by commonalities.

Alternative Imaginings of California

By 1850, approximately one thousand people of African descent resided in California. During the California Gold Rush (1848–59), people of African descent migrated to the state in varying degrees of freedom. Historians estimate that about one-half of the population was enslaved.[66] Southern enslavers, empowered by state and federal laws, smuggled hundreds of enslaved people into the gold mines in the hopes of making a quick fortune from stolen labor.[67] The free Black settler community in California dreamed of achieving political and economic liberation through their settlement on what they imagined was free soil. The legal reality, however, moved Black settlers to build an activist network that forced local governments to uphold the state constitutional ban on slavery. Black political imaginaries challenged the ambitions of Californios and Anglo settlers and, in turn, reinforced their political partnership.

In northern cities, such as San Francisco and Sacramento, where a majority of the Black population settled, an activist Black middle class developed in the 1850s. Black settlers contested the category of settler and attempted to claim a more active role in the settler project. Notably, in 1858, the abolitionist community in San Francisco aided Archy Lee, whom Charles Stovall, an enslaver, trafficked from Mississippi to Sacramento in his quest for freedom.[68] In southern cities, the Black population was small—Los Angeles had just forty Black residents in 1852.[69] In contrast to the well-off Black middle class in San Francisco, Black residents in Los Angeles fostered a tight-knit, working-class community and attempted to carve their space in the gente de razón society.[70] Regardless of its small size, a Black activist network also emerged in LA, which famously aided Biddy Mason in her effort to free herself and her children from enslaver Robert Smith in 1856.[71]

Mifflin Gibbs attempted to transform California into the freedom frontier he imagined. Born in 1823 into a Black, middle-class family in Philadelphia, Gibbs migrated to California in 1850. Prior to moving west, Gibbs was active in the Underground Railroad, abolitionist circles, and civil rights movements.[72] He even went on the abolitionist speech circuit with Frederick Douglass in Rochester, New York. Upon learning of the discovery of gold in California, Gibbs decided to migrate west and seize the opportunities he imagined the land offered.[73] Upon arriving in the southern Sierra Nevada gold fields in late 1850, he tried to use his skills as a carpenter to make a comfortable life, but anti-Black racism, backed by the law, made this impossible. Gibbs left the gold mines and moved to San Francisco, where he opened the Emporium for Boot and Shoe with Peter Lester, a Black settler.

Peter and Nancy Lester had known Gibbs in Philadelphia before they also migrated to California in 1850 with their children. Peter Lester was born in South Carolina and grew up in Philadelphia. Nancy Lester was born in neighboring New Jersey and later moved to Pennsylvania. In Philadelphia, they made a family together and participated in abolitionist politics. In 1850, the Lesters uprooted their family because they imagined California as a frontier where they could make a new home and become full members of a settler society. Upon realizing that California did not provide the freedom they imagined, Peter and Nancy Lester transformed their San Francisco home into an activist headquarters. There, they held legal clinics in which they explained that, despite the claims of Anglo men, slavery was illegal in California.[74]

Portrait of Mifflin Gibbs in a three-piece suit taken in 1901. Courtesy of the Library of Congress.

Lester and Gibbs were part of the team that paid for Archy Lee's legal counsel in 1858.

Gibbs and Lester made the Emporium into a successful business. Their success, however, did not protect them from violence. On one occasion, a pair of white would-be customers entered the Emporium and beat Lester with a cane. In his memoir, Gibbs lamented that during the assault, Lester chose not to fight back because doing so risked deadly violence. Afterward, their inability to give testimony resulted in a miscarriage of justice.[75] This instance of racial violence was likely the Anglo settler's attempt to squash Black success that challenged his white settler imaginary.

Such violence was common in California because the ban on Black testimony meant impunity for white assailants. In December 1850, this kind of violence targeted Sarah Carroll, a prosperous Black woman. In the US Census, Carroll was categorized as a free mulatto.[76] William Potter, a white man, robbed Carroll of gold coin amounting to $610, a gold breast pin with a diamond, and six chemise buttons. While details of the actual robbery are scant, Carroll reported the crime and Justice of the Peace Charles Sackett ordered Sacramento law enforcement to arrest Potter. Potter was caught and brought to court. Despite having Carroll's property, the very same judge discharged Potter as "he prov[ed] himself a white man and [there was] none but colored testimony against him."[77]

As Lester's and Carroll's cases demonstrate, Black men and women faced dire circumstances because they could not testify against white men. Thus, Black settlers took action to protect their community members. Black activists, including Mifflin Gibbs and Peter Lester, formed a western branch of the Franchise League and began a petition campaign to end the prohibition on Black testimony.[78] On March 22, 1852, Representative Patrick Canny of Placer County brought the Franchise League's petition to the California Assembly, stating, "The Free Negroes of San Francisco prayed for a change in the laws to authorize them to give testimony against white men." The assembly rejected the resolution by a vote of forty-seven to one.[79] Californios assemblymen Andrés Pico, Ygnacio del Valle, and José Covarrubias—who believed that Black men and women were neither entitled to such rights nor able to challenge patriarchal authority—voted to reject this resolution.

A year later, in 1853, assembly member W. C. Meredith of Tuolumne County presented another Franchise League petition demanding the repeal of the testimony statute. This time, George Carhart of Colusa County ordered the clerk not to file the petition under official business because it would tarnish the Assembly Journal.[80] The votes were not recorded, but Californio Assembly members Andrés Pico and José Covarrubias were among the men who did not object to this motion, once again upholding Californio and Anglo settler imaginaries.

As Anglo-Americans and Californios throughout the state used the testimony prohibition to assert their superiority over people of African descent, they began to employ the law to construct Chinese immigrants as racialized others unfit for citizenship rights. During the first five years of statehood, about twenty-five thousand Chinese men immigrated to California. The loss of the First Opium War (1839–42), as well as subsequent natural disasters, famine, and the Taiping Rebellion (1850–64), produced a myriad of hardships for Chinese families. California's specter of gold drew many Chinese men eastward to the state. Chinese immigrants imagined California as a place where they could build fortunes and return to China.

For some Anglo settlers, Chinese laborers did not have a role in their political imaginaries. Just a month after the California Assembly members rejected the Franchise League's petition to change the testimony law, Governor John Bigler addressed the state legislature. His speech rested on one point—Chinese immigration to California needed to stop.[81] Bigler asserted that Chinese immigrants threatened the state's prosperity and safety because a majority of them were coolies (unfree, contracted laborers) who did not intend to settle in the state.[82] Unfit for and unwilling to be citizens, Bigler imagined Chinese immigrants as a threat to white settler society.

While many Chinese immigrants initially intended to return to their home countries with wealth that would change their families' lives, once in California, they began to imagine themselves as part of and beneficial to the American settler project.[83] In a defiant response to Bigler's message, a pair of Chinese merchants, Hab Wa and Long Achick, declared that they had assimilated into American society by learning English and Anglo-American social customs, that Chinese immigrants were not coolies, and that some Chinese men had, indeed, already become citizens. The letter closed by stating that "very good Chinamen were in [California] and if allowed" more men would come with their families and would acquire American habits, language, ideas, religion, and "become citizens."[84] In California, Chinese immigrants imagined themselves as a part of the Anglo-American settler project. Despite such public statements, Anglo and Californio settlers did not incorporate Chinese immigrants into their political imaginaries because they neither possessed the traits of whiteness nor gente de razón. The *Daily Alta California* editors wrote that the Chinese were "mentally inferior to whites" and unlike "the negro, [and] less fit to become . . . servants."[85]

Anti-Chinese prejudice manifested itself as violence.[86] In 1853, George Hall, an Anglo settler, attempted to rob Ling Sing and three other Chinese miners. During the robbery attempt, Hall killed Sing while the other miners escaped with injuries. A court convicted George Hall of murdering Sing on the basis of the testimony the three other Chinese miners offered.

After this conviction, Hall filed an appeal with the California Supreme Court. In 1854, California Supreme Court Justice Hugh Murray reversed Hall's conviction because "Chinese testimony was inadmissible" according to a state law that provided "no Black or Mulatto person, or Indian, shall be allowed to give evidence in favor of, or against a white man."[87] Justice Murray noted that the "racial identifiers" of the Chinese indicated that Indians and "Asiatics" were "the same type of human species." Murray continued, explaining the intention of the California legislature, by clarifying that "black" "excludes all races other than the Caucasian." With this decision, Judge Murray expanded the legal construction of "black" to include people with Chinese ancestry and transformed Chinese immigrants into nonwhite noncitizens.[88] When confronted with alternative imaginings of settler society, Anglo and Californio legislators and judges doubled down on codifying a white settler society.

Chinese immigrants challenged the ban on testimony and the racial categorization imposed on them by the *People v. Hall* case. In 1855, a Chinese merchant living in San Francisco, Lai Chun-Chuen, openly published a sixteen-page letter, "Remarks of the Chinese Merchants," that responded to Bigler's continued anti-Chinese rhetoric and the 1854 *Hall* decision.[89] First, Chun-Chuen addressed the common misperception that all Chinese immigrants were coolies. Chun-Chuen assured the reader that Chinese men worked for themselves.[90] Next, Chun-Chuen distanced the Chinese from racialized "Indians and Negroes," arguing that the Chinese possessed more in common with "whites" because they came from a civilization that "for many thousands of years" had philosophers, a civil government, military institutions, and a wealthy and famous "civilization."[91] Therefore, Americans were wrong in considering Chinese immigrants "equal with [the] uncivilized race of men," meaning the Indigenous.[92] According to Chun-Chuen, Chinese immigrants were members of a superior society and entitled to settler privileges in California.

In the same year that Chun-Chuen claimed whiteness, Mifflin Gibbs and Peter Lester called for a California Colored Convention.[93] The first Colored Convention occurred in Philadelphia in 1830 and grew into the first civil rights movement in the United States. Gibbs's and Lester's participation in Colored Conventions in eastern cities prepared them to launch a movement in California.[94] The California Colored Convention announcement was a call to action. Black Americans had "migrated to the shores of the Pacific" to better their condition, only to encounter a "continuous series of outrages, injustices, and unmitigated wrongs." Now, they needed to devise a strategy "to obtain [their] inalienable rights and privileges in California"—to realize their political imaginaries.[95]

On November 20, 1855, fifty-four delegates gathered in Sacramento for the state's first Colored Convention. The fifty-four Black men represented ten northern gold-mining counties.[96] William H. Yates served as the president of the convention. Yates was born into slavery in Virginia and, after earning his freedom, moved to Washington, DC, where he worked as a porter for the US Supreme Court. As a porter, he earned the money to manumit his wife, Emeliner, and their children.[97] As a free person, he had assisted fugitive slaves on the Underground Railroad in Pennsylvania. Upon moving to California in 1851, he quickly became a leading abolitionist in San Francisco.[98] The secretary of the convention, Reverend Jeremiah B. Sanderson, had been a member of the abolitionist movement in Massachusetts and, after arriving in California in 1854, had started a campaign for public education across the state.[99]

At the convention, the delegates espoused moderate liberation politics to prove their competency for citizenship and utility to the settler state. Adopting a "propriety" tone, the delegates declared that they had assimilated into whiteness and, therefore, were fit for citizenship.[100] In his opening remarks, President William Yates reflected: "If there are feelings of liberty within the breasts of those present, who but the Caucasian taught them to us?"[101]

Over the course of three days, the delegates planned a campaign to extend testimony rights to Black settlers. They decided that they would first grow their organization and, second, continue the petition campaign but, third, would organize Anglo-American support. To recruit support, the delegates published the "Address to the People of California," which aimed to convince Anglo-American settlers that the testimony ban was "an injury to the white man" because it also subverted justice for them.[102] Moreover, Black settlers in California deserved the right to testimony because they had provided labor, in the sum of $3 million, to the state. If that were not enough, the Black settlers had "acquired most of the [Anglo-American's] manners and customs."[103] The delegates argued that they had proved themselves worthy of citizenship rights by assimilating into whiteness and contributing to the settler state.

After the convention concluded, delegates Jonas Townsend and Mifflin Gibbs started the state's first African American newspaper, the *Mirror of the Times*, which would serve as the public engine of this burgeoning civil rights movement. Newspapers already published descriptions of cases in which Anglo men committed crimes but did not suffer legal consequences because of the testimony ban.[104] Now the *Mirror* would provide editorial content to drive the movement. Given their anti-Black prejudices, Californios likely never read the *Mirror*, nor were supportive of Black claims to citizenship rights.[105] While there are no letters or speeches mentioning the testimony rights and Black Americans, it is likely the Californios did not give these rulings a second's thought given their legislative record.

In 1857, the US Supreme Court delivered the *Dred Scott* decision, effectively transforming all people of African descent into noncitizens. In light of this decision, free Black California residents rethought their strategy. Black Californians paused their testimony campaign in light of diminishing returns, and the statutes remained on the books until 1862. (The state legislature would change the statute in response to another petition campaign.) Mifflin Gibbs, Peter and Nancy Lester, and as many as eight hundred free Black settlers migrated to the British colonies of Vancouver Island and

British Columbia in search of gold, permanent freedom, and citizenship in another settler state that did not exclude them on the basis of race.[106] Anglo-American and Californio lawmakers, with the help of the US Supreme Court, had successfully created a legal framework that squashed alternative settler imaginaries. The remaining free Black settlers and Chinese immigrants would have to live in California as racialized outsiders.

Californios at a Crossroads

As Black and Chinese settlers attempted to expand who could legitimately claim a settler identity, elite Californios traveled north to San Francisco to testify before the US Land Commission in an effort to retain their land claims guaranteed by the Treaty of Guadalupe Hidalgo. In 1851, as California senator William Gwin introduced legislation that required all Mexican land grant claimants to prove their landholding was legitimate. Congress voted in favor of the 1851 US Land Act, which, in addition to imposing an immense financial burden on Californios, established a verification process that reinforced Anglo-American settler assumptions that Californios were unsuitable landholders due to their inherent incompetence.[107] In the Anglo-American majority city of San Francisco, Californios experienced the consequences of the testimony laws they coapproved as legislators.

In 1857, Manuel Domínguez, a Californio who had participated in the California Constitutional Convention, traveled to San Francisco to give testimony in a land claims case. Domínguez claimed a vast land grant known as Rancho San Pedro.[108] A prominent Californio, Domínguez held numerous political positions and was serving as an LA County supervisor when he arrived in San Francisco. Before Domínguez could take the stand, however, the lawyer for the plaintiff made a motion to prohibit Domínguez from giving testimony against his client on the grounds that his "Indian blood" made him an incompetent witness. The judge accepted the lawyer's claim and dismissed Domínguez, stripping him of one of his citizenship rights and gente de razón status.[109]

Pablo de la Guerra, upon learning of the San Francisco court's treatment of Domínguez, delivered a protest speech to the state senate.[110] Serving as a Democratic senator, de la Guerra reminded his fellow senators that Californios had "accepted the American rule with all candor and single heartedness"—in other words, as collaborators—yet they were "treated as a conquered and inferior race." De la Guerra reminded his fellow senators

Portrait of Manuel Dominguez. Dominguez wears a three-piece suit as an indication of his gente de razón status. It is likely that he looked like this when he appeared in court. Photo courtesy of University of Southern California Library and California Historical Society.

that this was not appropriate treatment for members of the gente de razón settler class. Aware of how Anglo settlers were marking Californios as racial others, he criticized Anglo statesmen for treating Californios as an inferior class just because they "spoke Spanish."[111] Rather than advocate for getting rid of the law, de la Guerra asserted the Californios' membership in settler society, arguing that such treatment should be reserved for members of "conquered and inferior race[s]"—meaning Indigenous, Black, and Chinese residents.

De la Guerra was not the only Californio outraged by the treatment of Domínguez. The leading liberal, Spanish-language newspaper, *El Clamor Público,* edited by Francisco P. Ramírez, described the San Francisco court's treatment of Domínguez as "anti-republican and anti-liberal." Ramírez, while lamenting the court's treatment of Domínguez, also condemned Domínguez, stating he "excluded himself from the enjoyment of citizenship by lending his signature to the approval of the law."[112] In contrast to de la Guerra, in *El Clamor Público,* Ramírez framed Domínquez's experience in the San Francisco court as a civil rights issue rather than a violation of the settlers' alliance. Ramírez, unlike the elite Californios in the state legislature, did not identify as a ranchero or gente de razón settler and supported the Black and Chinese testimony movement.[113]

In light of the attacks on their claims to citizenship, elite Californios recommitted to their alliance with the state Democrats. Elite Californios had no desire to support policies that did not allow them to dominate people they viewed as inferior. As Anglo-American settlers in the northern part of the state challenged Californio citizenship, in the south, the Democratic state party continued to treat Californios as a crucial voting bloc and made overtures in Spanish. During the 1857 election, the party printed a pamphlet entitled "A Los Votantes Californios y Mexicanos," which advised on the three-way race for governor. John B. Weller ran on the Democratic ticket, Edward Stanly ran on the Republican ticket, and George Washington Bowie ran on the Know-Nothing ticket.[114] The pamphlet encouraged Californios to vote for the Democrat Party because "the welfare of the country" was at stake and Democratic candidates "Don Juan G Downie [*sic*]," "Don Abel Stearns," and "Don J. Lancaster Brent" would squash out "the cancer that gnaws at the heart of their community."[115] The pamphlet's use of "Don" signifies that the party performed Californio cultural norms to earn their votes. In response, Californios continued to support the Democratic ticket, and Weller became governor with a notable 90 percent of the vote in Los Angeles, Santa Barbara, and San Diego.

At the end of the decade, Californio support for the Democratic Party began to fracture. Notably, Pío Pico allied with the California Republican Party, which ex-Whigs and ex-Free Soilers created in 1854 because the party opposed using filibusterism—the strategy of inciting revolution to annex territory to the United States—in Latin American and "greaser laws," which aimed to strip Spanish speakers of their citizenship rights.[116] As early as October 1856, Pío Pico penned a public letter in *El Clamor Público* and argued that because the Republican Party consisted of men who respected the gente de razón status, they should vote for John Frémont, the Republican presidential candidate. Pico asked his fellow "hijos del país" to recall that during the military occupation of Los Angeles, Frémont was the only US official to treat Californios with "consideration and benevolence" and that he accepted the terms of the Treaty of Cahuenga.[117] Thirty-two Los Angeles-based Californios signed on to Pico's letter; his brother Andrés Pico did not.

Allying with the Democrats did not serve Pío Pico. In 1859, Pío Pico was apprehended by a marshal and dragged to a San Francisco court. There,

Judge Ogden Hoffman ordered him to give testimony.[118] According to *El Clamor Público,* Pico did not know why he was arrested until he arrived in the courtroom and was ordered to fulfill a summons he initially failed to keep due to ill health. The court did not free Pico until a Southern California lawyer, Lancaster Brent, filed a writ of habeas corpus.[119] In this instance, a Northern California judge arrested and forced an elite Californio to give testimony for the benefit of the court, demonstrating dominance over the group.

Despite these attacks on Californio citizenship in the northern part of the state, the majority of elite Californios continued to work with the Democrats because they made overtures in Spanish and supported laws that allowed Californios to dominate inferior peoples in the southern part of the state. In 1860, as state and national politics fractured over slavery and the settlers' alliance fractured over racial regimes, Californios were again at a crossroads. In a public letter, Enrique Ávila, a prominent Californio from Los Angeles, wrote to Californios, explaining the ins and outs of the Los Angeles political landscape and what was at stake in this election.[120] Antonio Coronel and Ygnacio del Valle were two of the six elite Californios who signed onto the public letter.

A staunch Democrat, in the letter, Ávila explained that the hijos del país were "extremely democratic [*sic*]" and that their votes had "sustained" the party ticket in the last election.[121] In return, the Democrats helped elect "Don Andrés Pico a Californio for Senate, Don Tomas Sanchez a Californio for Sheriff, Don Cristóbal Aguilar and Don Antonio Coronel for supervisors." According to Ávila, the Californio-Democrat alliance still held, and the Republicans, which was the squatter's party, would not "protect" Californio interests as a landed class.

Ávila closed the letter stating the "Republican Party spoke too highly of the 'negro.'"[122] He warned the Californio voter that the Republicans "want[ed] to do with the negro what the Mexican government did with the Indians and the missions in California." According to Ávila, emancipation would transform enslaved people into "the plague of society" as he thought secularization had done for the Mission Indians. As the decade closed, despite Pío Pico's efforts, Ávila and other prominent Californios believed the only way to prevent the destruction of their patria chica and their gente de razón privileges would be to vote for the Democratic Party.

As Pico's and Ávila's letters make clear, at the end of the decade, Californios had created a political quagmire for themselves. Californio visions of patria chica had survived the first decade of US rule because elite Californios, like de la Guerra and Domínguez, supported laws that upheld the privileged status of whiteness and rejected Black and Chinese political imaginaries. However, in doing so, Californios tethered their aspirations of patria chica to a Democratic Party whose Anglo members increasingly failed to view their gente de razón allies as counterparts.

CHAPTER THREE

"The Whole Californian Population Is Disaffected with Our Institutions"

The 1850s Southern California Land Conflict

During the 1850s, just east of the San Gabriel River where present-day Whittier and Pico Rivera are located, Pío Pico resided in a two-story adobe, *El Ranchito*, surrounded by a beautiful garden. Pico inhabited El Ranchito after the US-Mexico War ended and remained there until flood waters damaged the adobe house in the 1860s. Prior to its destruction, Pico welcomed prominent Anglo-American and Californio guests to El Ranchito for social gatherings and walks through the rows of fruit trees and vines that covered the nearly ten-thousand-acre land grant.[1] El Ranchito, like all ranchos, was a small country where Pío Pico's patriarchal authority ruled supreme. El Ranchito depended upon the labor of at least one hundred Indigenous men and women who worked and irrigated the fields, raised herds of cattle and horses, and maintained the household. One observer remarked in 1859 that Pío Pico ran his estate as if he were a "feudal lord."[2]

Throughout the nineteenth century, elite Californios such as Pico, managed their ranchos on the edge of the Indigenous world while dealing with numerous challenges. After the heyday of the Gold Rush, tens of thousands of Anglo-American settlers traveled south and attempted to settle on what they imagined was free land. In this chapter, I contend that these settlement attempts, which threatened the foundation of the gente de razón settler society and the tense status quo between Californio and Indigenous communities, sparked a Southern California land conflict. Elite Californios and Indigenous bands asserted their claims to the land while Anglo-American settlers weaponized US institutions to open lands to their settlement. Most notably, in response to Anglo-Americans' demands, in 1851, the US Congress created the US Land Commission to nullify Californio property rights enshrined in the Treaty of Guadalupe Hidalgo.

Initially, prominent Californios interpreted these challenges as reneging on the alliance made at Cahuenga. In turn, elite Californios in Southern California pursued long-established strategies, such as a political campaign for state division, to protect their lands from Anglo-American settlement. However, the increase in Californio and American incursions into the Indigenous

Antonio Coronel's home, El Recreo, ca. 1870. El Recreo projected Coronel's power and wealth. The adobe is surrounded by an orchard, which conveys Coronel's proper utilization of the land. Not pictured are the laborers who maintained the rancho. Photo courtesy of University of Southern California Library and California Historical Society.

world prompted the Cupeño, Cahuilla, and Luiseño to adopt timeworn tactics, such as strategic raids and alliance-making, to expel Anglo and Californio settlers. In 1851, Antonio Garra, the leader of the Cupeño, attempted to organize a pan-Indigenous uprising to thwart the new waves of colonization. In turn, elite Californios set aside their campaign for state division and worked with Anglo-American settlers to suppress Indigenous power. With this decision, elite Californios did not abandon their efforts to protect their settler society; rather, they chose to suppress Indigenous power to protect their already-established patria chica as they had done numerous times before. In their attempt to suppress Indigenous power, Californios unintentionally legitimized the white settler state and compromised their own claims to the land.

The Indigenous World of Southern California

To understand the 1850s Southern California land conflict, one needs to understand the Indigenous world during Spanish and Mexican colonization. Prior to and after European colonization, in present-day San Diego, Riverside, and San Bernardino Counties, Kumeyaays, Cahuillas, Mojaves, southern Paiutes, and Yokuts traded with each other. In the late eighteenth century, Spanish Franciscans established missions on the territories of the Kumeyaay, Cupeño, Luiseño, Cahuilla, Tongva, and Chumash (present-day San

Diego, Los Angeles, and Santa Barbara). At first, individual bands established friendly trade relations with Spanish padres, which fell apart after the priests directed the building of more missions, destroyed foodways, and enslaved and harmed Indigenous peoples. During the centuries-long conflict for territorial control and political and economic autonomy, Indigenous actors came together to destroy the missions.[3] Notably, in 1775, allied Kumeyaay villages destroyed the San Diego Mission, killing three Franciscan priests.[4] The mission was later rebuilt.

After Mexican independence, power relations once again evolved. In 1833, the Mexican government adopted a policy of secularization in Alta California. As written, the law required missions to be converted into pueblos and private lands, which were to be distributed among the Indigenous who had labored in one of the twenty-one missions. Under the secularization law, Indigenous communities could form pueblos and elect an alcalde who served as the political head. The law established the position of an ex-mission administrator, tasked with redistributing the land and maintaining Indigenous laborers to tend to the vineyards, fields, and herds of cattle on rancho lands. The governor nominated prominent Californios as ex-mission administrators.

In 1835, Pío Pico became the administrator of Mission San Luis Rey, located in present-day Oceanside, a city in San Diego County.[5] Pico, like other ex-mission administrators, distributed lands to members of his compadrazgo networks and forced Indigenous laborers to work without compensation. Throughout Southern California, the Pico brothers were known for whipping Indigenous laborers on their ranchos.[6] Julio César, a Luiseño at San Luis Rey, described Pico as "the very worst" Californio administrator.[7] A group of Luiseños told Eugene Duflot de Moras, a French explorer who visited Alta California in 1840, they were "miserable" and "those in power rob[bed them]."[8]

Despite the Picos' efforts to control them, the Luiseños at the Temecula village of the ex-Mission San Luis Rey formed a pueblo and elected Pablo Apis as alcalde. In 1836, Apis sued Pico for mistreatment and the misappropriation of property. The Luiseños utilized Mexican political institutions to assert their political power and land claims. In retaliation, Pico had Apis arrested. When a horde of Luiseños demanded Apis's release outside the prison, Pico balked and released the Luiseño alcalde. Rather than cower to Indigenous power, he later enlisted San Diego troops to arrest Apis and other Luiseño men.[9]

As the Luiseños attempted to use the Mexican legal system to reclaim their lands in the decade after secularization, other Indigenous bands took advantage of the political instability and raided ranchos throughout San Diego County.[10] In 1837, Kumeyaay raiders burned Pico's Rancho Jamul, about twenty miles from San Diego, killing four people and kidnapping two. As big a blow as this was to Pico, he could not quell the attacks, as he was in prison for his role in a Southern California rebellion against the governor of Alta California. A few years later, during the summer of 1839, a group of three hundred Indigenous raiders threatened the Estudillo family's Rancho Otay, located in current-day San Diego County. Outnumbered, the Estudillo family abandoned the rancho and retreated to the presidio of San Diego, never to return.[11]

About seven years later, just after the Capitulation at Cahuenga, Cahuilla, Kumeyaay, and Mojave bands increased the raids they conducted in San Diego, Santa Barbara, and Los Angeles to expand the Indigenous world in light of the Californios' weakened position.[12] Given the terms of the Treaty of Cahuenga, elite Californios expected the US Army to protect their ranchos. On June 22, 1847, prominent San Diego Californios J. J. Warner and José Antonio Estudillo wrote to military governor Richard B. Mason requesting protection for Californio land and livestock from raids led by Cupeño chief Antonio Garra.[13] In response, Colonel J. D. Stevenson summoned Garra to Los Angeles. After negotiations, Garra agreed to end raiding on the condition of receiving good treatment from the US Army. To the Californios of San Diego and Los Angeles, Colonel Stevenson's actions demonstrated that the US Army was a valuable ally, in that it protected their land claims from Indigenous challenges. However, the arrival of tens of thousands of Anglo settlers at the end of the US-Mexico War and statehood would strain these agreements.

The 1851 US Land Act

Throughout California, the existence of vast Californio ranchos in places such as Sonoma, Monterey, Los Angeles, and San Diego undermined Anglo settlers' dreams of acquiring land. Given their cooperation during the war, elite Californios assumed that Anglo-American settlers would respect their landholdings and aid them in their efforts to contain, if not shrink, the Indigenous world. Newly arrived Anglo settlers, unbeholden to the military alliance made at Cahuenga, demanded the end of Californio and Indigenous landholding.

Even before statehood, Anglo settlers demanded that the government open Mexican land grants to settlement. They argued that unsophisticated

Californio landholding hindered Anglo settlement. As early as 1847, the *California Star* published a letter by "PAISANO" (meaning peasant of Spanish origin), which criticized Californios' "unbounded" grants for making Anglo settlement impossible.[14] The PAISANO letter demanded the creation of a land grant certification system that would open land to Anglo settlers as the federal government did in Oregon. Later, in 1848, another *California Star* column, this time by "Sober Second Thought," condemned the military government for upholding Mexican land claims. The writer described Californio officials as using their position "for the most dishonest, unjust, and infamous schemes ever carried on under the sacred name of law and courts of justice."[15]

Government reports, not just settlers, characterized Californio landholding as uncivilized. In 1849, at the demands of Anglo-American settlers, military governor Richard Mason ordered Henry Halleck, one of the era's preeminent legal military minds and the serving military secretary of the state in California, to write a report that would guide the state government in its regulation of private and public lands.[16] On April 13, 1849, Halleck published the *Report on Land Titles in California,* which reinforced the idea that the Mexican land grant system was unsophisticated and that Californios were prone to corruption and incapable of landholding according to Anglo-American agrarian republican ideals.[17]

In his report, Halleck substantiated that a majority of Mexican titles were illegitimate because they relied on *diseños*—maps that documented the parts of a land grant according to geographical markers—rather than precise units of measurement. Halleck explained that a large number of diseños were hastily drawn and "frequently contain double the amount of land included in the grants."[18] Halleck concluded that Californios' "carelessness" and incompetence resulted in a large amount of "unapproved" grants.[19] If the titles were honored by the US government, Halleck argued, the "growth and prosperity" of white settlements, like San Francisco, would be jeopardized.[20] To abet Anglo settlement, Halleck suggested the creation of a tribunal tasked with adjudicating the validity of Californio grants. Halleck did not address the fact that such a tribunal would violate the Treaty of Guadalupe Hidalgo.[21]

In addition to casting doubt on Californios' land claims, Halleck characterized Californios, especially ex-Alta California governor Pío Pico, as inherently corrupt. Halleck wrote that, according to a "very respectable authority," Pico illegally distributed land grants "*after* the United States had taken possession of the country." Halleck based this accusation on an 1848 letter

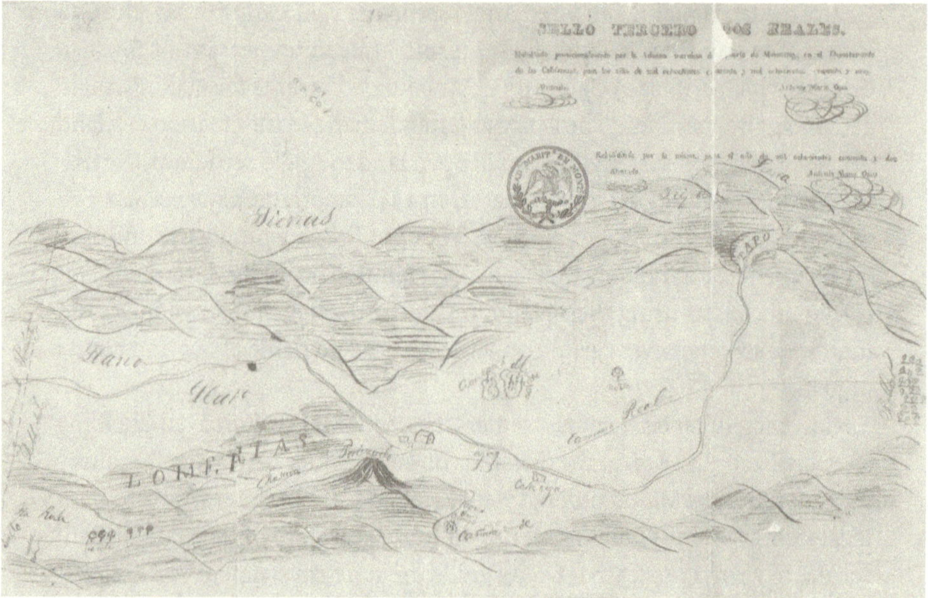

Diseño del Rancho Simi. The de la Guerra family claimed Rancho Simi. This diseño is emblematic of the maps created to confirm the Mexican land grants. Geographical markings delineate the boundaries of the grant. The diseño has an official government stamp, meaning the Mexican government approved the grant. Courtesy of the Bancroft Library.

from Colonel J. D. Stevenson, which, before accusing Pico of illegal behavior, described the ex-governor as unintelligent and "about five feet seven inches, corpulent, very dark, with strongly marked African features."[22] Halleck's accusations against Pico further legitimized racializing language about Californios as incapable of landownership.[23]

Halleck's report emboldened Anglo-American settlers' calls for a new property regime because it supported their prejudgments of Californios as unintelligent and racially debased.[24] Anglo-Americans had already begun constructing Californios as a racially inferior class incapable of landownership in popular travel literature.[25] For example, Lansford Hastings wrote in *The Emigrants' Guide to Oregon and California* that "ignorance" was one of "the chief ingredients" of the Californio character and that they possessed complexions from "the African black, to the tawny brown of our southern Indians."[26] Halleck was upholding the already-established aspersions made against Californios. After the publication of Halleck's report, the *Daily Alta California* followed suit and criticized the protection of Mexican land claims because it perpetuated Californio disuse. The paper claimed that if lands were made available to "patriotic" Anglo-American settlers, they would "make gardens of the waste."[27]

After California became a state in 1850, Anglo settlers called on the US Congress, a body that had little interest in upholding Californio property rights, to take action. Before ratifying the Treaty of Guadalupe Hidalgo, US president James K. Polk recommended that the US Senate strike out Article X, which explicitly protected land grant claims. Polk reasoned that the article would invalidate Anglo-American landholding in Texas.[28] Upon learning that the US Senate struck out Article X, Mexican officials demanded an explanation and required the Protocol of Querétaro to be added to the treaty. The Protocol of Querétaro declared that the US government's revisions did not "annul" land grants in ceded territories and did not change the spirit of the treaty's original terms.[29] However, when President Polk sent the treaty to Congress on July 4, 1848, for official proclamation, he did not include the protocol. Speaking on the matter six months later, US secretary of state John Clayton claimed the United States had no obligation to uphold the protocol and, therefore, or recognize Mexican land claims.[30]

California's first senators, John C. Frémont and William Gwin, answered Anglo-American settlers' demands to enact policies that made Californio and Indigenous lands available to Anglo-American settlers. In December 1850, four months after the Squatter Riots erupted in Sacramento, Senator Gwin read a squatter's letter that demanded the US Senate open land grants to preemption.[31] Gwin declared that if the Senate did not act in regard to land titles, a "great injustice will be done" against the inhabitants of California, meaning Anglo-American settlers. At the end of the speech, Gwin introduced "An Act to Ascertain and Settle the Private Land Claims in the State of California," which would create a three-person committee, the US Land Commission, tasked with verifying Mexican land grants. The bill relied on Henry Halleck's report and required strict scrutiny of all land claims created during Spanish and Mexican rule. In defiance of the terms of the Treaty of Guadalupe Hidalgo, the Land Commission process would require a land claimant to file their grant with the commission within two years or their lands would enter the public domain.

During the bill's debate, Missouri senator and John C. Frémont's father-in-law, Thomas H. Benton, criticized the bill for the onus it imposed on Californio land claimants. He argued that the Treaty of Guadalupe Hidalgo required the senators "to maintain and protect the people in the free enjoyment of their property."[32] Benton reminded his fellow senators that some of the people who had helped conquer California would suffer because of what the bill required. They were all the more remiss if they forgot that "conquered people have rights."[33] Benton warned that Californios would not submit to such a law, which ran the risk of jeopardizing the alliance between elite Californios and the US government, so he proposed an alternative bill, which would better protect land claims but still required claimants to prove their validity.[34] Benton was an avid supporter of Westward Expansion but did not want to alienate prominent Californios and endanger Anglo-American settlement. Given that his son-in-law, Frémont, had signed the Treaty of Cahuenga and now claimed a land grant, he knew the value of the alliance with prominent Californios.[35] In addition to his personal motivations, Benton did not support squatters, which proslavery Democrats like himself interpreted as supporting Free Soil (land where slavery did not legally exist) interests. Like many other Democrats of the day, Benton supported expansion policies that did not run the risk of weakening enslavers' rights.[36]

Despite Benton's warnings, Gwin's act became law on March 3, 1851. On behalf of settlers' requests, the US Congress had established a legal mechanism that made Californio property rights conditional.[37] Before the session was over, the US Senate acted to open Native territory to settlers. John C. Frémont, California's second senator, introduced a bill that would extinguish Indigenous claims in the Sierra Nevada Mountains by treaty.[38] Senator Frémont wanted to dispossess Indigenous nations and legally open the California gold country to Anglo-American settlers.[39] The US Senate did not pass Frémont's bill.[40] Instead, the US Senate allocated $50,000 to the Department of the Interior to send Indian agents to California, where they would negotiate treaties with individual tribes in order to open lands to Anglo settlers.[41]

Challenging Anglo-American Settlement

In July 1851, Pablo de la Guerra wrote to lawyer Eugene Cassidy, asking what the 1851 US Land Act meant for Californios. Cassidy explained the legal process and disclosed to de la Guerra that he feared the law and its administration would prove to be "a legal confiscation of the old estates in California" due to an onerous process and "monstrous fees."[42]

Confronted with this challenge to their ranchos, land grant holders in Los Angeles and San Diego revived their calls for state division and a return to territorial status for Southern California in July 1851. On July 5, in the *Los Angeles Star*, an anonymous writer, "Niebla" (fog), called for the separation of Southern California from the north and a return to territorial status.[43] Days later, San Diego sheriff Agoston Haraszthy, an Austrian immigrant who had assimilated into elite Californio culture, printed a public letter calling for a state division convention.[44] Both calls argued that the new laws placed an undue burden on land grant claimants and that territory status would exempt property owners from exorbitant taxes and the Land Commission process. The call for state division was a Californio attempt to save their ranchos and power without compromising Anglo-American settlement in the north. English-language newspapers discounted the calls for division as insignificant grumblings.[45]

In August 1851, Californios in Southern California began organizing a convention.[46] They argued that landholders of the south "had no voice" even though they were "permanent" settlers engaged in agricultural work for the whole state. Their biggest grievance was that land claimants would have to mortgage their ranchos to pay their Land Commission bills and taxes.[47] Juntas in Santa Barbara, Los Angeles, and San Diego met to plan next steps. On August 30, 1851, a junta of land claimants, including prominent Californios Joaquin Ortega and Pedro Carrillo, met at the San Diego courthouse. After the meeting, the junta printed a public address in English-language newspapers throughout the state. The statement declared that San Diego citizens "almost unanimously" supported division and made clear that the primary reason for wanting territorial status was the rancho.[48] Statehood had placed an insurmountable onus on land claimants because property taxes were based on the cash-flush northern mining economy, and Southern California land claimants, who were engaged in agriculture, could not pay their taxes. The junta wanted to return Southern California to territory status until it was ready to enter the Union as a state.[49] The San Diego junta announced a convention would be held in Santa Barbara, a middle point for the disaffected landholders and a center of Californio power.[50] In the weeks that followed, juntas in Los Angeles, San Luis Obispo, Santa Barbara, and as far north as Santa Cruz met and elected convention delegates.[51]

On October 20, 1851, at least thirty-one delegates gathered at the Convention for State Division. Prominent Californios, including Antonio de la Guerra, José Antonio Carrillo, and Antonio Coronel, attended the meeting.[52] José Antonio Carrillo, as convention president, pledged to exhaust all legal means possible to dissolve the political connection between the northern and southern regions. The delegates formed a seven-person Central Committee based in Los Angeles that would pursue division by sending petitions to the legislature.[53]

Just as the committee was ready to make its case for division before the state legislature, Southern California rancho owners faced another threat.

Earlier in 1851, Cupeño chief Antonio Garra began organizing a pan-Indigenous movement to rid the western-southern edge of the Indigenous world of Californio and Anglo settlers. Garra was outraged over the increasing settler incursions into Cupeño land. To oust Californio and Anglo settlers from the Indigenous world, Garra hoped to lead a series of pan-Indigenous coordinated attacks on Santa Barbara, Los Angeles, and San Diego in November, beginning with an attack on Warner's Ranch. Garra attempted to recruit Kumeyaays from San Pasqual and Santa Ysabel, Quechans and Cocopas, Luiseños from San Luis Rey and Temecula, multiple Cahuilla bands, and even fighters from Baja California.[54]

José Juan Warner was born in Connecticut and migrated to Alta California by way of St. Louis and Santa Fe. In Alta California, Warner established himself as a businessman by opening a trading post in Los Angeles. In 1837, Warner married Anita Gale, an adopted daughter of the Pico family, and became a member of the Pico compadrazgo network.[55] In 1844, Pío Pico granted Warner Rancho San Jose del Valle y Los Aguas, which José Antonio Pico had previously abandoned due to Indigenous resistance. By giving the grant to Warner, Pío Pico kept the land in the family. Warner established Warner Ranch and established a working relationship with Garra and the Cupeño to keep the property safe from Indigenous raiding. During the Gold Rush, however, Warner opened his ranch to immigrants taking the Southern Trail from New Mexico to Los Angeles, violating his agreement with Garra.

Before the attack on Warner's ranch was to commence, Garra sent messengers to two prominent Californios, José Ortega and Joaquin Estudillo. The message was an invitation to join the effort to remove the Anglo-American settlers from the region. Garra's message to Ortega argued that the uprising would end the "damage" wrought by American taxes.[56] Garra courted the Californios for two reasons. First, he assumed that the Californios wanted to stop the changes brought on by the Americans. Second, prior to the arrival of Anglo settlers, the Indigenous had worked out a stable, albeit tense, relationship with the Californios. For Garra, this was his last chance to preserve a world where Californio patriarchs and Indigenous chiefs could make alliances that sustained their small counties in a borderlands landscape. Garra hoped attacking Warner's Ranch would stymie, if not end, American settlement.[57]

Ortega and Estudillo refused to join Garra's uprising. Their imaginings of patria chica did not allow for collaboration with—or taking political cues from—Garra, who they considered a gente sin razón. As elite Californios,

Ortega and Estudillo would negotiate and collaborate with other settlers to squash Indigenous challenges.

The attacks commenced on November 21, 1851. First, Cahuillas attacked Dominga Noca's house, which was full of Americans. Then, as the sun rose, Garra led an attack on Warner's Ranch. They set fire to the buildings and took all of the cattle. Warner estimated that he lost $59,000 in property.[58]

As news of the raid spread, Californio and Anglo-American settlers panicked. In the wake of an Indigenous attack on ranchos, Californios paused their state division campaign. San Diego Sheriff Harasthy, who penned the public letter that announced the state division movement, raised a militia and wrote a letter to the governor, asking for assistance.[59] In Los Angeles, prominent Californios formed a commission with the US Army and issued a proclamation, calling all able-bodied men to gather at Rancho del Chino. Having built his identity on suppressing Indigenous resistance, Andrés Pico raised a company of fifty Californios and led them to Chino.

As Californio and Anglo-American men gathered at Chino, a prominent Californio member of the commission, Agustin Olvera, wrote a letter to Juan Antonio, chief of the Mountain band of Cahuilla and ally to elite Californios. In the letter, Olvera asked Juan Antonio for intel on Garra's motives and assistance in suppressing the revolt.

Like they had done during the US-Mexico War, elite Californios called on Juan Antonio for help. They called on Juan Antonio time and time again. As late as May 1851, José Lugo called on Juan Antonio to assist in guarding his rancho from a band of thieves—Anglo-American men allegedly from Texas, who were robbing ranchos throughout the San Bernardino Valley. Juan Antonio and his men captured and killed the thieves.[60]

Garra, hoping to garner Juan Antonio's support, sent a letter requesting a meeting. However, Juan Antonio had already decided to ally with the Californio and Anglo settlers, but agreed to meet with Garra. On the pretext of responding to the letter, Juan Antonio met with Garra and quickly took him as his prisoner. On December 20, Juan Antonio released Garra to the US Army, which held a court martial for him. During the trial José Warner served as Garra's interpreter.[61] We should retroactively judge Warner serving as Garra's interpreter as a miscarriage of justice but we would be remiss if we did not also interpret this as a demonstration of the US Army's lack of authority in the area and its reliance on people who spoke Spanish—and perhaps had familiarity with other native languages—to control the Indigenous world. On January 12, 1852, the US government executed Antonio Garra for "levying war against the government."[62]

Garra's failed uprising, however, transformed politics in Southern California. Just as Garra was executed, an Indian agent, O. M. Wozencraft, arrived in the region and made treaties with the leaders of the Luiseño, Kumeyaay, and Cahuilla bands, including Juan Antonio.[63] As other scholars have pointed out, these treaties were not signed under appropriate circumstances because the terms were not faithfully explained to the various Indigenous polities named in the treaties. In Treaty K signed by the Cahuilla (spelled "Kah-wé-as") and Wozencraft on January 7, 1852, the United States retained "the right of way" over said territory, regardless of Indigenous claims. Juan Antonio and other Indigenous representatives agreed to such treaties because agents promised to protect their world from errant Anglo settlers.[64]

This treaty was similar to others signed throughout the state, which three federal Indian agents—Redick McKee, George W. Barbor, and O. M. Wozencraft—made with numerous Indigenous polities throughout California from May 1851 until January 1852. In making treaties, the agents were attempting to clear as much land as possible for Anglo settlers.[65] McKee, Barbor, and Wozencraft also met with Anglo settler communities and relayed the terms of peaceful cohabitation as stipulated by the treaties in an attempt to end the violence settlers sparked as they encroached on Indigenous land.[66] By the end of January 1852, the Indian agents had signed eighteen treaties with leaders who represented thousands of Indigenous individuals from 125 tribes.

As treaties with sovereign nations, the eighteen treaties required approval by the US Senate. In the winter of 1851–52, settlers sent letters to Washington, DC, expressing disdain toward the commissioners who "had given the Indians large bodies of the finest farming and mineral lands in the state" and complained that their claims were located within the new treaty boundaries and that the land they had improved and cultivated would be lost without compensation.[67] California Senator, John Weller, in directing his fellow senators, explained that he "was opposed to the ratification of the treaties," because they would result in too many "Indians in the midst of the white population."[68]

Given the discontent with the treaties, on July 8, 1852, the US Senate resolved to neither advise nor consent to the treaties made by the Indian agents.[69] There is no record of the debate and the Senate filed the treaties into secrecy until 1905. Again, American settlers compelled the federal government to open lands to settlers despite previously made agreements. These treaties are now known as the Eighteen Unratified Treaties. Indigenous chiefs, like Juan Antonio, had signed these treaties with the expectation of maintaining control over their territory and that the US government would curb Anglo and Californio violence.

Californios and the US Land Commission

In the wake of Garra's revolt, Anglo settlers characterized Californios as un-American and disloyal. The *San Diego Herald* published Garra's letters to José Ortego and Joaquin Estudillo to cast doubt on Californio loyalty to the United States despite their role in ending the uprising.[70] Before Garra was executed, the *Daily Alta California* printed a letter by "Philo," which offered commentary on the uprising. Philo argued that this was not just an "Indian War" because "the whole Californian population is disaffected with *our* institutions" and "our *tax system*." Philo claimed that even though Andrés Pico led fifty Californio men to fight Garra, "*none* [went] without being *forced*" because of their "deep deadly hatred . . . against Americans."[71]

A month later, the *Daily Alta California* walked back the accusations against Ortega and Estudillo. The paper "denied the assertions" against them while conceding that by printing the accusations without comment, they had helped cement the idea that the two men had acted against the American government.[72] The same issue included a letter by José Joaquin Ortega in which he claimed "fidelity to the flag under which [he] live[d]" and refuted the allegations made against him. Ortega explained he allowed a band of Diegueno Indians (Kumeyaay) to hold their annual bird celebration on his rancho just as he was leaving for Santa Barbara for the state division convention. He did not communicate with Garra or any messenger of Garra's; in fact, he told the Kumeyaay to "behave," as he knew Garra felt aggrieved by the Americans. In printing the letter, it seems that the *Daily Alta California* did not believe that all Californios were antagonistic to the "Americans."

Regardless of Ortega's letter, Anglo settlers viewed Californios and the Indigenous as united in their hostility to the white settlement. To the chagrin of Californios, they were lumped together with Indians. Rather than revive the movement to divide the state, prominent Californios opted to participate in the Land Commission established by the 1851 US Land Act.

Over the course of two decades, the Land Commission heard 813 cases and awarded 604 patents. A majority of Anglo-American landholders who had purchased land grants in the north after the war had received their patents by 1861.[73] In contrast, Californios, mostly in Southern California, spent an average of seventeen years legally and financially embroiled in the Land

Commission process while contending with Anglo-American challenges to their land claims and citizenship.[74] As a result of the prolonged legal fight, by the end of the 1870s, many Californios lost their ranchos.[75] The 1851 Land Act was a legislative tool of colonization that culturally, if not legally, invalidated Californio property rights established by the Treaty of Guadalupe of Hidalgo.

In the month after Garra's revolt, a Los Angeles junta led by Antonio Coronel decided to demonstrate their willingness to participate and uphold US government institutions. They authored a petition requesting that the Land Commission hold sessions in Los Angeles, not just in San Francisco.[76] This petition demonstrated Californios' willingness to participate in the Land Commission process while also attempting to make the process easier for themselves.

As the Land Commission process unfolded in courtrooms, newspapers, and private correspondence, Anglo-Americans of all classes continued to paint Californios as incompatible with the white settler state and cited their inability to partake in English-language court proceedings as evidence of their inferiority. The Land Commission courtroom was a space where lawyers, land agents, and squatters challenged the Californio's settler identity by characterizing Californio land grant claimants as inferior to white settlers and antagonistic to white settlement. The courtroom became a site of racial othering.

Elite Californios, like Pablo de la Guerra, participated in the Land Commission process. Their participation inadvertently promoted a discourse that cast Californios as incompetent and corrupt landholders and Spanish fluency as indicative of inferiority.[77] In 1852, de la Guerra hired Henry Halleck, the author of the infamous land report, to defend his family's numerous claims in front of the Land Commission. After the creation of the US Land Commission, Halleck cofounded a law firm—Halleck, Peachy, and Billings—with Frederick Billings and A. C. Peachy to litigate land claims cases.[78] Halleck's decision to litigate on behalf of Californio land claimants was opportunistic. The Peachy, Billings, and Halleck firm represented one hundred and twenty claimants at a rate of fifty dollars to $1,500 per case.[79] Pablo de la Guerra and Henry Halleck developed a professional and personal relationship to their own advantage. For discounted legal service fees, de la Guerra obtained clients for Halleck's firm.[80]

The two exchanged letters from the 1850s to the 1870s, in which Halleck depicted Californios as incompetent and corrupt, reflecting Anglo-American sentiments. In a letter dated January 18, 1852, Halleck explained the Land Commission process to de la Guerra and instructed him to send his cases to

San Francisco, as the commissioners established their headquarters there. Halleck made clear that by locating their offices in the north, where most Anglo-American claims were located, the commissioners put Californios, with claims mainly in the south, at a disadvantage. Halleck then wrote about Californios, stating: "You know, as well as we do, that many of the Californians are so ignorant . . . that they allow themselves to be imposed upon by the first one who talks with them, and thus leave their true friends in the lurch for any trouble or expense."[81] Halleck admitted that he was "disgruntled with the old Californians." After this rebuke, Halleck asked de la Guerra to convince other Californios to hire him. Perhaps as a performance of his gente de razón status and duties of the compadrazgo system, de la Guerra convinced others to hire Halleck.[82]

In other letters, Halleck blamed Californios for unpatented claims, even though Halleck described the 1851 Land Act as "illegal."[83] In 1853, the Land Commission rejected de la Guerra's petition for Rancho El Rincon. Halleck initially blamed de la Guerra for his unconfirmed grant, writing that it was his "own "lazynous [*sic*]" for "not proceeding according *to* [his] own laws in making their grants, and [for] making false and antedated papers, and then swearing to them."[84] Although Halleck described the Land Commission's rulings as unjust, he still cited Californios as the reasons for the rejections, not the law or the commissioners.[85] I have not come across a record of de la Guerra directly challenging Halleck's characterizations of Californios in personal letters.

Like Halleck, lawyers and newspapers cast Californios as simple-minded and corrupt. Robert Greenhow, a government attorney tasked with collecting testimony for the US Land Commission, described Californio witnesses as having "never thought of anything" prior to the US invasion and stated that "the truth can rarely be expected" from Californios.[86] In August 1852, the editors of the *Sacramento Daily Union* argued that "the original land holder" needed to be supplanted by a "practical cultivator of the soil."[87] Early in 1853, the *Daily Alta California* published a series of letters that stereotyped Californios as "unprincipled men" who occupied the land "against the government of the United States."[88] These papers upheld the myth that only Anglo-American settlers could properly cultivate the soil, not Californios. Anglo-American squatters did not envision Californio landholders as part of their white settler state.

Just a year after passing the Land Act in 1852, the US Senate decided that all Land Commission cases would automatically be appealed and heard by the US Supreme Court. This dramatically lengthened the time it took a claimant to receive a patent, rendering land claims vulnerable to squatters, accusations of corruption and incompetence, and subject to exorbitant lawyer fees. After this change, 46 percent of Californio claimants went bankrupt trying to keep their land claims.[89]

Compounding the challenges of the 1851 US Land Act, Anglo-American squatters challenged Californio political power in Santa Barbara during the 1852 state elections. As elected officials, elite Californios were responsible for overseeing elections and established a polling place in the Santa Barbara courthouse. On Election Day, however, Anglo-American settlers set up a second polling place to challenge the legitimacy of Californio political power. When the polls closed, election officials refused to count the votes from the second, illegal voting place. In response, Anglo-American residents accused Californios of election fraud and the *Daily Alta California* published a letter from "a gentleman in Santa Barbara" who accused Californios of illegal activity but failed to provide details. Tellingly, the "gentleman" closed his letter with a threat, stating "that the squatters . . . are going to Santa Barbara and [will seize] upon Mission lands and private ranches."[90]

The accusations of voter fraud continued into 1853. In response, a junta of elite Californios led by José Covarrubias and the Carrillo brothers published a public letter in English and Spanish newspapers.[91] In the letter, the junta declared that they had first hoped to ignore the accusations, as they were gentlemen, but such slander and threats required comment. The junta addressed the accusations of electoral misconduct by explaining that the only out-of-the-ordinary thing they had done on Election Day was place the ballot box in a space of the courthouse that had three-foot-thick adobe walls to protect voters and officials. The letter revealed that they needed to protect Californio voters because on the eve of a past summer election, an unknown assailant attempted to assassinate Pablo de la Guerra. The junta stressed that all their conduct was legal, unlike that of the Anglo squatters who had organized an illegal polling place. In concluding the letter, the junta made clear its intentions. They did not wish "to create distinctions between the native born Californians and Americans" and offered to put this incident behind them so they could move forward as "collaborators of one government."[92]

In an effort to move forward as one government, elite Californios began to challenge the legislation—not on the grounds that such laws were unjust but that they violated protections established by the Treaty of Guadalupe Hidalgo. In April 1855, the California Senate attempted to accelerate the dispossession of Californio land claimants with "A Bill Concerning Ejectments," which would circumvent treaty property protections and the Land Commission process by creating a legal route for squatters to obtain lands by preemption.[93] State senator Pablo de la Guerra challenged this assault on Californio property, all the while performing his gente de razón status. De la Guerra delivered a speech in the California capitol, which resulted in a "manifestation of applause" and the bill's death. Had this speech failed, de la Guerra was prepared to travel to Washington, DC, and appear before Congress on behalf of all Californio land claimants.[94] Commentary on de la Guerra's speech reveals the racial assumptions about the Californios he defied. The *Daily Alta California* wrote that "Don Pablo possesse[d] the most perfect command of the English language" and that he "astonished" all with the "lucid and logical" argument and his "eloquence."[95]

Later in 1855, California state senator William Shaw, who also served as the leader of the San Francisco Settlers' Association, presented a bill that would require land grantee holders to pay squatters for the "improvements" they made on lands they illegally resided on. This bill was a cloaked attempt at confiscation because the fee that land grant holders would have to pay to squatters for "improvements" was often more valuable than the land. During the debate over Shaw's "Squatter Bill," Santa Barbara Representative José Covarrubias suggested renaming the bill "An Act to Annul the Treaty of Guadalupe Hidalgo" because it would violate the property rights of treaty citizens. Despite the political support for squatters' interests, the bill died in the California Senate because of its obvious unconstitutionality.[96]

As the Santa Barbara representatives pushed back against legislation that violated Californio property rights, in 1855, a junta of elite Californios in Los Angeles took matters into their own hands.[97] After four years of bringing their land claims to the Land Commission, many Californios were in danger of going bankrupt due to high lawyer fees. A junta, led by Abel Stearns, created a *Subscripcion* (subscription) to raise funds for Californios who struggled to pay their exorbitant lawyer fees. Stearns donated the most, $500, to the fund. Pío Pico, Manuel Dominguez, Ignacio Del Valle, and Agustín Olvera also donated to the Subscripcion.[98] The junta printed a Subscripcion flyer to garner support. The handout declared that the 1851 Land Act not only violated the Treaty of Guadalupe and Californios' "sacred rights," but it also imposed increasing costs on the land claimants that "intend[ed] to affect a general confiscation of [Californio] properties."[99] The plea also noted the accusation of "titles of being fraudulent" damaged Californios' character, compromising their gente de razón status.

Despite this condemnation of the Land Act, Californios still collaborated with Anglo-American settlers to maintain the social order, as they had done with Garra's Uprising. In July 1856, Los Angeles was roiled by a threat of extralegal violence in response to Deputy Constable William Jenkins's shooting and killing of Antonio Ruis. In the days following the incident, elite Californios sought to take matters into their own hands and held a meeting, as they were not confident that justice would be served. The rumor quickly spread that groups of Anglo-American and Californio men had taken up arms and were ready to duel. Under the cover of night, one to three hundred of "the lowest" Sonorans and Mexicans gathered on a hill ready to fight.[100] One account claims that they gathered on a hill and shot their rifles; another account claims that "maledictions" were exchanged between Anglo-American and Californio men.[101] After firing their weapons, the "Mexicans" marched to the Los Angeles Plaza, only to disperse.

During this incident, Pío Pico welcomed Anglo-American women to take refuge in his house.[102] As he had during the Garra Uprising and many times before, Andrés Pico mounted his horse to project Californio power. Andrés Pico, coordinating with Anglo-American mayor Stephen Foster, assembled a group of men and formed a cavalry that rounded the troublemakers and brought peace back to the city.[103] The Picos, interested in maintaining a gente de razón society, once again used the performance of violence to restore order.

State Division, Again

Three years later, in 1859, assemblyman Andrés Pico revived the state division movement and presented a bill to split California. Pico coauthored the bill with fellow Democrat assemblymember Henry Hancock. Hancock was originally from New Hampshire but had assimilated into Californio settler society and claimed a Mexican land grant. The bill proposed creating the Territory of Colorado at the present-day northern boundary of San Luis Obispo County. When he introduced the bill, Pico cited unfair land and tax policies as the reason for reverting to territorial status. The reasons for state division were the same as in 1851. Under territorial status, the US Land Act would not apply, and Californios would have a better chance at maintaining their land claims. In crafting the bill, Pico did not outright reject US authority; he did, however, attempt to remove a specific settler institution from Southern California to maintain patria chica.

The Chivalry, the proslavery branch of the state Democratic Party, publicly supported the bill because they viewed it as a way to extend slavery to California.[104] Pico welcomed Chiv support. Even though their reasons and goals differed, they both sought to control labor and land, albeit under different systems—the rancho and the plantation. When speculating on the outcomes of the bill, the *San Francisco Herald*, a Democratic paper, claimed: "Californians are so exceedingly dark-complexioned" and "little removed from the black race" it would be difficult "to detect the difference between them and Indians."[105] Given their allies' racial beliefs, the *San Francisco Herald* thought that Pico risked his own enslavement as a nonwhite supporter of the bill. However, Pico and other prominent Californios believed that their gente de razón status afforded them positions of authority and that local political alliances superseded outsider racial logics. Pico imagined state division as a means to return to pre-1848 Californio society, which would benefit elite Californios and could benefit the Chivs.

In a letter to Abel Stearns, Pico wrote that the resolution would return Southern California to territory status and pause the Land Commission process. By introducing the bill, Pico believed that state division would bring the "salvation of our properties and our happiness" and hoped to become territorial governor.[106] In September 1859, the Southern California electorate approved the bill three to one.[107] To become law, the California state legislature and the US Congress needed to approve the referendum. Neither legislative body took action on the referendum. The Californio gambit at state division stalled as the nation moved toward a civil war. Once again, Pico and other elite Californios would have to strategize how to hold onto power.

PART III | Colonized Colonizers

CHAPTER FOUR

"Star Spangled Banner, God, and Your Native Land!"

Californio Politics During the US Civil War and Reconstruction

On Christmas Eve 1861, it began to pour in Los Angeles. It then rained for over a month from Oregon to Mexico.[1] A swollen Los Angeles River washed away cattle, fields, and vineyards. The rains were so heavy that the Los Angeles, San Gabriel, and Santa Ana Rivers transformed into inland lakes that lingered for months.[2] Elite Californio families lost tens of thousands of cattle and fruit trees, falling further into debt. The Great Flood of 1862 remade the Southern California landscape, as the US Civil War, which began on April 12, 1861, had already begun to reshape not just the national but also the California political landscape.

Confronted with environmental calamity, elite Californios once again had to prove their usefulness to the Union if they were to hold on to political power during the civil conflict. This chapter follows the many prominent Democratic Californios in the hopes of retaining their power, leaving the party, and joining the Union Party.[3] Notably, during the 1864 election, the de la Guerra and Pico families encouraged Southern California to vote for the Union Party and presidential candidate Abraham Lincoln. Californio campaigning worked; in Southern California, Lincoln won, which demonstrated their utility in a state polarized by secession politics.

In addition to recalibrating their political alliances, during the US Civil War, elite Californios attempted to perform state-sanctioned violence against "threatening Indians"—just as their ancestral patriarchs had done. In 1863, the US Army created the Native Californian Cavalry at the request of prominent Californio Romualdo Pacheco. Young men of prominent Californio families, such as José Ramon Pico and Antonio María de la Guerra, joined the Native Californian Cavalry. The chapter argues that Pico and de la Guerra's enlistment was primarily an effort to demonstrate their gente de razón status and distance from "threatening Indians," not just an attempt to prove their Union loyalty. At a time when the US government questioned Californio loyalty and belonging, Pacheco imagined that if Californios mustered into the cavalry, they could first perform their gente de razón status and then their loyalty to the United States by subduing Indigenous communities, just as their forefathers had done.[4] My analysis of the Native Californian Cavalry diverges from other scholars' analysis of the battalion, in that I interpret Californio enlistment as a reflection of their desire to protect their homeland (patria chica) from an Indigenous threat, rather than a Confederate threat. The Californio attempt to control Indigenous power with ritualized, state-sanctioned violence was a way to project their belonging to the United States as gente de razón settlers. Mexican settlers had used ritualized, state-sanctioned violence to assert their belonging in elite and gente de razón society before and after the US-Mexico War. While the US Army was concerned with Confederate designs on the North American Southwest, Californio inhabitants joined the cavalry to remove the Indigenous communities from California. Tellingly, in Southern California, the Cavalry focused on suppressing the Indigenous communities of the Indigenous world, and in Northern California, the Cavalry focused on suppressing the Hupa in northwestern California.

The chapter then covers Californio responses to Reconstruction. Black activists from San Francisco to Los Angeles and Anglo-American Republicans attempted to forge a biracial democracy in the state by expanding the franchise and opening land to nonwhite settlers. Californios interpreted the efforts to establish a biracial democracy and increase federal intervention as a threat to their patria chica. Because of their racial prejudices and land-grant anxieties, Californios returned to the Democratic Party to squash the Black American and Republican efforts to remake the California social order.[5] Elite Californios, like Antonio Coronel, supported the state Democratic campaigns to reject the Fourteenth Amendment, which established birthright citizenship and the Equal Protection Clause, and the Fifteenth Amendment, which prohibited a state from denying a citizen's right to vote "on account of race [or] color" in the state legislature. The California legislature did not approve the Fourteenth and Fifteenth Amendments, which became a part of the US Constitution by the actions of twenty-eight other states. Motivated by their fears of Reconstruction, Californios returned to the Democratic Party and, once again, supported legislation that furthered their transformation from gente de razón settlers to colonized colonizers and dealt an existential blow to their patria chia.

Californios During the US Civil War

During the 1860 presidential election, a majority of Californios cast their votes for the Democrats despite the efforts of Pío Pico and Francisco Ramirez of *El Clamor Público*. In Californio-dominated Los Angeles, Southern Democrat presidential candidate John C. Breckinridge received 682 votes while Republican candidate Abraham Lincoln received 356 votes.[6] Abraham Lincoln won the state and the presidency without the support of Californios. Anti-Republican sentiment was so strong in Southern California that the *Los Angeles Star* lauded local Democratic victories as a local conquest and a "disapprobation upon Squatter Sovereignty and negro worshippers."[7]

Democratic celebrations in Southern California inspired rumors of Californio secession as the threat of civil war loomed. In this tense political climate, Andrés Pico responded to Enrique Ávila's 1860 public letter, which expressed support for the Democrats and maintaining the institution of slavery, in February 1861. Pico detailed the potential pitfalls facing prominent Californio families if they continued to support the Democrats. Pico believed that the United States was headed to civil war and maintained that it was necessary for prominent Californio patriarchs to "be very united" in their response to the crisis.[8] He insisted that they support the Union and that they "do something for *our* country." Pico asked Ávila to relay this message to his compadrazgo network. Despite having led a campaign for state division less than two years before, Pico now believed that the Californios' best chance at maintaining their property and power in Southern California depended on what they did for their country. One can imagine that by writing "*our* country," Pico meant both his patria chica and the United States. Despite Pico's counsel, a majority of Californios did not make clear where their loyalties lay. Pablo de la Guerra, for instance, instructed his family to withhold their opinions about the looming civil war.[9]

When the US Civil War began in April 1861, a group of prominent Californios in Los Angeles made their support for secession clear by joining the Los Angeles Mounted Rifles, which would travel east and fight with the Confederate States of America (CSA). The Los Angeles Mounted Rifles was the only militia from a Free State to fight on behalf of the CSA.[10] Of the seventy-six men who signed up, eleven were Californios.[11] Notably, Tomás A. Sánchez, a prominent Californio patriarch and the Los Angeles County Sheriff, enlisted.[12] In his capacity as sheriff, Sánchez distributed rifles and sabers sent by the federal government before the war to the enlistees headed to the Arizona Territory. Upon hearing about Sánchez' actions, Californios Andrés Pico and Romualdo Pacheco attempted to retrieve the weapons to no avail.[13]

A prominent Californio like Pico, Pacheco held land grants in San Luis Obispo and entered local politics in 1850 at the age of nineteen. His mother, Ramona Carrillo de Pacheco, was a member of the prominent Carrillo family.

Her brother was José Antonio Carrillo and her sister, Maria Antonia Carrillo, married José de la Guerra. In 1831, when Pacheco lost his father, patriarch José de la Guerra took in the widow and her sons. Fourteen years separated cousins Romualdo Pacheco and Pablo de la Guerra, but for a period, they grew up in the same house. Six years later, once José de la Guerra approved the marriage, Ramona Carrillo de Pacheco remarried to John Wilson, a sea merchant from Scotland who made a small fortune in the Pacific. Wilson sent the teenager Pacheco and his younger brother to the O'ahu Charity School in Hawaii to learn English from British and American instructors who taught Hawaiian British and Hawaiian American children. Fluent in English and Spanish, Pacheco returned to Alta California during the US-Mexico War. In 1853, at the age of twenty-two, Pacheco ran for San Luis Obispo County judge and won. In 1857, Pacheco ran for the state senate as a Democrat and won. After returning from England to visit his half-brother, John Wilson, Pacheco ran for public office in 1861 as a Union Party candidate.[14]

Sánchez's actions worried US Army officials, who began to surveil Californios. US general Winfield S. Hancock, stationed in Los Angeles to coordinate military control of the Mojave Trail in the Indigenous world, reported on Californio activities to his superiors in San Francisco and Washington, DC. Hancock expressed worry about Californio loyalty, since he thought they had "nothing to lose" and "were ready for change" that could secure their ranchos. Hancock warned that the Californio leaders had "great control over the people," insinuating that they could lead a separatist, if not secessionist, movement.[15] He reported on May 13 that a Union flag was raised over the Los Angeles courthouse, signaling support.[16]

Despite receiving Hancock's reports of Union support in Los Angeles, in June 1861, the California surveyor general E. F. Beale publicly demanded that Andrés and Pío Pico "define their relations to the Union and the Federal Government."[17] Andrés Pico responded in the *Los Angeles Star*. He declared that he "unconditionally and at all hazards, was for the Constitution and for the Union." Moreover, he reasoned that his vote for Abraham Lincoln was a "faithful testimonial of [his] political opinions."[18] This public declaration convinced Beale to not treat the Picos as enemies.

The issue of federal patronage finally convinced many Californios to support the Union. To destroy Democratic power in federal administration, President Lincoln replaced fifteen hundred officeholders with loyal Republican men. This strategy was so effective that Lincoln devastated the Democratic patronage network in California.[19] In 1860, sitting president James Buchanan had approved Pablo de la Guerra for a diplomatic position in Latin

America. When the paperwork came to President Lincoln's desk in March 1861, he denied de la Guerra the post because he had held juntas for the Northern Democrat candidate Stephen Douglas during the 1860 election.[20] Lincoln had made clear what Democrat support meant for Californios, pushing the final holdouts to reconsider their political alliances.

After two years of civil war, Andrés Pico and Romualdo Pacheco began to successfully rally Californio support for the Union Party during the 1863 elections. It became clear that joining the Union Party would not only project Californio support for the Union, but it was also a safer bet at retaining power. Pico and Pacheco convinced Pablo de la Guerra to run for Southern California district judge as a Union Party candidate against Benjamin Hayes, a Democrat and long-time Californio ally.[21] Pico and Pacheco's plan worked—Californios and the Union Parties of Los Angeles, San Bernardino, San Luis Obispo, and San Diego elected de la Guerra because he was neither a secessionist nor a Democrat.[22] De la Guerra's successful election projected Californio political power.

In addition to participating in electoral politics, during the US Civil War, prominent Californios committed state-sanctioned acts of violence against Indigenous Californians to demonstrate their utility to the Union.[23] While he had not answered the first call for volunteers in 1861, a year later, Andrés Pico offered to lead a militia against the Owens Valley Paiute-Shoshones and Western Shoshones. The Great Flood had washed away many of the crops and livestock the Paiutes depended on. Once the waters receded, Anglo-American settlers, who entered the valley in 1861, grazed their cattle on already damaged Paiute lands. This encroachment made it all the more difficult for the near-starving Paiutes to survive. To end the encroachments on their lands, hundreds of Paiutes and Shoshone mounted a campaign. In early April 1862, they killed Anglo settlers' cattle and informed the settlers that they needed to leave the valley as it belonged to the Paiute.[24] In retaliation, Anglo settlers asked for military assistance. Commanding colonel James Carleton sent volunteer soldiers stationed at the Drum Barracks to Owens Valley to remove the Paiute and Western Shoshone.[25] As he had done many times in the past, Pico offered his horse and sword to suppress Indigenous power as a demonstration of his gente de razón status and fealty to the United States.[26] His offer was denied. During the Civil War, the US Army pursued the Paiute and their allies until they were removed to a reservation at Fort Tejon, over two hundred miles away.

At the end of 1862, Romualdo Pacheco proposed the creation of a Californian Native Cavalry to the US War Department.[27] The cavalry of Native

Californians, meaning Californios, would use their horseback skills to prevent Indigenous attacks on the US Army in the Southwest desert. In January 1863, the US War Department approved the Californian Native Cavalry.[28] Like Pico, most Californios who ignored the initial call to take up arms against the Confederacy enlisted in the Cavalry to project their dominance over the Indigenous world and belonging to the settler state. The US Army created the Native Californian Cavalry to suppress Native politics and power in the Indigenous world, not to stymie Confederate designs in the Southwest. The Cavalry received orders to suppress the Apache and other tribes—not secessionists. As such, Californios' enlistment was an opportunity to project their power over the Indigenous in this borderlands region.

Initially, the War Department asked Andrés Pico to serve as General of the Cavalry, but he declined due to his poor health.[29] It was rumored that he could no longer spend hours on horseback. Instead, elite Californio Salvador Vallejo served as the general of the Californian Native Cavalry. Known for his animosity to the squatter class and thereby to the US government, Vallejo's enlistment surprised the press.[30] In his testimonio, Vallejo declared that he joined the Native Californian Cavalry to restore the Union to its proper size so that it could stop the spread of European despotism.[31] The French installation of Emperor Maximillian in Mexico during the Second Franco-Mexican War (1861–1867) troubled Vallejo and other prominent Californios—they did not want to see the country conquered by an antirepublican government.[32] Vallejo and other Californio cavalrymen volunteered to ride into the desert because they imagined their presence in the desert would impede French designs on Mexico. Given that Vallejo, like the Picos, had made a name for himself by suppressing Indigenous autonomy in current-day Napa Valley, we must also interpret Vallejo's willingness to lead the Cavalry as a demonstration of his gente de razón settler status.

While Vallejo served as general, other prominent Californios vied for various leadership positions within the Californian Native Cavalry. However, Anglo-American US Army officers denied Californio requests for leadership roles. In turn, Californios called on their compadrazgo networks to gain the positions they desired.[33] Andrés Pico wrote to Republican governor Leland Stanford on behalf of his nephew, José Ramon Pico, who enlisted and wanted to serve as a company captain and organize recruitment efforts in his hometown of San Jose.[34] In his letter to Stanford, Andrés Pico cited his Republican credentials, which seemed to do the trick. Governor

Stanford granted José Ramon Pico the Captain position for Company A of San Jose.

Antonio María de la Guerra asked his better-connected brother, Pablo, to write letters requesting that he be made a colonel.[35] As a result of Pablo de la Guerra's letters, Antonio María de la Guerra joined the cavalry as a colonel. De la Guerra used his leadership role to project his patriarchal authority. He recruited his nephews, Porfirio Jimeno and Santiago and José de la Guerra, into Company C, the Santa Barbara unit.[36] This upcoming generation of Californio patriarchs hoped to forge their power and defend their patria chica in the same way that their forebearers had in Alta California—through family networks and military service.

Like his uncle, José Ramon Pico used his position to project his power and influence. On March 21, 1863, with great pomp, Pico held a recruitment assembly at the San Jose Plaza. He gave a stirring speech that English-language newspapers praised alongside his horse-riding skills.[37] Pico called on the "Sons of California" to assist the United States in squashing the "unholy rebellion." It was their duty to help the Union "become the finest and mightiest Republican nation on earth." He closed his speech with a rallying cry of "Star Spangled Banner [*sic*], God, and your native land!"[38] Pico saw his destiny tied to the United States and imagined the Native Californian Cavalry as a way for Californios to fight for their patria chica. With this speech, Pico recruited about one hundred men.

By 1864, hundreds of Californio men had joined the cavalry.[39] The economic hardship sparked by the Great Flood of 1862, which all but destroyed the cattle industry, likely convinced Californios that military service would restore their political and economic stature. Despite the bombast and the eagerness of the Californio soldiers, Companies A, C, and D did not receive orders to move into the Indigenous world until March 1865, a month before the war would end.[40] The companies received orders to march into the hot and dry desert to open the Mojave Trail for Anglo settlers and to protect them from Apache, Chemehuevi, and other Indigenous strikes.[41] One wonders if Californios interpreted the orders to subdue the Apache and Chemehuevi in the Mojave as a continuation of the centuries-long efforts to quash Indigenous sovereignty in the Mojave Desert and, therefore, as an assertion of their gente de razón settler identity, or merely as a part of the war effort.

José Ramon Pico and Antonio María de la Guerra did not leave for the Arizona Territory, or the Indigenous world, until July 1865, months after the US Civil War had concluded.[42] The biggest threats the Cavalry faced were heat, thirst, and disease, all of which resulted in a high number of deserters.

Before the Cavalry saw any action, colonel James F. Curtis recalled them back to Los Angeles in January 1866, as their three-year enlistment had come to a close. The companies began a two-month march back to Southern California. During a mission to find Apache men to fight, José Ramon Pico fell off his horse and his gun discharged into his upper right thigh—all without even sighting an Apache soldier. He came home in a military ambulance. The Cavalry soldiers did not subdue Indians as they had hoped; instead, they came home tired, injured, and sick from a three-year-long campaign of waiting in the desert. The region remained out of US control until Apache leader Geronimo surrendered in the mid-1880s.[43]

Despite the disappointing outcome for the Cavalry men, prominent Californios, once again, proved their usefulness to the Union at the ballot box. The state Union Party called on prominent Californios to help President Abraham Lincoln win reelection in 1864. Andrés Pico obliged and, days before the election, he marched through the streets of San Jose with the Native Californian battalion. Pico delivered a speech in Spanish to a large Californio audience demanding that they "vote for the Union ticket and thus prove their devotion to *their* country and the cause of freedom."[44] His speech echoed his nephew's sentiments of patria chica and republicanism a year earlier. A writer for the *Daily Alta California* praised Pico's efforts, claiming that the "four hundred Spanish American voters" in San Jose voted "for the straight Union ticket." During this election, President Lincoln won California with Californio support.[45]

Rejecting Reconstruction

As young Californio men enlisted in the Native Californian Cavalry, older prominent Californios, such as Antonio Coronel, revived their public support for the Democratic Party when it became clear the war would destroy slavery. These elite Californios did not envision a California where settlers of African descent had citizenship rights and access to political power. The *Los Angeles Star,* which had a Spanish section called *La Estrella,* reported that Lincoln's Emancipation Proclamation had robbed "every master of his servant and every household of its property."[46] In July 1863, the California Democratic Party issued a party platform that condemned the Emancipation Proclamation, which freed all enslaved peoples in territories in rebellion on January 1, 1863, declaring it a "fanatical attempt to place the negro on a social and political equality with the white race." Elite Californios Antonio Coronel, Cristobal Aguilar, and Enrique Ávila participated in this meeting and signed off on the platform.[47]

Two months later, the Unionist-led state legislature repealed the ban on Black testimony in response to Black American activism. Despite the exodus of Black American activists to British Columbia following the *Dred Scott* decision, Black American communities in Northern California grew, particularly in San Francisco.[48] According to the 1860 Census, 4,086 people of African descent lived in California. Beginning in late 1862, the San Francisco-based Franchise League held meetings with Unionist politicians, and in January 1863, just nine days after Emancipation went into effect, California senator Robert Perkins introduced two bills to end prohibition on Black testimony. Crucially, the bills did not allow for Chinese or Indigenous testimony. On this assurance, the California Assembly voted for the bill without much debate. In the Senate, however, Democrats began to unveil their postwar attack on biracial democracy, a central goal of Reconstruction. Charles C. Dudley, a Union Democrat, decried the bill. He argued that if they allowed five thousand Black men to vote, then they would have to allow sixty thousand Chinese men to vote, and this would elevate members of inferior races "to the terms of equality with the white race."[49]

When the war ended in April 1865 with a Confederate surrender, Californio, Anglo-American, and Black American settlers reconsidered their political strategies. In light of Republican-sponsored legislation in California and Washington, DC, and Black settlers' challenges to white settler society, many elite Californios revived their alliances with the Democrats because they upheld Californio cultural norms by advocating for a racial order that would keep Black and Indigenous people in subordinated positions.

In January 1865, the US Congress passed the Thirteenth Amendment, which ended slavery but did not automatically extend citizenship rights to people of African descent. In response, Black activists in San Francisco called for the Fourth California Colored Convention on June 30, 1865, in *The Elevator*. The call revived the California colored conventions movement of the 1850s and put forth new demands—"the elective franchise, access to public education for children of African descent, and economic freedom." In other words, they demanded "equality before the law."[50]

Philip Bell founded and served as the editor of *The Elevator*, the official "organ" of the Executive Committee of the state's Colored Convention.[51] Born in New York City, Bell had participated in the Colored Conventions movement since 1830 and had the reputation of a leading African American journalist. In 1860, he migrated to San Francisco and established a real estate business. Bell imagined California as a state where Black Americans could participate in the settler project.[52]

The Fourth California Colored Convention met in Sacramento from October 25 to 28, 1865. Thirty-five men from twenty-five northern counties participated in the convention.[53] Due to a small Black population, pro-Southern sentiments, and limited newspaper distribution, the counties of Los Angeles, San Diego, San Bernardino, and San Luis Obispo sent no delegates.[54] On the first day of business, the delegation called on William Yates to deliver the opening message. Yates had served as the president of the 1855 Colored Convention. Since migrating to California in the 1850s, Yates had established himself as a political leader and regular writer for the *Pacific Appeal* and *The Elevator*. Yates encouraged the men present to practice patience as the fight for equal rights would be long and arduous.[55]

On the first day of business, the delegates decided that their main goal would be to obtain the right to vote in California, as this was the first step to becoming "equals before the law."[56] In Sacramento, the delegates laid down the groundwork to achieve this; they created county committees and a fund-raising apparatus. Over the course of three days, they also decided they would campaign to amend the School Law, ensuring children had access to education; improve access to business opportunities; and encourage respectable behavior as a demonstration of their eligibility for citizenship rights.[57]

As part of these efforts, the convention printed "The Report of the Committee of Industrial Pursuits," which echoed the prosettler sentiments of the 1850s Colored Conventions and called on "the colored people of the Pacific States and Territories, [to] secure farms [and] purchase homesteads" as settling land in the West was the crucial "right of every American citizen."[58] Belonging to the United States as full-fledged citizens meant participating in state making as a settler. In addition to encouraging Black settlement, the report also encouraged Black Americans to perform settler labor by building the transcontinental railroad. In doing so, they would contribute to the removal of Indigenous peoples and end "the too frequent incursions of hostile Indians."[59] By advocating for Indian removal, the delegates not only adopted the logic of settlement, they also encouraged Black settlers to assert their power, belonging, and distance from the Indigenous, just as Anglo and Californio men did. The delegates promoted Black settlement as crucial to the effort to transform the West amidst Indigenous and Chinese threats to the settler state. Under the leadership of Phillip Bell, *The Elevator* published the convention minutes, committee reports, and public addresses.[60]

As Black Americans began their campaign to shape Reconstruction in California, Anglo-American Democrats denounced Reconstruction and revived old tactics to stop it. At the 1865 Democrat state convention, the party declared that it was "impracticable to maintain republican institutions based upon the suffrages of negroes, Chinese, and Indians." The party believed that if interracial democracy became a reality, it would result "in the degradation of the white race and the speedy destruction of the government."[61] The party also called on prominent Californios. In the summer of 1865, Pablo de la Guerra received a letter from a representative of the California Democratic Party asking him to join a meeting to discuss a winning ticket for the next election.[62] De la Guerra liked what he heard and returned to the Democratic Party and ran for the district judge of Santa Barbara.

Californios rejoined the party as elected Democrats blocked Reconstruction in the state. In December 1865, California assemblymember William Holden, a Democrat, introduced a resolution to "vote and oppose" all measures that extended the vote to Black men.[63] The resolution passed with a forty-one to thirty-eight vote but died in the Federal Relations Committee. Assemblymembers introduced five additional resolutions to limit the citizenship rights of people of African descent, all of which died in the Federal Relations Committee because of their questionable constitutionality.[64]

In response to these attempts, Bell, as editor of *The Elevator*, demanded the recognition of people of African descent as settler citizens who migrated to California ready "to labor, to develop the resources of the land [and] to remain and make this State their permanent home."[65] In his rebuke of this proposed legislation, Bell not only made clear that people of African descent were prepared to participate in the settler project, but he also made the case that they were deserving of citizenship, unlike Irish and Chinese immigrants who were "alien to our [Anglo- and Black American] language, heathen in their worship, and naturally liscnetions [*sic*]."[66] These claims not only challenged Irish and Chinese immigrant claims to citizenship and the land but Californio claims because they, too, spoke another language and were Catholic.[67]

The Democrats were not alone in their aversion to extending the franchise. The editors of the *Daily Alta California* warned of the perils of extending the electoral franchise, stating that California inhabitants would suffer if they had to "engage in the hazardous experiment of putting ballots in the hands of persons who have no just conception in their value, force or effect."[68] The editors viewed the policies of Reconstruction as a threat to the white monopoly of governance and feared that expanding the right to vote to Black Americans would open the citizenship door to Chinese immigrants.[69]

The reconstruction policy of Congress, as illustrated in California, 1867. This satirical political cartoon depicts what many in California, if not the nation, feared. If Black men could vote, they feared that the racial hierarchy in America would become inverted. Courtesy of the Library of Congress.

As the California public debated the demerits of extending the franchise to people of African descent, in Washington, DC, the congressional Joint Committee on Reconstruction, in an attempt to resolve the numerous civil rights issues across the post–Civil War nation, drafted the Fourteenth Amendment, which includes the Citizenship Clause and the Equal Protection Clause, and distributed it to states for ratification. In June 1866, Republican governor Frederick Low of California faced a conundrum when he received the amendment. The California legislature had gone on recess, and Low considered calling a special session but worried about the national embarrassment that would follow if the state legislature refused to ratify the amendment, which seemed likely. Before his term ended, Low delivered a message to the Senate, asking legislators to approve the amendments and protect California's progressive reputation, but he did not send the bill to the body for a vote.[70] Instead, Low left the fate of the amendments to the California electorate and the next governor.[71]

Given the political stakes, the 1867 state elections became a referendum on Reconstruction.[72] The state Democratic Party exploited Californio fears about their own racial identity by presenting Reconstruction policies as an inversion of the racial hierarchy. Californios, whose political power had been weakened by the 1850 Land Act, accepted the Democratic argument that Reconstruction was the culprit and allied with the party in the hopes of returning to positions of power.

At the California Democratic Convention, the party, after much debate, called on Antonio Coronel to collect Californio votes in exchange for running as the Democratic candidate for state treasurer. During the debate, some delegates argued that Coronel's Spanish fluency disqualified him from the position. Anglo-American settlers viewed the Spanish language as a marker of racial inferiority alongside one's physical appearance, religion, or class status. It was not until delegate Solomon Sharp convinced the delegates that the convention needed to nominate a Californio to win "the southern counties['] support" that Coronel received enough votes.[73] Rather than leave a party that viewed his mother tongue as a marker of inferiority, Coronel accepted the nomination after being assured by party insiders that he would receive the support of the northern counties.[74] The party would rely on Coronel to convince Californio voters to obstruct Reconstruction, even if some of its members believed that Californios possessed characteristics that disqualified them from participating in electoral politics.

Coronel boosted a Democratic ticket that included Henry Haight for governor. Haight had been a Republican who campaigned for presidential candidates John Frémont and Abraham Lincoln in 1855 and 1860, respectively. After President Lincoln issued the Emancipation Proclamation in January 1863, Haight joined the Democratic Party. During the 1867 State Democratic Convention, Haight accused radicals in Congress of attempting to override states' rights and argued that Black suffrage would ruin California by creating the possibility for Chinese suffrage, another group Haight considered ill-equipped to participate in democracy.[75]

Democratic candidates exploited Californios' racism to win votes and obstruct biracial democracy. In 1867, the party printed and distributed a flyer, "A Los Hijos Del Pais [*sic*]." The address printed Haight's promise to oppose all attempts that would force his supporters "into a state of political equality with negroes."[76] With this flyer, the Democratic Party deftly exploited Californios' racial anxieties and prejudices.

In a speech delivered in support of Henry Haight, Coronel clarified his stance on the "Chinese Question." Coronel declared that "the Chinese have come to this country and enjoy . . . all the benefits" but they did not have the necessary traits to enjoy the spoils of California.[77] In another speech, he accused President Lincoln and the Republican Party of establishing "military despotism, [and] giving supremacy to the Negro over the white in ten of the most beautiful states in order to obtain their votes." He warned of a "storm" that threatened to "ruin" California and the United States if radical Republicans remained in power. Coronel viewed Reconstruction as an attempt to remove "all rights of the whites," which would lead to "the ruin of the country."[78] Californios received these speeches with open ears. In San Buenaventura, according to a letter written by Coronel's goddaughter Soledad Coronel, Antonio Coronel left women "crazy" because his speech had "raised them to the heavens as no other speech had done."[79] While his records do not document the impact of Black political activism on his political decisions, Coronel's speeches indicate he viewed Black enfranchisement as a transposition of the racial hierarchy. As Democrats questioned his racial superiority, Coronel asserted his position at the top of the hierarchy by designating other groups to the bottom.

During the 1867 election, elite Californios hosted multiple juntas *democráticas* to support Democratic Party candidates. In Santa Barbara, elite Californios, including Antonio Coronel and the de la Guerra family, organized a large junta in August 1867. At the junta, which brought together nonelite and elite Spanish speakers, Samuel Axtell, a candidate for the US House of Representatives, delivered a speech translated by Juan de la Guerra.[80]

To endear himself to the audience, Axtell first acknowledged the patriarchal authority and patronage of the de la Guerra family, "who honored [him] by presiding over this meeting, together with close to a hundred of his relatives and fellow friends, all from his childhood."[81] Rather than denigrate Californio cultural customs, Axtell respected and performed them. Throughout the speech, Axtell directly appealed to the Californio audience by expressing a settler affinity and desire to maintain the status quo of localized white and Californio political control in the state. Axtell then acknowledged the contributions of the California Native Cavalry and applauded the men who had "abandoned their fertile fields and peaceful houses to suffer the fatigue and privations of the camp for the [Civil War] war effort." Axtell presented the audience with many reasons to vote the "radical-red-republican" party out.[82]

The bulk of Axtell's speech asserted that Black suffrage threatened Californios' political dominance. Axtell explained that "the Republican Party falsely calls itself Unionist" only to place political "power in the hands of the negroes who were once their slaves." By interpreting Reconstruction as a betrayal of racial hierarchies, Axtell inferred that the Republican Party threatened the social position and political power of all elites in California, not just in the South. In his closing remarks, Axtell insinuated that if Californios voted "for the party of revenge," they would help the Republican Party "carry out infamous acts." Axtell pledged to protect the California racial order and the Californios' position within it. If they voted for him, he would do everything to oppose the suffrage of "los negros, Chinos y Indios."[83]

In 1867, the Democrats won a majority of the electoral races on an anti-Reconstruction, anti-Black, anti-Chinese platform. Henry Haight won the governorship with 49,895 votes, compared to Republican candidate George Gorham's 40,359 votes.[84] Sam Axtell won a seat in the US House of Representatives with 57.3 percent of the vote. Antonio Cornel won his bid for state treasurer.[85] Coronel was the only Californio to win a statewide office during this election in which the Democrats gained a twenty-two-seat majority in the state assembly and a majority in the US House of Representatives. The Democrats would control Reconstruction in California.

The success of the California Democratic Party in 1867 depended on Coronel's campaigning and financial support. In multiple letters, Democratic Party members praised Coronel's campaign speeches.[86] In addition to calling on Coronel to deliver speeches to Californios, his records indicate that he paid at least $1,100 to the state Democratic Party for the 1867 campaign.[87] Despite Coronel's contributions to Democratic victories and his obstruction of interracial democracy in California, Anglo settlers were wary of his and other Californios' claims to whiteness because they spoke Spanish. Just a month after the election, Coronel received a letter from James Alex Forbes, the former British consul under the Mexican Republic, informing him that there was a rumor going around Santa Clara County that he would resign as the state treasurer because "his English [wa]s not equal to the importance of his post."[88] The *Red Bluff Independent*, a newspaper based in Sonoma County, wrote that Coronel "can scarcely speak a word of English," which meant that "the people of California have no use for Coronel."[89] While the party leadership utilized Coronel's mastery of Spanish to earn Californio votes, party members cited his mother tongue as evidence of his inability to hold an elected office. By voting to reject Reconstruction, Californios empowered the efforts to strip all non-Anglo inhabitants of citizenship and political power. Spanish would become a marker of racial inferiority.

On December 5, 1867, Governor Haight delivered his Inaugural Address, which set the tone for the state's rejection of Reconstruction. He opened with support for the Union and the US Constitution and quickly followed with a condemnation of Congress for warping the meaning of the Civil War. Haight declared that the war was fought to preserve the Union, "not to destroy the liberties of any portion of the people, or create a negro empire on our southern border.[90] Haight also gave his opinion on extending the franchise, saying: "The policy . . . of admitting the Blacks to the right of suffrage belongs to each State to determine for itself."[91] Haight declared that "the people of this State have expressed their opposition both to negro and Chinese suffrage [and] it [was] good for both of those races that the elective franchise should be confined to the whites."[92] Under Haight's leadership, the California legislature refused to ratify the Fourteenth Amendment. The amendment became part of the US Constitution in July 1868 due to the votes of other states. California did not ratify the Fourteenth Amendment until 1959.

As governor, Haight also acted to obstruct the ratification of the Fifteenth Amendment, which prohibits state or federal governments from denying a citizen's right to vote on the basis of race. In an eight-page Executive Department report delivered to the Senate, Governor Haight requested the body "formally reject" the Fifteenth Amendment because the franchise was a state's rights issue.[93] Haight also argued that "if the [fifteenth] amendment is adopted, the most degraded Digger Indian within our borders becomes at once an elector, and so far, a ruler."[94] For Haight, extending the franchise threatened white control over politics and the white settler project. On January 7, the Senate and the Assembly voted to "recede from the amendment."[95]

While the Fifteenth Amendment became a part of the US Constitution on February 3, 1870, the California legislature, again, did not vote in favor of the amendment until April 3, 1962, nearly one hundred years later. Californio votes led to the state's rejection of Reconstruction.

Challenging Nonwhite Citizenship

Even though Anglo-Americans welcomed Californio support for policies that hindered Reconstruction in the state, they did not accept Californios' gente de razón status as white and challenged their citizenship. In 1869, Pablo De la Guerra ran for reelection as Santa Barbara district judge. He had held this position since he ran as a Unionist in 1863 and after the US Civil War, returned to the Democratic Party. After the 1869 election, the *Sacramento Daily Union* commented on the race, stating that de la Guerra "is a man of overwhelming personality, and has doubtlessly beaten Walter Murray," the Republican candidate.[96] Indeed, de la Guerra won the judgeship. But, a month after the election, in November 1869, Anglo-American politicians contested de la Guerra's electoral victory on the grounds that he was not a US citizen.[97] In December 1869, Santa Barbara judge James Maguire dismissed the case against de la Guerra, and Governor Henry Haight commissioned him as district judge of the first district.[98]

Despite being commissioned as a district judge by Governor Haight, de la Guerra's political opponents continued to challenge his election on the premise that he was not a US citizen. Martin Kimberly, born in Connecticut and a settler in Santa Barbara where he raised sheep, challenged de la Guerra's citizenship in the California Supreme Court.[99] Eugene Lies, the Santa Barbara representative in the California State Assembly, gave the argument on behalf of Kimberly.[100] This was an Anglo-American attack on Californio power in Santa Barbara—a Californio stronghold even after the US Civil War. Archibald Peachy, formerly of the Peachy, Billings, and Halleck law firm that dealt with the family's land cases, represented Pablo de la Guerra in court.[101]

During his argument, Lies argued that de la Guerra "is not and never was a Citizen" of the United States.[102] He contended that when the California legislature passed the Act of April 20, 1863, Pablo de la Guerra was no longer eligible for the position of a district judge because the law stated, "No person shall be eligible to the office of District Judge who shall not have been a citizen of the United States and a resident of this State for two years and of the District one year." The state legislature passed this law to prevent Black citizens from running for public office, but now it was being used against a

Californio. In supporting the disenfranchisement of Black US citizens, Californios made their citizenship claims all the more vulnerable.

Lies also argued that prior to the signing of the Treaty of Guadalupe Hidalgo, de la Guerra was "an alien enemy." And when the US Congress ratified the treaty, "[de la Guerra] was simply a Mexican who might or not elect to become a citizen of the United States." Congress had to make Californios into citizens, yet Congress had not acted on the matter. Lies argued that regardless of what the Treaty of Guadalupe Hidalgo required, Californios' racial inferiority disqualified them from citizenship and cited Senator John C. Calhoun's infamous "War with Mexico" speech as the reason why the Senate did not transform Californios into citizens. In the speech, Calhoun stated the US Congress "ha[s] never dreamt of incorporating into our Union any but the Caucasian race the free white race. To incorporate Mexico, would be the very first instance of the kind of incorporating an Indian race; for more than half of the Mexicans are Indians, and the other is composed chiefly of mixed tribes. . . . Ours, sir, is the Government of a white race."[103] Lies echoed Calhoun's question, if Americans were "to associate with ourselves as equals, companions, and fellow-citizens, the Indians and mixed race of Mexico?" and that it was a "great mistake [to] suppose that all people are capable of self-government."[104] Reflecting Anglo-American settler sentiment, Lies not only accused de la Guerra of not being a citizen but also categorized all Californios and Mexicans as racially inferior.

De la Guerra's lawyer, Archibald Peachy, ignored Lies's racial argument and made a procedural argument. First, Peachy argued that conquest dissolves the relationship between a people and their former sovereign and transforms conquered people into subjects of the new power. As such, the American conquest of Alta California transformed Californios into US citizens. Second, Peachy argued that the Treaty of Guadalupe Hidalgo transformed Mexican citizens into US citizens. Third, the admission of California into the Union also conferred US citizenship on conquered Mexican citizens.[105] According to Peachy, Pablo de la Guerra did not become a US citizen just once but three times over. With these two opposing arguments in hand, the court now had to decide if de la Guerra was a citizen.

Justice Jackson Temple delivered his decision in October 1870. Temple ruled that since de la Guerra was "a white male citizen of Mexico," he had become a citizen under the Treaty of Guadalupe Hidalgo.[106] Given that Justice Temple categorized de la Guerra as "a white male citizen of Mexico," he refuted Lies's accusation that de la Guerra was an Indian or mixed race and, therefore, not a citizen. Rather than extend citizenship to all peoples, Temple made clear that when Congress admitted California into the Union, it bestowed upon California "the right to prescribe the qualifications of electors, and to exclude some of the inhabitants from certain political rights."[107] Temple empowered the California government to exclude certain groups from certain rights according to specific "qualifications," meaning racial, gender, and national identities. This decision, while maintaining Californios' citizenship, allowed for the legislature to exclude other groups from certain rights according to specific qualifications.

Despite the attacks made on their own citizenship, elite Californios denied Black Americans their citizenship rights as a way of demonstrating their distance from the racialized group and their proximity to whiteness. In 1870, prominent Californio Ygnacio Sepúlveda denied the request of Lewis Green, a Black American man, to register to vote. In the five years following the conclusion of the US Civil War, the African American population in Los Angeles grew to 109, with half of the population having been born in the state.[108] Like in Sacramento and San Francisco, Black Angelenos asserted their right to participate in the settler project and had begun to accumulate real estate. In 1872, six community members, including Biddy Mason and Robert Owens, bought property to establish the first African Methodist Episcopal (AME) Church in Los Angeles.[109] On April 12, 1870, the AME church held a celebration for the Fifteenth Amendment on the anniversary of the firing on Fort Sumter. At the celebration, Reverand J. E. M. Gillard, a member of the San Francisco activist community and a regular contributor to *The Elevator*, delivered a speech "on the future of the colored race."[110] Despite the hundreds of miles between San Francisco and Los Angeles, Gillard's appearance demonstrates that the Black community in Los Angeles was connected to the center of African American activism in the state. Days after Gillard's speech, Lewis Green, a barber originally from North Carolina and one of the wealthiest members of the community, attempted to register to vote. Los Angeles County clerk Thomas D. Mott refused to register Green.

It is likely that Green and other members of the African American community decided to test whether or not the Fifteenth Amendment would be upheld in Los Angeles.[111] It likely did not surprise Green to have his request denied, as throughout the state authorities were refusing to register Black voters.[112] In response, Green took the issue to the county court, where Judge Ygnacio Sepúlveda ruled that the county clerk could not uphold the Fifteenth Amendment because the California Constitution did not permit nonwhite men to vote. According to Sepúlveda, if the clerk had allowed Green to vote, he would have violated the state constitution.[113] Sepúlveda declared that state legislation needed to be enacted before Green, and other African American men, could vote. While making a procedural argument, Sepúlveda demonstrated his willingness to uphold the white monopoly on the franchise, signaling that he was a member of the white settler class. Despite Sepúlveda's ruling, the state legislature passed "An Act to Enforce the Fifteenth Amendment to the Constitution."[114]

On June 21, 1870, Green and two other Black American men registered to vote. County clerk Thomas D. Mott entered Green into the Los Angeles County Great Register and categorized him as "C" (for colored) and noted that he could vote due to an "amendment to [the] constitution."[115] After Green's success, at least fifteen additional African American men registered to vote in Los Angeles within a year. Despite Californio efforts to hold on to their citizenship rights and gente de razón settler status by denying Black claims to citizenship, Black Americans were carving out their own space in the settler society.

Meanwhile, Anglo-American settlers continued to challenge Californios in electoral politics, arguing that they were not qualified for citizenship. In 1876, Romualdo Pacheco won the election for a US Representative position by a handful of votes. Peter D. Wigginton, the Democrat candidate, challenged the votes on the grounds that the election was unfair. In newspapers, Democrats challenged Pacheco's electoral victory on the grounds that Spanish-speaking voters moved the election in Pacheco's favor.[116] Again, Anglo settlers asserted that the Spanish language was a marker of inferiority and, therefore, noncitizenship status. Despite this attempt to block Pacheco's victory, the California Supreme Court eventually ruled that Pacheco won the close election and ordered him to take his seat.[117]

Californios' political and military service during the US Civil War and their opposition to Reconstruction did not protect them from Anglo-Americans' efforts of disenfranchisement. In fact, Anglo settlers successfully denied Californios the right to vote, hold political office, and claim citizenship because Californios supported and enforced the very laws and logics that made such disenfranchisement possible. In their efforts to control the labor and lives of people they deemed inferior, Californios cosigned onto the laws that would complete their transformation into colonized colonizers.

CHAPTER FIVE

"Cutting Up the Large Ranchos in the Southern Part of the State"

The End of the Rancho and the Drafting of the 1879 California Constitution

After the torrential rains of 1862, the drought came. For nearly three years the entire state thirsted for water. By 1864, the once-grassy ranchos of Southern California had become a parched and sunbaked landscape.[1] Tens of thousands of cattle became emaciated skeletons, too malnourished and dehydrated to move.[2] At the peak of the drought, the twenty-five-mile road from Los Angeles to San Pedro "was covered with the carcasses of dead animals." In San Diego, rancho owners wondered what they were to do because there was "no rain, no grass [and the weather was] nearly as dry as August" even though summer was months away.[3]

This chapter contends that in the mid-1860s, environmental misfortune made it impossible for Californios to combat the consequences of the racist settler legislation they supported. Before the drought, elite Californio families owned tens of thousands of cattle, which enabled them to hold onto their vast land holdings and perform their gente de razón status.[4] During the Gold Rush, Californios sold thousands of cattle at fifty dollars a head in response to high demand.[5] As a result of such profits, prominent Californio patriarchs, such as Pablo de la Guerra, could pay the bills created by the 1851 US Land Act, high property taxes, and Anglo squatting. Holding on to their ranchos meant that elite Californios retained the ability to defer the effects of the racist settler legislation they helped implement.

During the second decade of California statehood, settler challenges to Californio land holdings intensified as environmental calamity struck. On May 20, 1862, US president Abraham Lincoln signed the Homestead Act, a victory for the proponents of free-soil settlement, which expanded the 1841 Preemption Act and opened western "public lands" to US citizens.[6] Under the Homestead Act, a citizen or intended citizen could claim up to one hundred and sixty acres of public land at one dollar and twenty-five cents per acre. Anglo-American settlers in California, however, interpreted the act as the opening up of Indigenous lands and yet-to-be ratified Mexican land grants.[7] More and more Anglo settlers trespassed and squatted on Californio and Indigenous lands under the assumption that these lands had been or would be transferred into the public domain. To expel Californios from their lands, squatters killed livestock and burned fields.[8] When the California Drought of 1863–65 destroyed the cattle industry, it also destroyed the Californios' ability to hold on to their lands and, in turn, to uphold their gente de razón status. In Santa Barbara, the cattle population plummeted from three hundred thousand in 1862 to seven thousand in 1865.[9] In Los Angeles, the cattle population declined by 71 percent. In addition to depleted cattle numbers, the financial return for each cow plummeted to one to two dollars a head. In one instance, a ranchero in Santa Barbara sold five thousand cattle for thirty-seven cents each.[10] Unable to pay lawyer fees, property taxes, and loan bills, elite Californios, like Pablo de la Guerra and Pío Pico, began selling land parcels and entire ranchos in the late 1860s. As this sell-off unfolded, Anglo-American settlers founded immigrant unions to encourage immigration from the eastern US and Europe aiming to realize their political imaginaries—a California comprised of Anglo families and their farms. These settler unions also helped facilitate the destruction of ranchos throughout Southern California and, in turn, the end of Californios gente de razón settler society.

As dreams of patria chica faded, Anglo settler dreams came into focus. The destruction of Californio dominance in the region and the expansion of federal authority after the US Civil War enabled Anglo-American settlers to close the Indigenous world in Southern California. As argued in previous chapters, Californio society tensely coexisted with an Indigenous world controlled by the Luiseño, Cahuilla, and Kumeyaay in Southern California. For decades, Californios had attempted to leverage their alliances with specific bands as evidence of their innate superior ability to control and subdue the Indian despite their inability to do just that. In contrast to the 1850s, in the 1870s, the settler government did not consider Californio interests or alliances and removed the Luiseño, Cahuilla, and Kumeyaay from their lands to reservations to facilitate Anglo settlement.

In cities, violence also erupted. In 1871, Anglo, Californio, and Mexican men targeted the Chinese of Los Angeles, killing nineteen Chinese men.[11] This event is now known as the 1871 Anti-Chinese Massacre. While the violence must be interpreted as an attempt to expel Chinese immigrants from the city, it is also important to consider the multiple factors leading to

This 1864 painting of the Church of the Mission of San Miguel depicts a sheriff capturing a group of outlaws on a drought-stricken landscape. Starving cows and a dry, grassless earth make up the background. Image courtesy of Claremont College.

Californio participation. Californios imagined that by, once again, collaborating with Anglo settlers to racialize and exclude the Chinese from settler society, just as they had done with Indians and Black Americans, they would revive their old alliance and maintain their position atop the social order. Despite Californio efforts, Anglo-American settlers in Los Angeles interpreted Californio participation in the massacre as evidence of their inferior status.

In the second half of the 1870s, white settlers founded the Workingmen's Party, a proworker, profarmer, and anti-Chinese political party. During the 1878 election, the Workingmen's Party proposed rewriting the state constitution to insulate white settlement from capitalist monopolies, antifarmer and antisettler land polices, and racial others, specifically the Chinese. The state elected to rewrite the constitution and, once again, men gathered to craft a document to protect settler interests. Unlike the 1849 California Constitution, however, the 1878 Constitution did not bear the signature of a single Californio. Despite their decades-long effort to maintain their settler society, by 1879, Californios had become a racialized, landless class, ousted from state making.

Drought, Debt, and the California Immigrant Union

This steep decline in income meant that rancho holders could no longer pay their property taxes, mortgages, and lawyer fees.[12] Thus, in the 1860s and 1870s, elite Californios sold off their lands to Anglo-American settlers in the hopes of retaining a fraction of their wealth.[13] Like so many of their compatriots, Pío and Andrés Pico were in debt in 1863. Since their income depended on the cattle trade, the drought made it impossible for the Pico family to pay their property taxes and lawyer fees. Making matters worse, in 1862, Andrés had accrued $60,000 in gambling debts.[14] With this mounting debt, Andrés transferred his cattle and land claims to his brother, Pío. Now completely in charge of the family estates, Pío Pico became delinquent on his 1864 Los Angeles tax bill.[15] Like other prominent Californios, he sold off parcels of his ranchos in the hopes of retaining the remainder of the titles. Pío turned to his compadrazgo network and sold off portions of his land claims to his extended family. In 1864, Pico negotiated a deal with his brother-in-law, John (Juan) B. Forster, who married his sister, Isadora Ygnacia, in 1837. Originally from England, Forster assimilated into Californio settler society and became Don Juan Forster. Rancho Santa Margarita was the largest patented land grant in California.[16] Pico negotiated a deal where he would transfer half of his Rancho Santa Margarita y Los Flores for $42,000. He hoped the money from this transaction would take the family out of debt while also keeping the lands within his compadrazgo network.

However, in 1868, lawyer Alfred Beck Chapman informed his client, Pío Pico, that according to the deed, he had transferred the whole of Santa Margarita to Forster. Forster had prepared the deed only in English, even though he knew his brother-in-law preferred to read Spanish, and assured Pico that the transaction included half of the rancho.[17] Sources from 1864 to 1868 indicate that Pico used his half of the rancho land without protest from Forster, meaning during these four years, both men proceeded as if the sale had encompassed only half of the rancho.[18] Months after the revelation, Andrés Pico confronted Forster, which caused a permanent estrangement between the two families.

In 1873, the case went to court, where Pico insisted that Forster had defrauded him. Forster insisted that the transaction with Pico was a legal one. The trial lasted for a month, but after twenty minutes of deliberation, a San Diego jury decided in Forster's favor.[19] The jury likely harbored anti-Californio sentiments, given that they were all Anglo-American settlers who had arrived in California within the last three years and had business interests in San Diego.[20] Compounding Pico's disadvantage, the court's translator, Rufus Porter, did not translate the Picos' remarks faithfully. This was such an issue that the presiding judge requested retranslations of the Picos' testimony.[21] Pico's situation was emblematic of other Californios—they had made alliances with settlers to control the land and labor of peoples they deemed inferior only to realize that their supposed allies had lumped Californios with the racially inferior and intended to dispossess them.

Like the Picos, the de la Guerras also fell into debt. The 1862 Great Flood pushed the de la Guerras into financial hardship. After the floods killed a majority of his cattle, Pablo de la Guerra tried to get a $50,000 low-interest loan from a San Francisco bank. He failed to get the loan because other cash-strapped rancheros rushed the banks trying to secure loans, which drove up the interest rates.[22] As the drought entered its second year and shortly after de la Guerra had been ousted from the California Senate because of his Democratic affiliation, the family sold off a portion of its prized Rancho San Julian claim in 1864, only to sell off the remainder of the rancho in 1867. In 1865 de la Guerra sold Rancho Simi. In August of 1872, the de la Guerra family sold off Rancho Conejo to John Edwards and Howard Mills. With this sale, the family, which had once claimed five hundred thousand acres, now held just twenty-four thousand acres.[23] Edwards and Mills sold parcels of Rancho Conejo to settlers hoping to transform the ranchos into communities, or small countries, that resembled the rural farming communities of the Midwest and East Coast. Emblematic of Californios' experiences with the elongated Land Commission process, the de la Guerra family received the US Land Patent for Conejo a month after the sale.[24] Without land and without cattle, prominent Californios lost their status as rancheros—a pillar of their gente de razón identity. The drought hastened what the 1851 US Land Act began—Californio dispossession and white settlement.

As Californios sold off their ranchos, Anglo-American settlers began to move into Southern California in greater numbers. Californios were now a minority population.[25] By 1870, non-Californios residents accounted for 62 percent of the Los Angeles population, with Californios accounting for 38 percent. Similarly, in Santa Barbara, Californio residents accounted for 37 percent of the county population.[26] San Diego's white population grew from seven hundred to 4,833 from 1850 to 1870.[27] Anglo-American migrants achieved this demographic shift with assistance from the railroad, settler unions, and state and federal governments.

In December 1869, California governor Henry Haight issued a call to the legislature to encourage the "right kind of immigration" to the state in his biannual message. Haight imagined the state populated by "immigrants of kindred races" who would establish permanent agricultural settlements and adequately develop the state's resources.[28] He asked the legislature to develop "measures" and allocate funds "to establish agencies in New York and Baltimore and Europe . . . to [attract] immigrants to this coast, and [secure] additional means for their safe and speedy transfer" to California. Haight declared that the legislature needed to act to ensure that California would not have a population of "races inferior in natural traits, pagan in religion, ignorant of free institutions and incapable of sharing in them without putting the very existence of those institutions in peril." In case his inferences were not enough, Haight clearly stated that he meant for California to have "a farming population from Germany and other European states."[29]

After Haight's speech, the California Senate introduced bills to encourage "the right kind of immigration," but the body failed to pass legislation that would allocate funds for immigrant recruitment.[30] In turn, a group of San Francisco businessmen stepped in and formed the California Immigrant Union to recruit "desirable American and European immigrants" from eastern states and Europe, primarily current-day Germany.[31] The organization, with volunteers and paid agents, would collect donations to print settler propaganda and "facilitate the travel" of "intelligent agriculturalist" to California.[32] Governor Haight, along with ex-governors John Downey, Milton Latham, and Leland Stanford, served on the honorary committee.

As part of its efforts, the California Immigrant Union published propaganda to encourage white settlement in California, such as the pamphlet *All About California and the Inducements to Settle There*.[33] The pamphlet declared that the Union's objective was to "encourage immigration from Europe and the eastern parts of the United States" to California and to establish permanent farming settlements in the state.[34] To entice the reader, the pamphlet portrayed California as an uncultivated Eden with "soil that yields the richest and most varied reward." *All About California* also presented the state as the embodiment of settler democracy, proclaiming that the state's homestead laws protected "poor men . . . from merciless creditors" and that education was available "to the children of the poorest citizens."[35] To encourage the growth of permanent settlements, the pamphlet encouraged its readers to bring together their funds with other settlers and create joint-stock companies to purchase entire estates, ideally ranchos recently lost by Californios, and divide them into family parcels. As Californios lost their land claims to debt, Governor Haight, whom a majority of Californios had voted for in 1867, and the California Immigrant Union encouraged aspiring settlers to imagine the state as a pristine landscape where one could leverage their whiteness as much as their labor to transform the old ranchos into a "fruitful flower-crowned paradise."[36]

In Santa Barbara County, the financially struggling Carrillo family sold Rancho Lompoc to the Hollister-Dibblee Land in 1863. The Carrillo family sold off this land grant while still embroiled in the Land Claims process. After the US Supreme Court approved the Rancho Lompoc patent in 1873, ten years after the Carrillos sold the grant, the Hollister-Dibblee Land sold the forty-three-thousand-acre rancho to the Lompoc Land Company, a joint stock company created to establish a settler colony in Santa Barbara County.[37]

In August 1874, the Lompoc Land Company founded a Lompoc temperance colony to encourage "desirable" settlement in Santa Barbara County and worked with the California Immigrant Union to recruit Anglo settlers from Indiana, Ohio, New York, and Tennessee, as well as Bavaria, where people had a "practical devotion to the principles of liberty."[38] To encourage agricultural family settlement, the Lompoc Land Company sold off parcels of land, immediately built schools and churches, and planned a town center. Lompoc was a successful colony and served as a model for transforming ranchos into agricultural towns.[39]

Just months after the announcement of the Lompoc colony, in January 1875, businessmen, with the assistance of the California Immigrant Union, formed the Centinela Land Company.[40] The company purchased two ranchos—Rancho Centinela and Rancho Sausal Redondo—to establish a colony "for the purpose of aiding immigration and assisting the immigrant."[41] Like the Lompoc Compony, the Centinela Company worked with the general agent of the California Immigrant Union, W. H. Martin, to recruit settlers.[42] On behalf of the Centinela Company, the California Immigrant Union printed a supplemental pamphlet to *All About California*, which advertised the Centinela Colony.

In San Diego, John Forster had similar ambitions. In 1873, even though he was in the midst of a case to prove he held the deed to Rancho Santa Margarita, Forster sent an envoy to Europe, Max Strobel, to recruit settlers.[43] When the case started, Strobel had recruited about one hundred hopeful settlers from Holland on the guarantee that if they improved the land, they would receive eighty acres of land.[44] Forster hoped these European emigrants would transform the rancho into a town, but Strobel died in the middle of negotiating the agreement, and Forster's colonization scheme fell through.[45] Despite Forster's failed attempts, numerous Anglo landowners engaged in colonization schemes that transformed Southern California ranchos into white settlements.[46]

Anglo Americans in California praised the California Immigrant Union and land companies for encouraging white immigration and destroying the rancho. The state Grange organization lauded the Union for encouraging white, agriculturalist immigration, which ranchos had impeded for years.[47] The *San Jose Mercury* claimed that the "colonization schemes [solved the] ranch problems and opened up . . . tracts of . . . for the benefit of the general public" and condemned rancho owners who still held on to their titles.[48] A syndicated letter printed in 1875 described the schemes as "the most practicable way of cutting up the largo ranchos in the southern part of the State."[49] A year later, the *Santa Barbara Weekly Press* praised the efforts because it meant "land for the people" and took Santa Barbara out of its state of "wilderness."[50] By characterizing Santa Barbara as a wilderness rather than a powerful Californio region shaped by the influential de la Guerra and Carrillo families, newspapers joined the California Immigrant Union and state politicians in undermining the role Californios performed in shaping the region's politics and economy and, therefore, justifying the eradication of the rancho.

Making Reservations

Since the passage of the 1862 Homestead Act, more and more Anglo-Americans descended on the Indigenous world and squatted on Luiseño, Cahuilla, Cupeño, and Kumeyaay lands on the assumption that Indigenous lands were a part of the public domain.[51] In turn, the US Bureau of Indian Affairs actively and intentionally pursued a removal policy to abet white settlement in Southern California.[52] In contrast to the decades when they called on prominent Californios, Anglo settlers now called on the US government to remove the Indigenous. No longer in control of the land, Californios were unable to negotiate with Indigenous leaders.

Indian Affairs superintendent agent B. C. Whiting proposed relocating the numerous Indigenous villages to open up the region to Anglo-American settlers. Whiting explained that the "real estate in the [region was] much sought after" and a reservation would limit the occurrence of violent conflicts between Anglo settlers and the Indigenous.[53] In response to the superintendent agent's reports, on January 31, 1870, US president Ulysses S. Grant signed an executive order that set aside San Pasqual and Pala as reservations.

After Grant's executive order, the Bureau of Indian Affairs ordered Luiseño, Cahuilla, and Kumeyaay villages to move to reservations at Pala and San Pasqual. The Luiseño, Cahuilla, and Kumeyaay refused to leave their lands; reservations did not factor into their political imaginaries. Some Indigenous leaders expressed concern about the political conditions at the reservations; others worried that they would lose their personal liberties or that they would become "slaves of the government."[54] Special Indian agent Augustus Greene reported to DC that "the Mission Indians of Southern California [were] retarding the settlement" because they resided on lands they did not cultivate. Green recommended that the US government remove the thousands of Luiseño, Cahuilla, and Kumeyaay to reservations, "to leave the land which they occupy to white settlers."[55]

By attempting to remove Indigenous communities to reservations, the Bureau of Indian Affairs sparked political conflict. In 1871, Anglo-American settlers signed a petition requesting that the executive order allowing for the creation of reservations be rescinded; they coveted the lands that would become reservations. Upon receiving the petition, President Grant withdrew his order to create a reservation on April 5, 1871.[56] The Cahuilla and Luiseño remained on their ancestral lands, but Anglo-settlers encroached on their lands and even built villages.

Overwhelmed by Anglo squatters, on May 8, 1873, the leaders of the Cahuilla and Luiseño sent a petition to the US Land Office in Los Angeles demanding that their ancestral lands be respected. The office refused to acknowledge the request. A year later, in May 1874, Cahuilla and Luiseño leaders sent another petition stating that Anglo-American settlers were encroaching on their lands and requesting that the US Land Office provide each Cahuilla and Luiseño family with a land title. Again, the office refused to act on the matter.[57]

In October 1874, the Bureau threw its weight behind the reservation system in order to free up Indigenous land. Special US commissioner Charles A. Wetmore visited Anglo settlers in San Diego and delivered a speech explaining how the reservation system would work. He stated that the reservation system would resemble the old mission system where on designated lands, the federal government and the Catholic church would "civilize" and teach agricultural skills to Indigenous "wards." The bureau agents imagined that the reservation system would transform the Indigenous into agricultural citizens. To facilitate Anglo settlement, the US government would conduct a survey to clarify which lands were available for homesteading and purchase.[58] Assured of their access to the land, the audience members wholeheartedly endorsed the plan, as did newspapers across the state.[59]

As part of the larger effort to remove the Indigenous to reservations, in September 1875, Anglo settlers, backed by the San Diego sheriffs, ejected hundreds of Luiseño from their village located on the Temecula Rancho.[60] At first, Olegario, the chief of the Temecula band of Luiseño, consulted with his Los Angeles–based lawyer to resolve the issue, but a month after the eviction, newspapers reported that Olegario had organized a group of fifty to sixty men to "burn stores and murder settlers" in retaliation.[61] The tension dissipated for reasons not preserved in the archive. In time, the federal government removed the Luiseño and established a military post to protect white settlers.[62]

On December 27, 1875, by executive order, President Grant established nine reservations in the Indigenous world.[63] While conflicts over land and political authority continued, the creation of reservations signified the transformation of the Indigenous world by federal power. Emblematic of this transformation was in 1877 when the Southern Pacific Railroad ran tracks from Fort Yuma through the Indigenous world and to River Station in Los Angeles. Anglo settlers could now traverse through and settle in the Indigenous world.

A New Constitution

As the US government removed Indigenous peoples to abet white settlement, Anglo-Americans and Californios engaged in acts of violence to assert racial boundaries between settlers. During the 1850s and '60s, both Anglo and Californio settlers tolerated Chinese laborers despite preexisting prejudices. But in 1871, racial tensions erupted in Los Angeles when Anglo, Californio, and Mexican residents killed nineteen Chinese men after a violent confrontation between two Chinese social organizations. The 1871 Anti-Chinese Massacre was, undoubtedly, a violent assertion of anti-Chinese prejudice in Los Angeles. However, given Californio and Mexican participation, the event was also a Californio and Mexican attempt to revive their alliance with Anglo-American settlers as enforcers of a racial hierarchy.[64]

In 1871, Los Angeles had 172 Chinese residents. Most Chinese inhabitants could only secure dilapidated housing on or around Calle de los Negros, a street considered to be a vice district.[65] Californios who owned land on the street rented out derelict rooms to Chinese residents to make easy money. For example, Antonio Coronel rented out rooms in the Coronel family house located on the corner of Calle de los Negros and Calle del Aliso.[66] As Californio and Anglo settlers increasingly associated Chinese residents with racial degeneracy and social upheaval, they meted out casual violence against Chinese individuals as a way of enforcing the socioracial order.[67]

On October 24, 1871, a long-standing conflict between two rival *tongs*, the Nin Yung and Hong Chow, culminated in a gunfight on Calle de Los Negros. Los Angeles Police officer Jesus Bilderrain, a son of Anglo and Mexican parents, first responded to the fight. A group of Californio and Anglo police officers—Esteban Sanchez, Robert Hunter, and Robert Thompson—joined Bilderrain to suppress the violence and restore order. During the initial gunfight, Ah Choy, a Chinese resident, and Thompson were killed. An Anglo-American officer, Thompson was married to a Mexican American woman, Rosario, who was pregnant with twins at the time of his killing. When news that Chinese gunmen had killed an Anglo police officer spread, approximately five hundred Anglo-American and Californio residents descended on Calle de Los Negros to punish the Chinese men who violated the socioracial order. Witnesses reported that men rushed to Calle de Los Negros once they heard that Chinese assailants "were killing the white man."[68]

Eager to avenge Thomas's death, Anglo, Californio, and Mexican men trapped Chinese men in the buildings of the Coronel block. Los Angeles sheriff James Burns deputized citizens and ordered them to shoot anyone who tried to escape the buildings. After three hours, the mob stormed the Coronel building and began assaulting Chinese men. The mob killed a twelve-year-old boy. The mob targeted a well-known doctor, Chee Long "Gene" Tong, who begged for his life in English and Spanish. After Tong was dead, his murderers cut off his fingers to pilfer his rings and looted his house.[69] The murderous mob's treatment of Tong demonstrates that they intended for their violence to correct Chinese transgression of the socioracial order.

As the violence continued to unfold, Antonio Coronel, who was serving as state treasurer, and José Cristóbal Aguilar, the Los Angeles mayor, who were near Calle de los Negros, refused to intervene. In fact, Mayor Aguilar mounted his horse and simply surveyed the violence. One can imagine the image Aguilar projected—an overseer of corrective violence. Aguilar was not alone; according to newspapers, many "respectable citizens" simply watched as the violence unfolded.[70] The Anglo-Californio-Mexican mob killed at least nineteen Chinese men and assaulted and robbed many more.

Four days after the massacre, and only due to the Anglo community's outrage, elite Californio and county court judge Ygnacio Sepúlveda ordered a grand jury to investigate the causes and consequences of the event.[71] The grand jury issued forty-nine indictments for murder, assault, and theft but only delivered eight convictions. Later, the California Supreme Court reversed each conviction on the grounds that the forty-nine indictments were "fatally defective."[72] Not a single person was criminally charged for their involvement in the Anti-Chinese Massacre. Aided by the courts, the Anglo-Californio-Mexican mob clarified the racial distance between Chinese and non-Chinese residents.

In response to the California Supreme Court's decision, one Chinese resident, Wing Chung, sued the City of Los Angeles for not taking the necessary action to prevent the massacre and demanded restitution for the damage inflicted on his store. Chung lost.[73]

Inspired by Chung's lawsuit, Antonio Coronel also sued the city for $5,000 in damages to his adobe slum. The court, which was unwilling to administer monetary justice for Chinese immigrants, was also unwilling to award Coronel the damages he requested. When Anglo residents heard of Coronel's demand, they expressed outrage, arguing that the Coronel House was a "festering ulcer" and a "disgrace to the city."[74]

A year later, the Los Angeles Common Council cited Coronel for maintaining a public nuisance, describing the house as "ill-governed and disorderly," where ill-reputed men and women gathered for "drinking, tippling, whoring and misbehaving themselves."[75] While Californio residents participated in the massacre to racially distance themselves from the Chinese, Anglo settlers in Los Angeles weaponized the meaning of massacre to create racial distance from the Californios, reviving racializing stereotypes of Californios as incompetent landowners who engaged in corrupt behavior. Californios could no longer successfully assert their racial superiority because of their declining political and economic status.

Throughout the state, working-class and landless Anglo-Americans, as well as European immigrants, had grown increasingly anxious about their economic positions during Reconstruction and the Long Depression (1873–79). In response, white settlers organized the People's Independent Party and began demanding a new state constitution. The prominent Californios of Los Angeles, such as Ygnacio Sepulveda and Reginaldo del Valle, remained loyal to the Democratic Party—they did not join the working man's cause.

During the 1875 state elections, the People's Independent Party campaigned on rewriting the California Constitution to protect individual rights, rather than the interests of capitalist and railroad companies, and ending government corruption to serve the interests of white farmers. At its core, the antiland monopoly movement was about restoring the settler state's promise of a white agrarian republic by removing corporate and racial menaces—Californio and Chinese immigrants—from the land.[76] Despite the significant support of California farmers, the People's Independent Party failed to achieve an electoral victory. In the 1875 election, the People's Independent Party nominated John Bidwell, an early Anglo-American settler of Alta California, as their gubernatorial candidate; however, Democratic candidate William Irwin won the race. While not a member of the People's Independent Party, Irwin ran on an antimonopoly, anticorporation, and anti-Chinese campaign but did not advocate for rewriting the state constitution.[77] After the 1875 election, the People's Independent Party vanished, but its supporters and their demands remained.

As the Long Depression lingered, Anglo-American and European immigrant laborers throughout California, especially in San Francisco where the local economy depended on the railroad industry, sought a scapegoat. During the first half of the decade, approximately one hundred and fifty thousand laborers, many from China and Ireland, migrated to San Francisco in pursuit of wealth. The economic downturn, however, caused employers, especially railroad companies, to cut wages and dismiss workers, mostly Irish laborers, resulting in a 20 percent unemployment rate. Due to racially stratified payrolls, which were enforced by railroad companies, Chinese laborers received lower wages for their labor and retained their jobs, bolstering the idea of the Chinese as an economic menace. Rather than blame the railroad companies, immigrant laborers, mostly Irish, blamed Chinese laborers for their economic plights. On July 23, 1877, when the Central Pacific Railroad Company announced wage cuts, San Francisco erupted into a three-day riot characterized by mostly Irish immigrants attacking Chinese men and property.[78]

Across the United States, strikes and demonstrations percolated. In San Francisco, destitute workers met in sandlots where they listened to labor and political leaders blame Chinese workers for the white workers' plight. The most vociferous speaker was Denis Kearney, a naturalized Irish immigrant.[79] Kearney was born in County Cork, Ireland, and after becoming an orphan at the age of ten, he became a shipboy and worked on ships until he arrived in San Francisco in 1868. In 1876, he became a US citizen. In the months following the July riots, Kearney developed a following consisting of mainly young, unskilled, unemployed European immigrant men who had recently become US citizens.[80] Kearney, along with Frank Roney, who fled Ireland due to his revolutionary politics, formed the Workingmen's Party of California (WPC) in October 1877.[81]

The WPC had four goals: one, to remove the Chinese; two, to remove the rich from government; three, to destroy the land monopoly; four, to elect workingmen into public office. Due in great part to Kearney's speeches, the party's slogan became "The Chinese Must Go!"[82] While we must recognize the impact of these recently nationalized Irish immigrants' anti-Chinese racism, we must also interpret their performance of violence against and the demand for expulsion of the Chinese as an attempt by to racially distance themselves from another laboring immigrant class and to bridge the racial gap between Anglo-American settlers. The WPC was born out of the inability of Irish immigrants to achieve the white settler dream, and its political goals were an assertion of that dream. Kearney, whom historians have described as a "self-made man" and "a producer in the Jacksonian sense," likely imagined California as a place where he could claim a higher spot on the socioracial hierarchy.[83] Like the Californios, Kearney and Irish immigrants attempted to demonstrate their superiority over an inferior class with corrective violence and political maneuvering.

During the first two months of 1878, men who had never participated in local politics formed the Workingman's Club No. 1 of Los Angeles and the Second Ward Workingmen's Club of Los Angeles.[84] The men had formed the clubs to address two issues: one, the employment of Chinese laborers resulted in the "suffering for the need of labor to earn an honest livelihood"; two, the presence of Chinese immigrants endangered the settler project in California because they prevented "citizen workmen" from "developing the unequaled resources of [the] State."[85] The Workingman's Party was an anti-Chinese party as much as it was a prosettler party.

During the 1878 statewide election, the Workingman's Party assembled a ticket of candidates that campaigned on an antimonopolist, anti-Chinese, and a prosettler platform. Prominent Californios in Los Angeles continued to support the Democrats due to the party's stance on landholding. Californios like Ygnacio Sepulveda, who still held onto his judgeship, and Reginaldo del Valle, the son of Ignacio del Valle, publicly endorsed the Democrats, refusing to be associated with a working-class party.[86] In the north, voters came out for the party, which picked up all thirty legislative seats in San Francisco. The Workingman's Party candidates won an additional thirty seats throughout the state. A measure for a constitutional convention, which also appeared on the 1878 state ballot, received 74,600 votes in support and 44,214 against.[87]

As a result of the electoral outcome, the state legislature called for 152 delegates, thirty-two of whom were to be elected by voters, to gather in

Sacramento in September 1878 to rewrite the constitution.[88] The major parties of California all ran tickets. The Non-Partisan Party was a coalition of traditional Democrats and Republicans. The Democrat and Republican Parties posted their own candidates in opposition to the Non-Partisan Party nominees. The WPC ran candidates, as did the new splinter party of Anti-Kearney Workingmen.[89] The delegation was made of seventy-nine representatives from the Non-Partisan ticket, fifty from the WPC ticket, thirteen from the Republican ticket, and ten from the Democratic ticket.

As the party that loudly advocated for a new constitution, the Workingman's Party had three goals when it came to rewriting the state constitution: first, to exclude the Chinese from the state; second, to end land monopoly and a predatory tax system; third, to limit the power of the state legislature. Regardless of their party, every delegate sought to rewrite the constitution to realize their settler imaginaries by protecting white farmer settlements from the land regulations, onerous taxes, and a strong legislature–the very mechanisms that contributed to the dispossession of the Californios.

Beginning in September 1878, the 152 delegates met in Sacramento to draft a constitution that would fix the perceived shortcomings of the 1849 constitution.[90] Unlike the 1849 Constitutional Convention held in Monterey, not a single Californio delegate was present at the 1878 convention in Sacramento. On Friday, October 4, 1878, the delegation offered nominations to fill vacant seats. Tulare delegate Joseph Brown, a Democrat originally from Kentucky, made a motion to welcome a Spanish-speaking delegate to the convention.[91] He nominated José Ramon Pico, the former captain of the Native Californian Calvary. Brown argued that Pico deserved a seat because the Pico family had played a central role in the state's history and that the family had even donated lands to the state. He stressed that Pico was "a gentleman of refinement and a scholar."[92] By characterizing Pico this way, Brown attempted to refute the racialized ideas his fellow delegates likely held about Pico. If presenting Pico as a refined gentleman, or gente de razón, was not enough to convince the other delegates, Brown argued that the "the Spanish and Mexican Population [that] amounts to twenty-three thousand" merited representation.[93] Brown closed his speech, declaring "that a family that has done so much for this State, . . . should occupy a position on this floor."[94]

The delegation was unconvinced by Brown's speech. A delegate from Northern California, James Shafter, a Republican originally from Vermont, responded, stating that he could not support Pico's nominations because he would be "exposed to considerable personal danger."[95] Shafter clarified that

Pico had brought his "lasso" and intended to use the weapon on his foes. While Anglo-Americans once relied on Californios' use of violence to control the Indigenous, Shafter now linked a propensity to violence as evidence of Californios' inability to participate in governance. Shafter continued, stating that it was not the responsibility of a republican government to afford privileged treatment to wealthy families, especially since the Pico family had claimed land by ill-gotten means. The delegation did not welcome Pico. In the span of thirty years, Californios had been ousted.

This was a delegation of white settlers. Tellingly, only two delegates had been born in California—two men in their twenties from San Francisco, meaning they were born after California became a US state. Thirty delegates had been born outside the United States, with a majority coming from Ireland. The remaining delegates originated from northern and southern states.[96] The would work together to create a constitution that protected the white settler state.

In addition to denying the Californio population representation at the convention, the delegates acted to exclude Californios from the political process by transforming California into an English-only state. The 1849 constitution had required the California government to translate and print all laws in Spanish.[97] From the 1850s to the 1870s, Anglo-American settlers cited Californios' Spanish-language fluency as a marker of racial inferiority.[98] During the debate on this provision, Northern California delegate William Tinnin, a Democrat originally from Mississippi, proclaimed that if one was not capable of speaking English, they were "not competent" to participate in the political process.[99] He finished by stating that the state government should not provide translations "for the benefit of foreigners." For Tinnin, Spanish speakers were incapable of participating in the political process because their Spanish fluency meant they were foreigners ineligible for citizenship.

Delegates from the Southern California counties protested the English-only amendment because local electoral politics and the judicial system still relied on the Spanish language. Delegate James Ayers of Los Angeles, a Democrat originally from Scotland, reminded his colleagues that the Treaty of Guadalupe Hidalgo required them to extend "equal rights and privileges" to Californios and, thus, they should not include an English-only provision in the state constitution.[100] Despite Ayers's and others' objections, the delegation approved the article forty-six to thirty.[101] The 1879 California Constitution required that "all laws of the State of California, and all official writing, and the executive, legislative, and judicial proceedings, shall be conducted, preserved, and published in the English language."[102] Californios had been excluded from the convention and, now, the delegates excluded Californios from governance.

The delegates also acted to exclude Chinese immigrants from the California economy and electoral politics. On the seventy-third day of the convention, the Committee on Chinese issued its recommendation, which was to create a legal environment that discouraged Chinese immigration to the state.[103] They could not ban Chinese immigration, as that was the purview of the federal government. The committee recommended empowering and requiring the state legislature to write laws that would exorcise California of "dangerous and detrimental" Chinese persons from all aspects of society. The delegates thought that allowing for state discrimination in this manner would not violate federal policy against racial discrimination and avoid US Supreme Court challenges to the US Constitution. It is essential to note that while the delegates sought to limit the legislature's power regarding property taxes, they were more than willing to empower the body, provided it enacted laws that protected white control of politics and established an apparatus to control and discipline Chinese bodies.

After much debate, the delegates crafted Article XIX, which transformed the Chinese into "aliens." Aliens were foreigners solely because of their race and, therefore, were unable to become naturalized citizens.[104] Section 1 of Article XIX empowered the legislature to regulate and provide protections "from the burdens and evils" caused by "aliens" who were "dangerous or detrimental to the well-being or peace of the State."[105] This section of the 1879 constitution transformed all Chinese immigrants into aliens whose very presence endangered the state.[106] Sections 2 and 3 of Article XIX forbade corporations and the state, county, and municipal governments from employing the Chinese in any capacity. However, section 3 permitted the employment of a Chinese individual as "punishment for crime."[107] Section 4 of Article XIX was a list of policy recommendations for the state legislature. The section declared that since "the presence of foreigners ineligible to become citizens of the United States [was] dangerous to the well-being of the State," the legislature was required to "discourage" such immigration by any means possible. The constitution also empowered municipal governments to remove Chinese immigrants from the state.[108] Years before the US Congress passed the 1882 Chinese Exclusion Act, these California delegates attempted to exclude Chinese immigrants from the state.

The writers of the 1879 constitution also attempted to reform the land and tax policies that the Workingman's Party cited as detrimental to Anglo settler livelihood. Article XVII, entitled "Land, and Homestead Exemption," required the legislature to "protect, by law, . . . a certain portion of the homestead and other property of all heads of family."[109] The second and third sections of the article required the legislature to prevent the development of large landholding in the form of ranchos and railroad land monopoly by discouraging "the holding of large tracts of land, uncultivated and unimproved" by individuals or corporations and compelled the state to sell public lands "suitable to cultivation . . . only to actual settlers."[110] The Workingman's Party sought to reform the tax system imposed by the 1849 California Constitution because property owners had to pay taxes on their mortgage and their equity. While this tax system successfully drove Californios into debt and off their land, the "double tax" now inhibited white settlement.[111] After much debate, the delegates established a board of equalization to assess property tax structures, transferred the mortgage tax obligation to lenders, and raised the taxes on railroad property.[112] This constitution attempted to make the Californio rancho a legal impossibility while abetting white family settlement.

On May 7, 1879, the California electorate approved a new state constitution with a vote of 77,959 to 67,134.[113] With the 1879 California Constitution, Anglo-American settlers had created a document that consolidated and protected Anglo settler power. Less than a year after its ratification, a federal court nullified Article XIX on the grounds that it violated the Burlingame Treaty, which established protections for Chinese immigrants; the Fourteenth Amendment of the US Constitution; and the US Civil Rights Act of 1866.[114] Still, Chinese immigrants and Chinese Americans experienced discriminatory treatment in many parts of their lives. Anglo-American settlers, in pursuit of their settler dreams, accomplished their goals of reforming the state property tax system to aid white settlement, ousting Californios from government, and excluding the Chinese from the state.[115]

Conclusion: A Landless Class

After the ratification of the 1879 constitution, prominent Californios found it increasingly difficult to participate in politics as they had once done. White settlers no longer required Californio cooperation. The Pico family acutely experienced the transition from political elite to colonized class. In the last decades of his life, Pío Pico was determined to maintain his status as an important political and business figure. As Californio political power waned, Pico decided to create a landmark that would embody Californio power and wealth—he would build a grand and modern hotel, the Pico House, in Los

The Pico House in December 2023. Built in the 1870s, the Pico House hides in plain sight as is evidenced by the scooters parked in front. Photo by author.

Angeles. In 1869, Pico purchased the Carrillo house located at the northwest corner of La Plaza in Los Angeles (close to Calle de los Negros) and invested over $100,000 to build an extravagant three-story, European-style hotel.

The Pico House opened on June 19, 1870. Pico built this hotel to cement his legacy as a founder of California. In newspaper reporting on the hotel, Pico is credited with bringing modernity to La Plaza, but it was not enough to make the pueblo modern.[116] The *Los Angeles Star* described the plaza as "a filthy, neglected . . . waste spot" and "an eye sore to the community."[117] Newspapers proposed that the only solution was to erect an iron fence and transform the center of Californio Los Angeles into a manicured park. Anglo-Americans continued to associate Californios and all other nonwhite inhabitants with an inability to properly utilize the land.

As Pico embarked on this business venture, he was embroiled in the legal fight to save Rancho Santa Margarita y Los Flores. When Pico lost Rancho Santa Margarita in 1873, he fell into debt. To stay afloat, Pico took out a mortgage on the Pico House with a San Francisco bank, Savings and Loan Society. The cash helped him to hold onto his remaining properties for a while. But in 1883, Pico lost the Pico House when the bank took him to court for foreclosure. Even though Pico had evidence that he paid the mortgage in full, the court ruled against him, and he lost the hotel. In attempting to build a monument to the Pico family, Pío had miscalculated and collaborated with men who had no intention of treating him as an equal and hastened his family's demise. He remained in litigation, desperately trying to save other properties until his death in 1894.[118] Newspapers memorialized Pico as "the last governor of Mexican California," as well as a conman who nefariously claimed and granted Mexican land grants.[119]

Despite his decades-long relationship with the Democrats, Antonio Coronel did not run for reelection as state treasurer when his term ended in 1871. There is no record of Coronel's reasons for this decision, but the growing hostility toward Californios, the attacks on his Spanish fluency, and the critiques of his proprietor practices may have convinced him to abandon political office. During the last two decades of his life, Coronel no longer sought political office but continued to privately campaign and fund the Democratic Party in Los Angeles.[120]

In his last years, similarly to Pío Pico, Coronel tried to ensure that Californios and their patria chica did not fade from people's recollections of the past.[121] He advised author Helen Hunt Jackson as she wrote her novel *Ramona* (1884), a Southern California romance novel that centers on a Scottish Native young woman, Ramona. The novel, which was published the year Antonio Coronel died, became a sensation and began the cultural reinterpretation of Spanish and Mexican history often described as the Spanish Fantasy Past. This romantic and inaccurate portrayal of Spanish and Mexican society ignores the Indigenous reality of colonization while venerating Californios.

A cultural ideology, the Spanish Fantasy Past obscures the Indigenous and Mexican history of the state and, in turn, spins a historical narrative from Spanish settlement to the US conquest to an Anglo future that does not offset racial and class anxieties by centering nonwhite actors. Beyond *Ramona*, the Spanish Fantasy Past took hold of the California landscape through Spanish colonial revival architecture and the state's history as reflected in the cultural romanticization of the Spanish missions from the 1880s to the 1920s.[122] Rather than project the idea that the Indigenous, Californios, and Mexicans are a part of the region's history, the Spanish Fantasy Past relegates all non-Anglos to a bygone, if not fantastical, era and promotes the idea that civilization only began with Anglo-American settlers.[123] As a result, the Spanish Fantasy Past obfuscates Californio as well as Indigenous, Black, and Chinese history in the region.

Much like the Picos and the Coronels, the impact of the de la Guerra family on the state has been forgotten. Pablo de la Guerra, who focused on maintaining his family's political power, resigned from district judgeship in 1873 due to failing health. Months later, in February 1874, de la Guerra died without the land grants he spent his fortune trying to retain. Although the plaza adjacent to Santa Barbara City Hall has borne the family name since 1853, the family's mark on California politics remains obscured by the Spanish Fantasy Past myth. Since 1924, the Plaza de la Guerra hosts a yearly Old Spanish Days Fiesta that highlights the Spanish founders of the city, not the Californio political leaders. Despite their decades of efforts when the Californio patriarchs died, so did their dreams of patria chica.

Epilogue

A Landscape of California Dreams

If you ride the Los Angeles Metro south from Campo de Cahuenga to its terminus in Downtown Los Angeles and exit through Union Station, you will find many of the sites that feature prominently in this book. Union Station, built in the Mission Revival style during the 1930s, is an iconic conduit of the Spanish fantasy past that stands on the site of Yaanga, a Tongva village, and the original Los Angeles Chinatown. As you leave the station from the north exit, you will pass, but perhaps not see, a small, inconspicuous plaque that states that Union Station was built "on an Indian Village and later Chinese town site" by three railroad companies.[1] There are no signs that acknowledge this site was once known as Yaanga, the center of Tongva power, or that LA Chinatown's residents were forced to move to its current-day location north of the station to make way for the trains that connected the city to Chicago and other eastern US cities. This book, in a way, was an effort to make this, and many other sites of historical consequence, legible to the reader.

If you continue walking and cross Alameda Street, you will find yourself at Olvera Street, just three hundred feet from Union Station. In the 1930s, Anglo boosters revamped Olvera Street as a tourist attraction that embraced the Spanish fantasy past. In doing so, the historic street lends itself to the romanization of Spanish California and the idea that the white settler state directly followed the Spanish colonial era while also glossing over the state's Mexican Era and promoting a historical narrative of linear progression that culminates in a prosperous Anglo future.[2] Original advertisements for the refurbished Olvera Street presented the site as "A Mexican Street of Yesterday in a City of Today." Such advertising relegates Mexican California and Mexican Californians to the past and asserts that the future belongs to California's Anglo inhabitants.[3]

At Olvera Street, you will find a number of monuments dedicated to the memory of pre-twentieth-century California—that is, if you notice them. You can take a picture standing next to a wooden cross (which families and children often do) that honors Felipe de Neve, the *Las Californias* governor who "founded" Los Angeles. At the northwest corner of the plaza, you can book your wedding at the Pico House, which casts an impressive shadow on

The plaque located at the Union Station north entrance mentions that the station was built on the old sites of an Indian village (Yaanga) and the Old Chinatown. The language of the plaque does not acknowledge the displacement of these two communities or the name of the village. Photo by author.

the plaza over the numerous plaques that refer to Pío Pico as "the last Mexican governor."

On the north side of the gazebo, you will find the *Pobladores* monument.[4] The rock monument includes a plaque that lists the names and casta statuses of the forty-four Mexican settlers who founded the pueblo. In the 1950s, Miriam Mathews, the first credentialed Black American librarian of Los Angeles, began the campaign to dedicate a monument to the Black and multiracial founders of Los Angeles. The city dedicated the monument, decades later, in 1981 during bicentennial celebrations. Since the monument went up, the Pobladores plaque has gone missing multiple times. People speculate that the plaque disappears as an effort to erase the black founders from the city's history. The plaque is replaced each time it is removed.

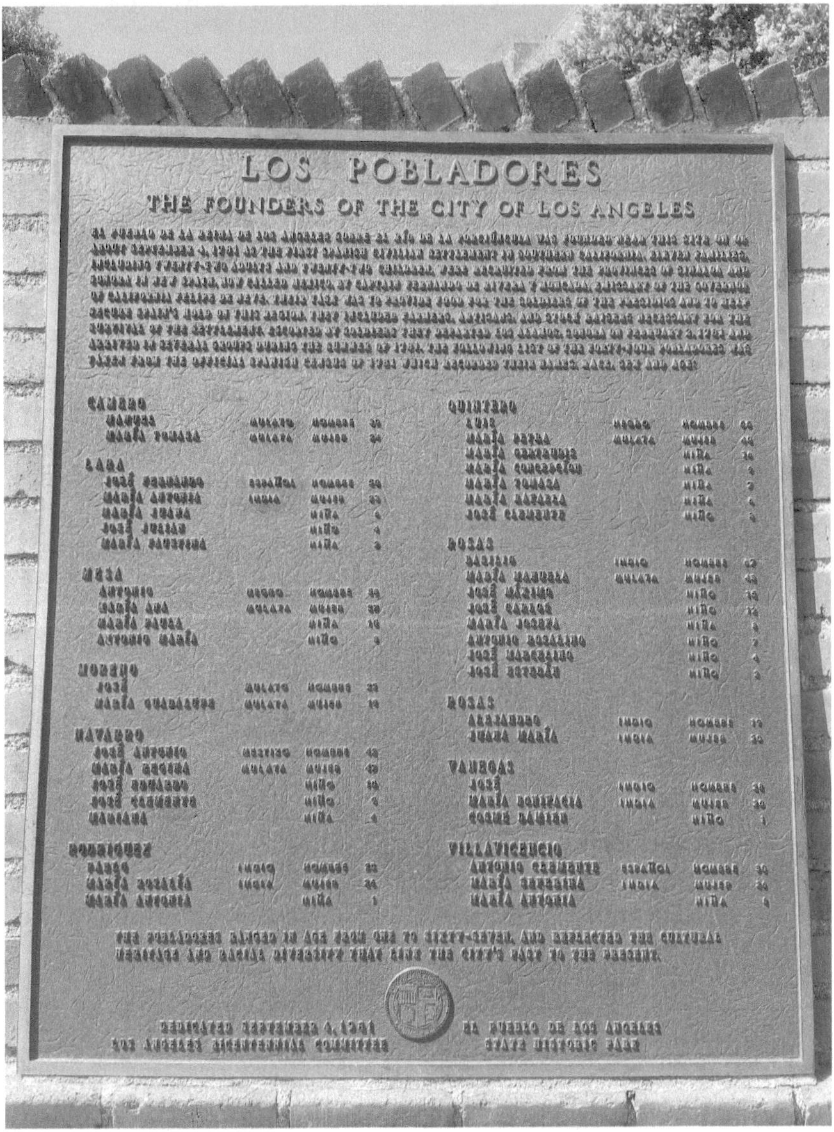

The Pobladores plaque documents the multiracial group of settlers who founded the pueblo in the eighteenth century. Photo by author.

Just a few feet from the Pico House lies Los Angeles Street, which was once known as *Calle de Los Negros,* you can see a plaque placed on the sidewalk that refers to the 1871 Anti-Chinese Massacre as "a mob of 500 locals" that targeted the city's Chinese inhabitants. The inscription excuses those involved by explaining Chinese residents were targeted because they were "not protected

The plaque that memorializes the Anti-Chinese Massacre is placed on the sidewalk, making it all the more difficult to see. The language of the plaque infers that the lack of legal protection, rather than their own racial ideologies, propelled non-Chinese residents to act on their anti-Chinese sentiment and violently persecute Chinese residents. Photo by author.

under law"—as if the laws were natural. These monuments embrace a historical narrative that casts nonwhite residents in a primitive and unruly town of the past, far removed from Anglo settlements of the present and future.

Notably, in 2021, the Los Angeles Mayor's Office Civic Memory Working Group issued nineteen recommendations for the city to "engage more productively and honestly with its past."[5] One recommendation was "to develop citywide commemorations, considering both ephemeral and permanent forms, to mark the 150th anniversary of the 1871 Anti-Chinese Massacre." The Civic Memory Working Group called for designs and selected a proposal by artist Sze Tsung Nicolás Leong and writer Judy Chui-Hua Chung. Their proposal consists of placing tree trunk sculptures throughout Downtown LA to mark and honor the known and unknown dead. Leong and Chung created the monument to invite people to "reflect" and "interact" with the city's forgotten history. This monument, in contrast to the plaques already in place, has the power to unveil the obscured history of the city's people. However, the city of Los Angeles has not fully funded this memorial, and the Department of Cultural Affairs has failed to raise $3,350,000 by its goal of summer 2026.[6]

If you linger on and around Olvera Street and the surrounding Los Angeles Plaza, however, you will notice that the site continues to be a gathering place for the Mexican and Indigenous communities. It is a contested space where the many, past and present, communities of Los Angeles attempt to carve out their political imaginaries and historical memories. On any given day, you can see Latine families from all over the city make their way to Olvera Street for taquitos at the legendary Cielito Lindo, for cultural and religious expression at La Placita church, and to take part in political events—protests often radiate from Los Angeles Plaza and into the city's downtown. If you drop by on a weekend, you can find the In Tlanextli Tlacopan, an Aztec dance group, performing. They perform traditional dances to assert the existence of Indigenous people and to refute the myth that "Spanish people just eradicated" Native people.[7] The men and women of In Tlanextli Tlacopan dance just feet from the space where a Junipero Serra statue once stood.[8] In June 2020, in solidarity with the national George Floyd protests, about one hundred Tataviam and Tongva protesters tore down the statue. At Los Angeles Plaza, the fight over historical memory continues.

As someone who grew up in Los Angeles, it was only through researching and writing this book that I noticed and began to understand the traces of the state's multiracial past on the landscape. Knowing this history allows one to appreciate the Pico House as an architectural marvel and reckon with the family's legacy in the city and state they helped shape. At the same time, this history also allows one to recognize Union Station as Yaanga, a train depot, and an assertion of the Spanish fantasy past. I hope that, by recovering the settler imaginaries of Californios alongside those of Indigenous Californians, Black American settlers, Chinese immigrants, and Anglo settlers, I have made clear that a myriad of people have made and remade California in an effort to realize their dreams of small countries. Californio political participation was crucial to the construction of California—a state with a legal structure that controlled the labor of nonwhite inhabitants but did not consider them citizens.

Just as reviving Californio settler imaginaries forces us to recast the history of California and the nation, it forces us to reconsider the historical construction of racial identity. The Mexican American identity, at least in California, has been informed by experiences of immigration, cultural displacement, and assimilation, as well as by experiences of colonization as the colonizer and the colonized. The Mexican American identity can also be a product of a settler colonial process—of claiming land and losing land. By recognizing Californios as state makers, this book has demonstrated that the development of the Mexican American identity has also been informed by displacement and a state of being made propertyless. All of these experiences contribute to the continued construction of Mexican and Latine individuals as perpetual foreigners, a racial script that remains powerful to this day.[9]

By recovering the political imaginaries of the varied settlers and Indigenous people of California, *Dreams of Small Countries* reframes the state's first thirty years as a multifaceted competition over which imaginary would take hold of the landscape. As I intended for this book to demonstrate, not one particular vision was inevitable—Californios, Black Americans, Chinese immigrants, and Indigenous Californians all tried to shape California. When elite Californios decided to ally with Anglo-American settlers, intending to save their patria chica, they inadvertently signed onto the white settler state. As a result, they lost the gamble and helped make the California we know today.

This brings us back to the Los Angeles Plaza, where we began this epilogue and where, in many ways, the stories of this book commence, conclude, and restart. If you were to continue your walk through this historically contested space and walk east down Spring Street, you would pass by the apartment buildings and businesses of New Chinatown. These stores and restaurants, where you can see Dodgers fans grabbing a bite before heading up to Chavez Ravine, stand on the sites of the city's first vineyards, which were planted by Indigenous laborers for Californio settlers. If you continue walking east, you will arrive at Los Angeles State Historic Park, known as the park for the people by the people. On this once-abandoned Southern Pacific Railroad station, which is now a cherished community green space, you will find native plants and the Zanja Madre, the original aqueduct that brought water to the Los Angeles pueblo. A proposed gondola project from Union Station to Dodger Stadium now threatens the park for the people by the people. From this historical and cultural junction, you could continue walking east toward the channelized Los Angeles River and see where the de Anza expedition shared a tobacco pipe with Tongva men. Beyond Los Angeles, you could continue travelling through the state's past and head north toward the famed Gold Country, now the famous Wine Country, or go south toward the Indigenous world. Whether you are a resident or visitor, and whether you're walking or driving, I urge you to see a California that has been and will continue to be shaped by countless dreams.

Notes

Abbreviations

ACC	Articles of Capitulation at Cahuenga, Seaver Center for Western History Research, Los Angeles
ACP	Antonio F. Coronel Papers, Seaver Center for Western History Research, Los Angeles
AGP	Archibald H. Gillespie Papers, 1812–1878, Charles E. Young Research Library, UCLA
ASP	Abel Sterns Papers, Huntington Library, San Marino
BDW	Benjamin Davis Wilson Collection, Huntington Library, San Marino
BHS	Benjamin Hayes Scrapbooks, Bancroft Library, University of California at Berkeley
BIAR	United States, Bureau of Indian Affairs Records, 1851 Aug. 9–Nov. 19, California State Archives and Library, Sacramento
BL	Bancroft Library, University of California at Berkeley
DVC	Del Valle Collection, Seaver Center for Western History Research, Los Angeles
GFC	Guerra Family Collection, Huntington Library, San Marino
PFP	Pico Family Papers, 1864–1876, Bancroft Library, University of California at Berkeley
SCWHR	Seaver Center for Western History Research, Los Angeles
VFP	Vallejo Family Papers, Bancroft Library, University of California at Berkeley

Introduction

1. Garcia, *Trees of Califas*.

2. Rebecca Earle's description of patria chica as a commitment to a project by a group whose members are united by a common sense and emotion, rather than a government system, has been extremely influential to this work. Additionally, theorist Benedict Anderson's argument that nations exist in people's thoughts and imaginaries has influenced how I theorize Californios' political imaginaries. Earle, *Return of the Native*, 10–12; Anderson, *Imagined Communities*; Nieto-Phillips, *Language of Blood*, 23; Gutiérrez, "Unraveling America's Hispanic Past," 81–83; Monroy, "Creation and Re-Creation of Californio Society," 180–81.

3. In this work, I use "Anglo" and "Anglo-Americans" to refer to people identified and self-identified as white US citizens interchangeably. I use "Anglo" and "Anglo-American" to designate whiteness and US citizenship. My use of "American" in Anglo-American by no means discounts the citizenship status of Californios but is based on other scholars' use of the term.

4. Given the unstable definition of whiteness, I consider "whiteness" to be both an ideology that values European, specifically Anglo-Saxon, traits, culture, belief systems, and behaviors as superior and as a broad, historically constructed identity that attempts to naturalize social, political, and material privileges. For scholarship on whiteness, see Fields, "Ideology and Race in American History"; Harris, "Whiteness as Property"; Roediger, *Wages of Whiteness*; Moreton-Robinson, *White Possessive*; Jacobson, *Whiteness of a Different Color*; Haney-López, *White by Law*; Montejano, *Anglos and Mexicans in the Making of Texas*; Foley, *White Scourge*; Gómez, *Manifest Destinies*.

5. Scholars have studied non-Anglo actors of settler colonialism and settler colonialism as a process that can absorb settler and colonized people of previous regimes. See Roberts, *I've Been Here*; Hernández, *City of Inmates*; Gómez, *Manifest Destinies*, 1–48; Wood, *Black Montana*; Dunbar-Ortiz, *Not a Nation of Immigrants*, xi–xxvii, 18–50; Alanzo, *Tejano Legacy*.

6. The term "colonized colonizer: is adapted from Troutt Powell's *A Different Shade of Colonialism*. Troutt Powell reconsiders the dualistic role Egyptians performed while simultaneously resisting British imperialism and attempting to colonize the Sudanese as the "colonized colonizer." I expound on this idea in Suárez, "Legal Confiscation."

7. Sánchez, *Becoming Mexican American*; Molina, *Fit to Be Citizens?*; Molina, *How Race Is Made in America*; de Genova, *Racial Transformations*; Ruiz, *From Out of the Shadows*.

8. Scholars have demonstrated that California was not a pristine wilderness when Anglo-Americans arrived in the state, but that it was a landscape intentionally managed by Indigenous Californians. Anderson, *Tending the Wild*.

9. The myth persists well into the twentieth century. Kevin Starr, one of the most read contemporary historians of California, wrote in 2005 that "the very acculturation of California into an American commonwealth had been the result of the gold rush." Starr, *California*, xi.

10. Another trend Bancroft established was describing Californios in racializing language. Shortly after this sentence, he describes Californios as "indolent." Bancroft, *History of California*, 82–83.

11. Turner, "The Significance of the Frontier in American History."

12. For seminal works of New Western History, see White, *It's Your Misfortune and None of My Own*; Worster, "Beyond the Agrarian Myth"; Deutsch, *No Separate Refuge*; Worster, *Under Western Skies*; Cronon, *Nature's Metropolis*. For an assessment of New Western History, see Wrobel, "Introduction."

13. Herbert Eugene Bolton first engaged with the borderlands concept in *The Spanish Borderlands*. More recently, in the essay "From Borderlands to Borders," Jeremy Adelman and Stephen Aron demonstrated the substituting of "borderland" for all of North America's "frontiers" "[has] enriched our understanding of the complexity and contingency of intercultural relations." In my work, I analyze California as a place shaped by the process of colonialisms and rely on Adelman and Aron's concept of borderlands to interrogate how the construction of nation-state borders hardened racial hierarchies and limited the autonomy of a variety of peoples.

14. The work on the US Southwest borderlands is vast. Select works that have influenced this book are Zappia, *Traders and Raiders*; DeLay, *War of a Thousand Deserts*;

Hämäläinen, *The Comanche Empire*; Blackhawk, *Violence over the Land*; Jacoby, *Shadows at Dawn*; Truett, *Fugitive Landscapes*; St. John, *Line in the Sand*.

15. Gutiérrez and Orsi, ed., *Contested Eden*; Hurtado, *Intimate Frontiers*; Haas, *Conquests and Historical Identities in California*; Torres-Rouff, *Before L.A.*; Pérez, *Colonial Intimacies*; Chávez-García, *Negotiating Conquest*; Saavedra, *Pasadena Before the Roses*; Pitt, *Decline of the Californios*.

16. Gómez, *Manifest Destinies*, 119.

17. My definition of "political imaginaries" is based on my reading of Anderson, *Imagined Communities*; Taylor, *Modern Social Imaginaries*; Castoriadis, *Imaginary Institution of Society*; Wiley, *Politics and the Concept of the Political*; Beavers, *Geography and the Political Imaginary*; Tullos, *Alabama Getaway*.

18. Patrick Wolfe demonstrated that a central aspect of the settler colonial process, throughout the world, is the elimination of the native. Wolfe, "Settler Colonialism and the Elimination of the Native." For scholarship that characterizes Anglo settler violence against the California Indigenous as eliminatory, see Madley, *An American Genocide*; Lindsay, *Murder State*; Akins and Bauer, *We Are the Land*, 125–60; Blackhawk, *Rediscovery of America*, 295–99; Heizer, *Destruction of the California Indians*.

19. Zappia, *Traders and Raiders*, 9.

20. Zappia, 11–15.

21. This estimation combines the estimated population decline of Indigenous Californians over the course of two centuries and should be understood as a minimum estimate. Madley, *An American Genocide*, 3; Lindsay, *Murder State*.

22. Throughout New Spain, Spanish settlers first constructed their identities in opposition to the Indigenous and developed an *español-indio* binary. Rather than an articulation of nationalism, the sobriquet *español* meant that one was a Spaniard with *limpieza de sangre*, an idea of blood purity based on Christian and Iberian ancestry. In Alta California, as a result of the Bourbon Reforms, a series of reforms instituted by the Bourbon Monarchy to reassert Spanish colonial power over New Spain, Español evolved to include soldiers with mixed ancestry in Alta California. Over time, *español* became *gente de razón*. Miranda, "Racial and Cultural Dimensions of 'Gente de Razón'"; Haas, *Conquest and Historical Identities*, 13–44; Pubols, "Becoming Californio," 22; Gutiérrez, "Hispanic Identities."

23. In her testimonio, María de la Angustias de la Guerra Ord used *blanco* and *gente de razon* interchangeably a handful of times. See Ord, *California Recollections of Angustias de la Guerra Ord*, 8, 14. Anglo-American settlers who assimilated into Californio society also used the terms interchangeably. See also Wilson and Caughey, *Indians of Southern California*, 29.

24. Mason, *Census of 1790*.

25. Bottoms, *Aristocracy of Color*; Waite, *West of Slavery*; Smith, *Freedom's Frontier*.

Chapter One

1. Crespí, *Description of Distant Roads*, 338–39.

2. Crespí, 339.

3. I use the English spelling of "Yaanga" rather than the Spanish spelling of "Yangna."

4. Crespí, *Description of Distant Roads*, 339.

5. Hackel, *Children of Coyote*; Haas, *Saints and Citizens*.

6. Martínez, *Genealogical Fictions*; Menchaca, *Mexican American Experience in Texas*, 7–38; Vinson, *Before Mestizaje*.

7. Weber, *Mexican Frontier*, 162–82.

8. Pubols, "Becoming Californio," 133.

9. Scholar Martha Ortega Soto argues that the Mexican government, as well as Mexican and Californio settlers, were primarily concerned with defending Alta California rather than developing an economy. Ortega Soto, *Alta California*.

10. Gutiérrez, *When Jesus Came*, 177–226; Pérez, *Colonial Intimacies*; Gómez, *Manifest Destinies*, 52–86.

11. Ord, Savage, and Perissinotto, *California Recollections*, 86–87.

12. Pérez, *Colonial Intimacies*, 16–48.

13. Scholar Miroslava Chávez-García describes this upward social mobility as being "whitened" in Alta California. Chávez-García, *Negotiating Conquest*, 67.

14. Gutiérrez, *When Jesus Came*; Monroy, *Thrown Among Strangers*; Almaguer, "Interpreting Chicano History," 486–90, 498–501.

15. Traditionally, *español/a* means a person born in Spain.

16. Mason, *Census of 1790*, 32, 80.

17. Here I build on the work of multiple scholars of twentieth-century Los Angeles. In *A Place at the Nayarit*, scholar Natalia Molina uses the term "cultural broker" to describe a person who has cultural capital and who shares their capital with someone of a different status. Molina builds on scholar Genevieve Carpio's term "racial broker," which describes Latine real estate agents who used their position to help aspiring Latine renters and buyers. By using "social broker" here, I am describing Californio women who share their privileged racial and family status with the men they married. Molina, *A Place at the Nayarit*, 77; Carpio, *Collisions at the Crossroads*, 195–200. The scholarship on gender in Alta California is also crucial to my use of "social broker." Bouvier, *Women and the Conquest of California*; González, *Refusing the Favor*; Casas, *Married to a Daughter of the Land*; Pérez, *Colonial Intimacies*; Saavedra, "Speaking for Themselves."

18. Pico carried on extramarital affairs with multiple women and had children with Ascencion Avila, a member of elite Californio society, and Felecita Romero, a servant. After his death, these children were treated as legitimate heirs. Salomon, *Pio Pico*, 188n30; Gray, *Forster vs. Pico*, 65.

19. Chávez-García, *Negotiating Conquest*, 52–122.

20. "Jamul" is a Kumeyaay word meaning "slimy water" or "foam." Salomon, *Pio Pico*, 29–31.

21. "Teresa de la Guerra," in Beebe and Senkewicz, *Testimonios*, 57.

22. Pubols, *Father of All*, 214, 215.

23. These are just three of the many grants that Pío Pico granted during his short term as governor. For a compiled list of land grants and which governor granted them, see "Appendix," in United States, District Court *Reports of Land Cases*.

24. Scholars have written on the political and economic motivations of Indigenous raids. See Zappia, *Traders and Raiders*; Guidotti-Hernández, *Unspeakable Violence*; Jacoby, *Shadows at Dawn*.

25. Zappia, 108.

26. Pico, *Don Pio Pico's Historical Narrative*, 86–88.

27. Pubols, *Father of All*, 16–17.

28. The de la Guerras also became linked to the Picos as José Antonio Carrillo was married to Estéfana Pico.

29. Pubols, *Father of All*, 76–88.

30. Cassidy, *Life and Times*, 52–54.

31. Cassidy, 59.

32. Camarillo, *Chicanos in a Changing Society*, 12; Pitt, *Decline of the Californios*; 10–13.

33. Pico, "Christmas in California Before the Gringos Came."

34. Pico, "Christmas in California Before the Gringos Came."

35. I use "hijos del país" because in a myriad of primary sources, elite Californios refer to themselves and their fellow Californios as "hijos del país."

36. For an extensive look at how Californios resisted Mexican authority and, also, attempted to integrate into the federal republican system, see Perez Tisserant, "Revolts in Mexican California."

37. For an extensive look at how Indigenous nations shaped the economies of Alta California, as well as Nuevo Mexico, during first half of the nineteenth century, see Zappia, *Traders and Raiders*, 104, 99–122.

38. Pablo de la Guerra to David Broderick (written by Joseph Lancaster Brent), 1857, Guerra Family Collection (GFC).

39. Petition quoted in Vallejo, *Recuerdos*, 1112.

40. Woolsey, "Capitalist in a Foreign Land"; Wright, *Yankee in Mexican California*; Wash, "If Walls Could Speak."

41. Davis, *Sixty Years in California*, 61.

42. Bidwell and Kennedy, *What Makes a Man*, 3.

43. Pubols, *Father of All*, 245.

44. Ide, *Who Conquered California?*, 8, 12.

45. Frémont led five expeditions into the West. During his third expedition, which began in June 1845, Frémont planned to survey the central Rocky Mountains, the Great Salt Lake region, and part of the Sierra Nevada Mountains. Before this expedition began, President James K. Polk gave Frémont the go-ahead to engage in military action if war broke out between Mexico and the United States. Chaffin, *Pathfinder*, 249.

46. During the 1840s, the Corps of Topographical Engineers had evolved to support Westward Expansion. The US government assigned topographical expeditions to examine possible water and land routes for future military movements. War Department, "General Regulations for the Army, 1841," Art. LXXV, quoted in Traas, *From the Golden Gate to Mexico City*, 7, 19.

47. Walker, *Bear Flag Rising*, 101.

48. Vallejo, *Recuerdos*, 1220.

49. Vallejo was not alone in this strategy. Haas points out that elite Californio Juan Bautista Alvarado spoke favorably of American government institutions and welcomed US occupation *if* Californios remained in control of local governance. Haas, "War in California, 1846–1848," 341; Vallejo, *Recuerdos*, 1223.

50. Vallejo, *Recuerdos*, 1131.

51. Bancroft, *History of California*, 43; Walker, *Bear Flag Rising*, 101.

52. Walker, 14.

53. Bancroft, *History of California*, 150–53.

54. Bancroft.

55. In the nineteenth century, Anglo-Americans began to construct stereotypes about Californios (and all Mexicans) because the Mexican colonial project impeded US colonization in the North American Southwest. Historian Daniel Weber pointed out that Anglo-Americans viewed Californios as "indolent, ignorant, and backward" when their presence threatened the US project, but once US authority was stable, Californios became provincial bumpkins. See Weber, "Spanish Legacy," 5, 11.

56. Vallejo, *Recuerdos*, 1250; Rosenus, *General M. G. Vallejo*, 118.

57. US Captain John Montgomery commanded a frigate that was anchored of the coast of Sausalito and had been anchored in the area long enough to have become cordial with Vallejo.

58. Vallejo, *Recuerdos*, 1196.

59. Sutter, quoted in Hurtado, *John Sutter*, 195.

60. Sloat, "To the Inhabitants of California," July 7, 1846, Papers on the Bear Flag Revolt, BL.

61. It was not until Castro and others convinced Pico of an American invasion that Pico agreed to collaborate. Ord, Savage, and Perissinotto, *California Recollections*, 110, Coronel, *Cosas de California*, 75–77.

62. "Letter from José Castro to Antonio Coronel, 1846 August 3," Antonio F. Coronel Papers (ACP).

63. Ord, Savage, and Perissinotto, *California Recollections*, 114.

64. Phillips, *Indians and Indian Agents*, 34.

65. François Gendreau, a Canadian man married to a Walla Walla woman, served as the captain of the Walla Walla detachment. Akins and Bauer, *We Are the Land*, 129–30, 199; Frémont, *Expeditions*, 209.

66. After the war, Frémont gave the Walla Walla one hundred horses as payment for their service. Frémont, *Expeditions*, 230–31.

67. Haas, "War in California," 341.

68. Pitt, *Decline of the Californios*, 33.

69. Coronel, *Cosas de California*, 77–78.

70. "Pronunciamiento de Varela y otras de California contra los americanos, September 24, 1846," reprinted in Bancroft, *History of California*, 5:310 n.

71. Haas, "War in California," 342.

72. In the sources, Varela's first name is also spelled as Servulio. Coronel, *Cosas de California*, 81.

73. "Pronunciamiento."

74. Dubois and Woodward, *Temecula Massacre*, 20.

75. Coronel, *Cosas de California*, 111.

76. San Pasqual is near a Kumeyaay village of the same name.

77. Dubois and Woodward, *Temecula Massacre*, 31.

78. José del Carmen Lugo, *Vida de Un Ranchero*, 40–42.

79. Dubois and Woodward, *Temecula Massacre*, 8; Phillips, *Chiefs and Challengers*, 81–88.

80. Phillips, 188.

81. Frémont, *Expeditions*, 238.

82. Pitt, *Decline of the Californios*, 35.

83. Treaty of Cahuenga, Art. I (1847), ACC.

84. Chávez-García, *Negotiating Conquest*, 82.

85. Gillespie's papers contain fourteen signed oaths in which Californios promise "not to bear arms and to keep the peace." Antonio Coronel signed one of these oaths. Oaths signed, AGP.

86. "Appointment from Stephen Foster to Antonio Coronel, 1848 April 10," ACP.

87. Newspaper reports on these raids document Anglo-American settlers referring to the Indigenous as members of the "horse thief" tribe. See *California Star*, March 27, 1847; *California Star*, April 10, 1847; *California Star*, May 1, 1847; "Noticias del Pais," *California Star*, March 27, 1847.

88. In addition to working as a US Indian agent, Vallejo pledged to not take up arms against the United States on August 2, 1846. Oath to United States, August 2, 1846, VFP.

89. Phillips, *Vineyards and Vaqueros*, 212.

90. Ord, Savage, and Perissinotto, *California Recollections*, 114.

91. Treaty of Guadalupe Hidalgo (February 2, 1848). Accessed at https://avalon.law.yale.edu/19th_century/guadhida.asp.

92. Griswold del Castillo, *Treaty of Guadalupe Hidalgo*, 36, 62.

93. Griswold del Castillo, 36, 43–44.

94. Population Schedules for California, Seventh Census of the United States, 1850; (National Archives Microfilm Publication M432, 1009 rolls); Records of the Bureau of the Census, Record Group 29; National Archives, Washington, DC.

95. For more on what Anglo-Americans thought about landholding in California, see Shelton, *Squatter's Republic*.

96. Prior to the admittance of California to the Union, there were fifteen Free States and fifteen slave states. Quoted in Ellison, "Struggle for Civil Government in California," 138.

97. *California Star*, December 11, 1847.

98. The supporters of California statehood were aware of the national tension that would be caused by the admittance of California into the Union as a Free State. Potter, *Impending Crisis*, 63–64.

99. Ellison, "Struggle for Civil Government in California," 138–39, 145–46.

100. Waite, *West of Slavery*, 166.

101. In 1849, the city of Los Angeles had a population of 1,610, meaning not even 1 percent of the population participated in this process. Census of the City and County of Los Angeles, California, for the Year 1850, cited in Foster, Stephen Clark, Thomas Savage, and Hubert Howe Bancroft, "Angeles from '47 to '49. As Seen by Stephen Clark Foster, Translator with Mormon Battalion, First Alcalde of Los Angeles under the US, Etc.," Ms., 1877, BL; Wilson, "Benjamin Davis Wilson's Observations," 125.

Chapter Two

1. "District of Los Angeles," *Weekly Alta California*, December 6, 1849.

2. In total, fifteen thousand people voted. The 1850 US Census counted 192,597 people; however, this number leaves out the Indigenous population, which is estimated to be at least one hundred thousand. 1850 US Census; *Daily Alta California*, November 15, 1849; *Weekly Alta California*, December 6, 1849.

3. Tennis, "California's First State Election," 373.

4. Perez Tisserant, "Revolts in Mexican California," 759–82.

5. In *Black Montana*, Anthony Wood argues that Black settlers in Montana viewed themselves as settlers crucial to the American settler project and performed an active and self-aware role in Native elimination and settler expansion because they believed that settlement in the West, not just Montana, "fulfilled the liberal demands of civic and political liberation." My analysis of Black settlers builds on this idea and analyzes Black settlers' actions in California under this lens. Wood, *Black Montana*, 1–25; Boutelle, *Race for America*, 1–20.

6. Lew-Williams, "Chinese Naturalization, Voting and Other Impossible Acts," 515–17.

7. Lew-Williams, *Chinese Must Go*, 17–24.

8. Two of the forty-one non-Californio delegates, John Sutter and Pedro Sainsevain (née Pierre Sainsevain) were from Europe but had resided in Alta California for a decade. Sutter's allegiances, as described in chapter 1, were not with the Californios; however, Sainsevain, who helped create a robust wine industry in Los Angeles, had assimilated into elite Californio society. Of the remaining delegates, seventeen hailed from slave states, the rest from Free States. For a list of delegates and their origins, see Browne, *Report*, 482–83.

9. The official translator for the convention was William Hartnell, the husband of Teresa de la Guerra.

10. Gwin, quoted in Browne, *Report*, 1.

11. Carrillo, quoted in Browne, 22.

12. Anglo-American settler Benjamin D. Wilson wrote in his memoir that he and Americans living in Los Angeles wanted to maintain a territorial government because the current system benefited them. The desire to split the state in two was an old Californio idea. The division of Alta California had been on the minds of Californios earlier in the 1840s and prior to US occupation, due to regional and federalism difficulties. This 1849 attempt was an effort to maintain and consolidate political power under US governance and perhaps an attempt to work around, if not protest, to the American government institutions in California.

13. Dimmick, quoted in Browne, *Report*, 23.

14. For examples, see Browne, 25, 31, 153, 400.

15. Gilbert quoted in Browne, 61. Article IX of the Treaty of Guadalupe Hidalgo reads, "The Mexicans who, in the territories aforesaid, . . . shall be incorporated into the Union of the United States and be admitted at the proper time (to be judged of by the Congress of the United States) to the enjoyment of all the rights of citizens of the United States, according to the principles of the Constitution; and in the meantime,

shall be maintained and protected in the free enjoyment of their liberty and property, and secured in the free exercise of their religion without restriction."

16. The formation of race in the United States had resulted in the interrelated construction of citizenship and whiteness. As constructed, American citizenship did not include people of African and Indigenous descent. See Fields, "Ideology and Race in American History," 143–77; Lopez, *White by Law*.

17. Botts, quoted in Browne, *Report*, 62.

18. Gwin, quoted in Browne, 63.

19. Foster, quoted in Browne, 63.

20. De la Guerra, quoted in Browne, 63.

21. Browne, 64–68.

22. Browne, 341; Cal. Const. of 1849, art. II, § 1.

23. Teft, quoted in Browne, 137.

24. Wozencraft, quoted in Browne, 138. In the 1850s, proexpansionist politicians who were opposed to slavery believed that if white free farmers settled the west, they would stop the growth of slavery. Foner, *Free Soil, Free Labor, Free Men*, 27–29; Almaguer, *Racial Fault Lines*, 38–41; Berwanger, *Frontier Against Slavery*, 68.

25. Browne, 149–52; Almaguer, 38; Berwanger, 69.

26. Chávez-García, *Negotiating Conquest*, 52–60.

27. Cal. Const. of 1849, art. XI, § 14.

28. Historian Laurel Clark Shrine demonstrated that extending property rights to married women was the case in the Florida borderlands, where the US government depended on women to create and maintain families, homes, and communities for territorial expansion, Shrine, *Threshold of Manifest Destiny*.

29. Scholar Andrew Gibb makes a convincing case for Angustias de la Guerra's role in shaping the 1849 California Constitution. Gibb, *Californios, Anglos, and the Performance of Oligarchy*, 160–69.

30. Teft, quoted in Browne, *Report*, 258.

31. Browne.

32. Browne, 274. The resolution was passed with the following wording: "All laws, decrees, regulations, and provisions, which from their nature require publication, shall be published in English and Spanish." Cal. Const. of 1849, art. XI, § 21.

33. Cal. Const. of 1849, art. XI, § 21.

34. As scholar Rosina Lozano has argued, in order for the United States to control the land, especially in the Indigenous world, US officials required Spanish-speaking settlers, like Californios, to create governments with bilingual politics. Lozano, *American Language*, 4, 46.

35. Tennis, "California's First State Election," 375.

36. For Southerners, the admission of a Free State meant the addition of senate and house seats from a Free State, meaning a blow to proslavery power in US Congress. Hamilton, *Prologue to Compromise*; Potter, *Impending Crisis*, 90–120; Stegmaier, *Texas, New Mexico, and the Compromise of 1850*; Maizlish, *A Strife of Tongues*; Waite, *West of Slavery*, 45–48.

37. *Daily Alta California*, October 19, 1850; *Sacramento Transcript*, October 21, 1850; *Marysville Daily Herald*, October 22, 1850.

38. "Matters on the Pacific Side," *Daily Pacific News*, November 1, 1850.

39. "Los Angeles Alcalde a 1st Alcalde of Santa Barbara 1850, March 4," GFC; Wilson, "Benjamin Davis Wilson's Observations," 125.

40. Wilson.

41. Wilson.

42. The junta was referring to Article XI, section 13, of the 1849 California Constitution, which dealt with property tax. The section reads: "Sec. 13—Taxation shall be equal and uniform throughout the State. All property in this State shall be taxed in proportion to its value, to be ascertained as directed by law; but assessors and collectors of town, county, and State taxes, shall be elected by the qualified electors of the district, county, or town, in which the property taxed for State, county, or town purposes is situated." During the debate on the section, Delegate Henry Halleck made a motion to make sure that state property taxes were agreeable to the southern region, but during the debate, no Californios spoke in favor or against this provision. Not until the text of the constitution was made available to California inhabitants did elite Californios speak out against it. Perhaps the lack of appropriate translations at the time of the convention resulted in delayed resistance to this taxation system or the junta had already decided to petition the US Congress for territory status. Cal. Const. of 1849, art. XI, § 13; Browne, *Report*, 256–57.

43. Tennis, "California's First State Election," 373.

44. Mariano Guadalupe Vallejo served in the first California legislature, but only after he disputed the outcome of the Sonoma County election. It was initially reported that Vallejo's opponent, Jonas Spect, lost by fifty votes. However, two batches of ballots were discovered totaling fifty-eight or fifty-nine votes in favor of Spect. (The impreciseness of the vote was how the totals are reported in archival sources.) The California Senate then counted the votes and declared that Vallejo won by eighteen votes. Despite the alliances he made with elite white US citizen settlers, Mariano Guadalupe Vallejo only served one term in the California Senate because the growing Anglo-American settler population in Sonoma County curtailed Vallejo's claims to political power. *California Senate Journal*, 1st Sess. 1850, app. A.

45. Antonio Maria de la Guerra also served in the California Senate from 1851–52. David Broderick to Pablo de la Guerra, 1853, GFC.

46. Coronel also served on the LA Common Council, the Water Board, and as County Assessor and Commissioner of Commons Schools.

47. *California Senate Journal*, 1st Sess., 1850, app. GG.

48. *California Senate Journal*, 1st Sess., 1850, 217.

49. Reséndez, *Other Slavery*, 264.

50. *California Senate Journal*, 1st Sess., 1850, 589.

51. In addition to the guardianship provision, sections 14 and 20 of the Act allowed for the convict leasing of Indigenous men by criminalizing autonomous mobility as "vagrancy." If convicted of being "a vagrant," any city official could "hire out such vagrant within twenty-four hours to the highest bidder, . . . for the highest price that can be had, for any term not exceeding four months." California legislators criminalized autonomous Indigenous individuals and incentivized convict leasing by requiring that all revenue from leased labor be "paid into the County

Treasury." Act for the Government and Protection of Indians, Cal. Stats. § 14 and § 20 (1850).

52. Smith, *Freedom's Frontier*, 109–29.

53. Madley, *American Genocide*, 158–62; Smith, "Remaking Slavery in a Free State," 28–63.

54. Antonio María de la Guerra, the only Californio senator during the third session, did not participate in the Senate vote.

55. On the foreign Miners' Tax, see Smith, *Freedom's Frontier*, 94.

56. Coronel, *Cosas de California*, 169, 183.

57. "An Act Concerning Crimes and Punishment," Cal. Stats. ch. 99 (1850). The California legislature had already banned Indigenous testimony in cases with white litigants with Section Six of the Act for the Government and Protection of Indians.

58. "An Act Concerning Civil Cases in the Courts of Justice in the State," Cal. Stats. ch. 5 (1851).

59. Carlin, "Courtroom as White Space"; Johnson, "Color of Truth"; Gonzales, "Toward a Critical Race Theory of Evidence."

60. Notably, Pío Pico did not join the Democratic Party. He opposed not the Democratic Party but all US governmental institutions, unlike his brother, Andrés. In 1853, he was elected to the Los Angeles Common Council but refused the position.

61. "The Election at Santa Barbara," *Daily Alta California*, January 1, 1853.

62. "Democratic State Convention," *Sacramento Daily Union*, February 27, 1852.

63. *Daily Alta California*, November 1, 1852.

64. The strongest Democratic counties were Monterey and Santa Barbara. These counties also had majority Californio populations. Dubin, *United States Presidential Elections*.

65. For an extensive look at Gwin and Chivalry politics, see Lynch, "Southern California Chivalry"; Waite, *West of Slavery*, 107–12. In their examination of commonalities between elite Californios and southern Anglo-Americans, scholars have cited the interest in seigneurialism as the linchpin. See Monroy, *Thrown Among Strangers*.

66. Campbell, *Making Black Los Angeles*, 30–35; Taylor, *In Search of the Racial Frontier*; Lapp, *Blacks in Gold Rush California*.

67. For more on how the California legislature aided enslavers in their efforts to bring enslaved people to the state, see Waite, *West of Slavery*, 41–61.

68. Lapp and Wilson Moore, *Archy Lee*; McGinty, *Archy Lee's Struggle for Freedom*.

69. Colman, "John Ballard," 200.

70. Campbell, *Making Black Los Angeles*, 39.

71. Demaratus, *Force of a Feather*.

72. Gibbs and Washington, *Shadow and Light*, 1–7; Foreman et al., *Colored Conventions Movement*, 337.

73. Gibbs and Washington, 36–38.

74. Forman et al., *Colored Conventions Movement*, 335.

75. Gibbs and Washington, *Shadow and Light*, 46.

76. Moore, "African-Americans Fight Racism in Early California," 12–13.

77. People v. W. H. Potter (1850) in David Snyder, *Negro Civil Rights in California: 1850* (Sacramento: Sacramento Book Collectors Club, 1969).

78. During the nineteenth century, those unable to vote utilized lobbying and petitioning because it was one of the only ways one could attempt to affect political change without the franchise. For more on the use of collective and individual lobbying and petitioning in the pre–Civil War United States, see Morgan, *Inventing the People*, 223–38; McKinley, "Petitioning and the Making of the Administrative State," *The Yale Law Journal* 127, no. 6 (2018): 1538–1637.

79. *California Journal of the Assembly*, March 22, 1852, 395.

80. Fisher, "Struggle for Negro Testimony in California," 314.

81. "Governor's Special Message," *Daily Alta California*, April 25, 1852.

82. Coolies were not a racial category; rather, they were an aggregation of American racial imaginings that produced an image of Chinese immigrants as racialized, coerced, and unfree laborers. For more on the meanings and construction of the coolie, see Jung, *Coolies and Cane*.

83. Historian Beth Lew-Williams presents a significant case that throughout the second half of the nineteenth century, Chinese immigrants and Chinese individuals born in the United States sought to become US citizens and despite the legal impossibility, some individuals had become US citizens. See Lew-Williams, "Chinese Naturalization, Voting, and Other Impossible Acts."

84. "Letter of the Chinamen to His Excellency Governor Bigler," *Sacramento Daily Union*, May 8, 1852.

85. "Saturday Morning, June 4, 1853," *Daily Alta California*, June 4, 1853.

86. For an extensive look of racially motivated violence against Chinese Miners in Gold Rush California, see Johnson, *Roaring Camp*, 185–236. For anti-Chinese violence throughout the nineteenth-century US West, see Lew-Williams, *Chinese Must Go*.

87. People v. Hall, Appellant, 4 Cal. 399 (1854).

88. *People v. Hall*.

89. Chun-Chuen, *Remarks*.

90. Chun-Chuen.

91. Chun-Chuen.

92. Chun-Chuen.

93. For more on the fight for testimony and the California Colored Convention as California's first civil rights movement, see Pfaelzer, "None but Colored Testimony Against Him," in Foreman et al., *Colored Conventions Movement*, 330–48. For more on how the Colored Conventions were an important forum of national civic activity and Black activism before the US Civil War see, Foreman et al., *Colored Convention Movement*, 21–71; Fischer, "Struggle for Negro Testimony," 315; Lapp, *Blacks in Gold Rush California*, 212.

94. Forman et al., *Colored Conventions Movement*, 337.

95. "Call to Convention," *Pacific Appeal*, April 12, 1862.

96. *Proceedings of the First State Convention*, 3–4.

97. Jones, *Birthright Citizens*, 7–9.

98. Lapp, *Blacks in Gold Rush California*, 99–100.

99. Lapp, "Jeremiah B. Sanderson," 321–33.

100. I use the term "propriety" as other scholars do to describe the politics of the delegates. Foreman et al., *Colored Conventions Movement*, 338.

101. Yates, quoted in *Proceedings of the First State Convention*, 6.

102. *Proceedings of the First State Convention*, 13.

103. "Address to the People of California," reprinted in Aptheker, *Documentary History of the Negro People in the United States*, 374–76.

104. For example, newspapers printed short articles about the *Levanter*, a case of maritime murder. In the fall of 1855, off the coast of Chile, James Gray killed shipmate S. Flood aboard the American clipper *Levanter*. Gray and Flood were white US citizens, and the only witness was an unnamed Black shipman. The clipper left from California, so many wondered if the US Federal Circuit Court would uphold the California ban on Black testimony when the alleged crime occurred on international waters and the victim was a white man. During the preliminary hearing, the US commissioner refused to allow the testimony of the Black shipman because of his alleged "incompetency." In November 1855, Judge Matthew McAllister of the California Circuit Court acquitted Gray because the unnamed Black shipman's testimony could not be used against a white man, thus extending the antitestimony law to international waters. "Negro Testimony in the U.S. Courts," *Placer Herald*, November 24, 1855; "Law Report," *Daily Alta California*, October 28, 1855.

105. While we don't know what Californios thought, we do know what leading abolitionists thought of the California Colored Convention. Frederick Douglass, who had worked with Gibbs in Philadelphia, refused to publish an account of the convention in his paper, the *North Star*, on the account of its propriety tone and the omission of any statements on slavery. William Lloyd Garrison also refused to publish the resolution and minutes in the *Liberator*. See Aptheker, *Documentary History of the Negro People in the United States*, 373.

106. Smith, "Dred Scott on the Pacific," 46; Howay, "Negro Immigration into Vancouver Island in 1858," 101–13; Edwards, "War of Complexional Distinction;" Kilian, *Go Do Some Great Thing*; Beasley, *Negro Trailblazers*, 78.

107. Suárez, "Legal Confiscation."

108. The land grant includes current-day Pacific Coast cities San Pedro, Torrance, Redondo Beach, Hermosa Beach, and Manhattan.

109. Moore, "We Feel the Want of Protection," 114; Heizer and Almquist, *Other Californians*, 131; Pitt, *Decline of the Californios*, 202.

110. Pitt, 202.

111. "Draft of Speech," GFC.

112. "Don Manuel Domínguez," *El Clamor Público*, April 4, 1857; "Defensa del Sr. Mr. Domínguez," *El Clamor Público*, April 25, 1857. Founded by Francisco P. Ramírez, *El Clamor Público* was the first Spanish-language newspaper printed in Los Angeles after the American occupation. Due to its liberal and Republican politics, Ramírez could not sustain funding for *El Clamor*, and it only ran from July 1855 and August 1859. Gary, *Clamor for Equality*.

113. "La Legislatura" and "Mr. Brent y el Senor Mr. Dominguez," *El Clamor Público*, May 2, 1875.

114. "A Los Votantes Californios y Mexicanos," ACP.

115. "A Los Votantes Californios y Mexicanos." In many of the Democrat pamphlets and flyers, the names of Anglo candidates were Hispanicized. For example, John Downey's first name became Juan Downie.

116. *El Clamor Público*, November 1, 1856.

117. *El Clamor Público*, October 4, 1856.

118. "Cronica Local," *El Clamor Público*, July 30, 1859.

119. "Cronica Local."

120. Avila penned the letter to Antonio María Pico, after which he printed the letter for the public with the support of other Californio Democrats. Antonio Coronel and Ygnacio del Valle were two of the six elite Californios who signed onto this letter when it became public.

121. "Enrique Avila a Antonio María Pico," 1860, ACP.

122. "Enrique Avila a Antonio María Pico," 1860, ACP.

Chapter Three

1. These descriptions are based on my personal visits to El Ranchito, currently known as Pío Pico State Park, and Pleasants, *In Pioneer Days*.

2. Pleasants, 1.

3. Zappia, *Traders and Raiders*, 67–68.

4. Carrico, "Sociopolitical Aspects"; Panich, *Narratives of Persistence*, 76.

5. Salomon, "Secularization in California."

6. For example, the day after becoming the administrator of ex-Mission San Luis Rey, Pío Pico ordered an Indigenous man publicly whipped to demonstrate his authority. Phillips, *Chiefs and Challengers*, 59.

7. Salomon, "Secularization in California," 365.

8. De Mofras, *Travels on the Pacific Coast*, 179.

9. Salomon, "Secularization in California," 360–65.

10. Zappia, *Traders and Raiders*, 112.

11. Phillips, *Chiefs and Challengers*, 69.

12. Zappia, *Traders and Raiders*, 104–5.

13. Phillips, *Chiefs and Challengers*, 355.

14. *California Star*, March 13, 1847.

15. *California Star*, April 8, 1848.

16. During the US-Mexican War, Halleck was in charge of fortifying US bases throughout Alta California. After the war ended in California, he became the military secretary of state. He served as a delegate at the 1849 California Constitutional Convention and was a prominent land claims lawyer. During the US Civil War, he served as senior commander for the Union Army in the western theater, general in chief, and wrote influential treatises on war conduct. For more on Halleck, see Marszalek, *Commander of All Lincoln's Armies*. For Halleck's reputation as a military studies expert, see McCurry, *Women's War*, 27–29.

17. Report on Land Titles in California, House Ex. Doc., 31st Cong., 1st Sess. 5, 118 (1850).

18. Report on Land Titles, 122.

19. Report on Land Titles, 122–23.

20. Report on Land Titles, 124.

21. Halleck did not write the only report on Mexican land grants. William Carey Jones, a lawyer, wrote *Land Titles in California* at the request of the federal government. Published a year after Halleck's report and running counter to the Anglo settlers' beliefs about Californios and their property, Jones's report did not influence Anglo-American settlers' opinions and legislators' action on Mexican land grants. In *Land Titles in California*, Jones declared Mexican land grants as "mostly perfect titles" and that "under the law which created them, they were equivalent to patents from our [the US] Government." He also insisted that the few fraudulent titles that existed could be quickly resolved by a congressional board and that private and public lands could be ascertained "with little difficulty." Jones, *Report on the Subject of Land Titles in California 1850*; Suárez, "Legal Confiscation," 29–59.

22. J. D. Stevenson to Governor Richard B. Mason, July 1848, in Bennett, *Reports of Cases Argued*, 579.

23. Halleck cites the claims of J. D. Stevenson and A. Bell rather than providing evidence of antedated documents.

24. Gates, "Adjudication of Spanish-Mexican Land Claims," 213–36.

25. See also Dana, *Two Years Before the Mast*; Lord, *At the Extremity of Civilization*.

26. Hasting, *Emigrants' Guide*, 113–14.

27. *Daily Alta California*, December 28, 1849, 1.

28. Griswold del Castillo, *Treaty of Guadalupe Hidalgo*, 43–44.

29. "Treaty of Guadalupe Hidalgo," February 2, 1848 (accessed at https://avalon.law.yale.edu/19th_century/guadhida.asp); Mawn, "Land Grant-Guarantee."

30. Griswold del Castillo, *Treaty of Guadalupe Hidalgo*, 96.

31. Cong. Globe, 31st Cong., 2nd Sess., 116 (1850). For more on the squatters in Sacramento, see Shelton, *Squatter's Republic*, 11–36; Suval, *Dangerous Ground*, 134.

32. Cong. Globe, 31st Cong., 2nd Sess., 427 (1850); Gates, "Frémont-Jones Scramble for Lands in California," 20.

33. Cong. Globe, 31st Cong., 1850, 2nd Sess., 53, 158 (1850).

34. Senator John C Frémont supported the alternative bill. After the war, Frémont purchased a large, private Mexican grant, Rancho Las Mariposas. Shortly after the purchase, gold was discovered on the land. Frémont's support for land claimants' rights contributed to his unsuccessful bid for reelection. Cong. Globe, 31st Cong., 2nd Sess., 158 (1850).

35. As Missouri's senator, Thomas Benton helped author one of the first Homestead Acts, supported the transcontinental railroad, and was an unwavering advocate of Indigenous displacement. Smith, *Virgin Land*, 36.

36. For more on the influence of squatters, free-soil ideology, and proslavery politics on land policy in California, see Suval, *Dangerous Ground*, 115–35.

37. Cong. Globe, 31st Cong., 2nd Sess., 816 (1850).

38. Hyde, *Empires, Families, Nations*, 464; Cong. Globe, 31st Cong., 1st Sess., 1816 (1850).

39. Banner, *Possessing the Pacific*, 168; "Speech of Col. Frémont in the United States Senate on the Indian Agent Bill," in Bigelow, *Memoir of the Life and Public Services of John Charles Frémont.*

40. Cong. Globe, 31st Cong., 1st Sess., 1816 (1850).

41. Banner, *Possessing the Pacific*, 186–87.

42. Eugene Cassidy to Pablo de la Guerra, July 28, 1851, GFC.

43. *Daily Alta California*, August 2, 1851.

44. *San Diego Herald*, July 24, 1851.

45. In July, nearly every article printed in English-language newspapers called for division and restoration of territorial status and also provided an editorialization on the support for the movement, which discounted the political power of the juntas organizing the movement. It is not until August 1851 that English-language newspapers, like the *Daily Alta California*, take the movement seriously, see *Daily Alta California*, August 9, 1851.

46. "Division of the State," *Sacramento Daily Union*, August 8, 1851.

47. *San Diego Herald*, August 28, 1851.

48. "Address of the San Diego Committee," *Daily Alta California*, September 12, 1851.

49. "Address of the San Diego Committee."

50. *San Diego Herald*, September 4, 1851.

51. *Daily Alta California*, October 26, 1851.

52. This is by no means an exhaustive list of Californios who attended the convention. Reporting on the convention concedes that the list of the attendees was inconsistent with some names only appearing on certain lists.

53. "Proceedings of the Convention of Delegates," *Daily Alta California*, October 27, 1851.

54. Phillips, *Chiefs and Challengers*, 100–102.

55. Pio Pico's mother took in Gale at the age of five.

56. Phillips, *Chiefs and Challengers*, 132.

57. In a statement explaining his reason for planning the revolt, Garra stated, "If the war was lost, all was lost." *Los Angeles Star*, December 20, 1851.

58. Phillips, *Chiefs and Challengers*, 109.

59. Phillips.

60. After the news of this event made its way to Los Angeles, Los Angele mayor, Stephen Foster, threatened to arrest Lugo for "inciting the Indians." Lugo avoided arrest by declaring that he only called on Juan Antonio because Foster had refused to answer his call for help. In 1852, confronted with increasing challenges to his rule over his patria chica, Lugo sold the rancho to a group of Mormons who would go on to establish current-day San Bernadino, and shifted to focusing on his land holdings in Los Angeles. Lugo's testimonio does not mention Garra's uprising, but the timing makes a compelling case for its role in his decision to abandon his land grant and consolidate his power elsewhere. Lugo, *Vida de Un Ranchero*.

61. "Our San Diego Correspondence," *Daily Alta California*, January 16, 1852.

62. "Our San Diego Correspondence."

63. The January 16, 1852, issue mentions the execution of Garra and the arrival of Wozencraft on the same page. "Treaty with the San Louis Rey," *Daily Alta California*, January 16, 1852.

64. "1851–1852—Eighteen Unratified Treaties between California Indians and the United States," US Government Treaties and Reports, June 8, 2016, https://digitalcommons.csumb.edu/cgi/viewcontent.cgi?article=1004&context=hornbeck_usa_2_b.

65. In recounting his conversation with Chiefs Julio and Prieto, representatives of one thousand Indigenous people in the Clear Lake area of California, Agent McKee stated he informed them that the under the treaties, the US government would "settle all your difficulties and prevent the Whites from injuring you." Given the intent to obtain the treaties, I believe that McKee told signatories this to compel them to sign the treaties; whether or not he meant it is a different story. MeKee, "Talks and Minutes of Council Proceedings of the Commissioners Meeting with California Indians," 1852, BIAR.

66. Entries in which a US Indian agent goes over the terms with Anglo-American settlers, Camp Rincon, August 14, 1851; Camp Lupi ya ma, August 18, 1851; Camp Dame, September 12, 1851; Camp in Scotts Valley, October 29, 1851; and Camp in Scotts Valley, November 3, 1851, appear in MeKee, "Talks and Minutes."

67. Quoted in Banner, *Possessing the Pacific*, 184.

68. Weller quoted in Banner, *Possessing the Pacific*, 188. Both houses of the California Legislature had voted down the treaties. California Senators William Gwin and John B. Weller opposed the treaties. "Majority and Minority Reports of the Special Joint Committee on the Mendocino War," 5, State of California, Appendix to the Journals of the Senate, of the Eleventh Session of the Legislature of the State of California (Sacramento: C. T. Botts, 1860).

69. *Journal of the Executive Proceedings of the Senate of the United States of America*, 418–20.

70. It is important to note that the *San Diego Herald*, which John James Ames, a settler from Maine, founded, was an independent paper. Under Ames, the *Herald* supported anti-Immigrant candidates and the extension of a white settler society in San Diego. Smythe, *History of San Diego*, 295–303.

71. "Letter from the South—the Indian War," *Daily Alta California*, December 12, 1851.

72. "Arrival of the Sea Bird—Letter from Los Angeles and San Diego," *Daily Alta California*, January 16, 1852.

73. After fighting had ceased in Alta California, wealthy Anglo-Americans, often lawyers; high-ranking army officers; and businessmen bought land grants from Californios. John C. Frémont purchased two land grants from Californios who sought to incorporate a fellow elite into their property system.

74. Morton and Salta, "Finding Aid to the Documents," 2.

75. Hornbeck, "Patenting of California's Private Land Claims," 442–45.

76. "From Los Angeles," *Daily Alta California*, February 26, 1852.

77. Suárez, "Legal Confiscation."

78. While serving as the military secretary of state, Halleck had used his position to help Frederick Billings and A. C. Peachy establish themselves in California. When Billings arrived in San Francisco, Halleck pulled strings to get Billings appointed as the San Francisco recorder and, later, the California attorney general. When Peachy arrived in San Francisco, Halleck helped him get the position of notary public.

79. For perspective on this fee, a pound of beef cost twenty cents per pound in the 1850s. Marszalek, *Commander of All Lincoln's Armies*, 78; Bastian, "I Heartily Regret," 317.

80. Numerous letters between Halleck and de la Guerra detail this arrangement. Bastian, "I Heartily Regret," 317.

81. Henry Halleck to Pablo de la Guerra, January 18, 1852, GFC.

82. Halleck to de la Guerra, May 28, 1853, GFC.

83. Halleck to de la Guerra, March 1852, GFC.

84. Emphasis original. Halleck to de la Guerra, May 23, 1853, GFC.

85. In a November 22, 1853, letter, Halleck describes the commission's behavior as inconsistent and not adhering to the law but does not go as far as holding the body responsible for denied claims. Halleck to de la Guerra, November 22, 1853, GFC.

86. Robert Greenhow to Caleb Cushing, December 15, 1853, in Bastian, "I Heartily Regret," 318.

87. "California Land Titles," *Sacramento Daily Union*, August 12, 1852.

88. "Senator Gwin's Supplemental Land Bill," *Daily Alta California*, May 31, 1852; "Senator Gwin," *Daily Alta California*, January 12, 1853.

89. Chávez-García, *Negotiating Conquest*, 125.

90. "The Late Election at Santa Barbara," *Daily Alta California*, December 27, 1852.

91. "The Election at Santa Barbara," *Daily Alta California*, January 1, 1853; "Eleccion de Santa Barbara," *Los Angeles Star*, January 15, 1853.

92. "The Election at Santa Barbara"; "Eleccion de Santa Barbara."

93. "Letter from the Capitol," *Daily Alta California*, April 19, 1855.

94. Halleck to de la Guerra, June 18, 1856, GFC.

95. "Letter from the Capitol," *Daily Alta California*, April 19, 1855.

96. Although Shaw's bill failed, prosquatter legislators continued their efforts to legally confiscate Mexican land grants for the benefit of Anglo-American settlers with the 1856 Settlers' Law. The law passed but the California Supreme Court ruled the law unconstitutional.

97. Elite Californios adopted a variety of strategies. Also in 1855, Juan Bautista Alvarado, a former governor of Alta California, convened a junta that discussed mass emigration to Sonora, Mexico, as a solution to high taxes, land issues, and increasingly discriminatory state laws. Torres-Rouff, *Before L.A.*, 104.

98. Landowners, "Subscripcion," 1855, ASP.

99. "Subscripcion."

100. The term "Mexican" here reflects the usage of the term in the sources. I believe the use of "Mexican" by Benjamin Wilson reflects the distinction elite Californios and their allies made between their property-owning gente de razón class and propertyless, racialized "Mexicans." Letter of August 2, 1852, BDW; Torres-Rouff, *Before L.A.*, 121.

101. In the August 2, 1852, letter, Wilson describes the men as "Mexicans," but in all likelihood the men who gathered on Bunker Hill were not only Mexican immigrants but also nonelite, dark-skinned Californios who were also treaty citizens. From the evidence available to scholars, and Wilson at the time, there is no way to determine whether the group was comprised solely of Mexicans.

102. Letter of August 2, 1852, BDW.

103. *Los Angeles Star*, July 26, 1856, 2; "Local," *Los Angeles Star*, August 2, 1856, 2; *El Clamor Publíco*, July 26, 1856, and August 16, 1856.

104. See "The Division of the State," *Southern Vineyard*, June 17, 1859; "Political Intelligences," *Daily Alta California*, May 23, 1859. For an analysis of the proslavery, Anglo-American Chiv support of the bill, see Waite, *West of Slavery*, 155–60.

105. Lynch, "Southern California Chivalry," 113.

106. Andres Pico to Abel Stearns, February 5, 1859, ASP; *El Clamor Público*, October 22, 1859.

107. Waite, *West of Slavery*, 158.

Chapter Four

1. Many newspapers document the start of the rain. For example, the *Daily Alta California*, December 24, 1861, issue contains at least two articles mentioning the beginning of the storm. The *Sacramento Daily Union*, December 24, 1861, remarks on the heavy rain and the American River nearly overflowing its banks.

2. "The Flood," *Los Angeles Star*, February 1, 1862; Brewer, *Up and Down California*, 20–31, 41.

3. During the Civil War, the Republican Party went by the Union Party to attract Union supporters who did not want to vote for Republicans.

4. My analysis of Mexican violence against Indians in borderlands spaces is based on Guidotti-Hernández, *Unspeakable Violence*, especially chapter 2; Prezelski, *Californio Lancers*; Lynch, "Southern California Chivalry"; Lynch, "On the Edge of Empires," 105–21.

5. During Radical Reconstruction, Republican congressmen attempted to craft federal legislation that assured Black participation in political life, especially in the form of electoral politics. Du Bois, *Black Reconstruction in America*; Foner, *Reconstruction*.

6. *Los Angeles Star*, November 10, 1860.

7. *Los Angeles Star*, November 10, 1860.

8. "Letter from Andrés Pico," February 16, 1961, DVC.

9. Cassidy, "Life and Times of Pablo de la Guerra," 162–65.

10. Waite, *West of Slavery*, 184.

11. Other Californio enlistees were Pedro Antonio Abila, Jose Maria Abila, Francisco Martinez, Manuel Cota, Francisco Cota, Jose Perez, Dolores Ruiz, Felipe Sanchez, Guadalupe Sanchez, and Jose Sanchez. Muster Roll of the Los Angeles Mounted Rifles, March 7, 1861, Military Department. Militia Companies Records, California State Archives.

12. Although he enlisted, Sánchez never physically joined the CSA Army or fought in the war.

13. Pitt, *Decline of the Californios*, 234.

14. Genini, *Romualdo Pacheco*, 16, 20; "Romualdo Pacheco," cited in Wasniewski et al. [United States, Congress, Office of the Historian], *Hispanic Americans in Congress*, 118.

15. United States War Department et al., *War of the Rebellion*, 477–86.

16. From the sources available, it is not clear what eased tensions in Los Angeles, but in his memoir, Joseph Lancaster Brent, a Californio ally and Confederate sympathizer, wrote that he convinced Californios not to revolt because they had much to lose. Brent's recounting causes one to wonder if he warned Californios not to join the secessionist causes because they had too much lose or if he told them that it was not their fight to join. Brent eventually left California to fight for the CSA. Brent, *Memoirs of the War Between the States*, 53–54.

17. *Los Angeles Star*, June 15, 1861.

18. *Los Angeles Star*, June 15, 1861.

19. Waite, *West of Slavery*, 171.

20. De la Guerra' service was so valued the state party nominated Pablo de la Guerra as an elector for Stephen Douglas at the convention. Eugene Casserly to Pablo de la Guerra, September 17, 1860, GFC.

21. Albert Heyward to Pablo de la Guerra, June 24, 1863, GFC.

22. Interestingly, the Santa Barbara Union League did not support de la Guerra, calling him a "doughface," a term used to describe Northerners who supported the Southern secessionist cause. Pitt, *Decline of the Californios*, 237–39. In a letter, Eugene Lies explained that the Californio vote had given de la Guerra the edge. Eugene Lies to Pablo de la Guerra, October 30, 1863, GFC.

23. Prior to the Civil War, Pacheco and Pico were generals in the state militia. While these positions were highly symbolic, Pico and other prominent Californios raised militias to suppress Indigenous actions in the Indigenous world when conflicts arose.

24. United States War Department et al., *War of the Rebellion*, 46.

25. The US Civil War did not stop state-sanctioned violence against Indigenous polities in California; in fact, the war exacerbated violence against Native communities throughout the trans-Mississippi West. Madley, *American Genocide*, 290.

26. Gray, *Forester vs. Pico*, 94–96; Madley, 310.

27. The evidence that Romualdo Pacheco thought up the Native Californian Cavalry is not concrete. However, many historians have cited Pacheco as the creator. I have also chosen to consider Pacheco the creator because even though Pacheco did not leave behind many archival sources, there are a handful of sources that corroborate his founding role. See *Sacramento Daily Union*, January 28, 1863; Orton, *Records of California Men*, 104; Gray, *Forester vs. Pico*, 94–96; Prezelski, *Californio Lancers*, 24; Lynch, "Southern California Chivalry," 194.

28. Orton, *Records of California Men*, 304.

29. Despite accusations of disloyalty in 1860, Pico's work for the Union now compelled US Army officials to describe him as patriotic. G. Wright to L. Thomas, in Orton, *Records of California Men*, 304–6.

30. Pitt, *Decline of the Californios*, 232; Prezelski, *Californio Lancers*, 29; Lynch, "Southern Californio Chivalry," 195.

31. Vallejo, *Notas históricas sobre California*, 154–55.

32. The French presence in Mexico also bothered the de la Guerras. Pablo de la Guerra believed that the Confederates and the French were working together to conquer the US-Mexico borderlands. See Albert Hayward to Pablo de la Guerra, June 24, 1863, GFC.

33. Initially, Anglo-American officers in the US Army did not fill leadership positions with Californios because of their prejudices. In his reporting on the Native cavalry, Colonel Curtis often describes the Californio servicemen as thieves, having bad morals, and creating bad morale. Curtis's prejudice was so overt, his superiors chastised him for it. Prezelski, *Californio Lancers*, 85, 89–94, 97, 99.

34. Prezelski, 32.

35. Antonio María de la Guerra to Pablo De La Guerra, May 26, 1864, GFC.

36. Antonio María de la Guerra also recruited Californio men living in the Monterey area, including José Antonio Sánchez, brother of Tomás Sanchez, who fought on behalf of the Confederate Army. Pitt, *Decline of the Californios*, 231.

37. Four companies made up the Native Californian Cavalry: Company A of San Jose, Company B of San Francisco, Company C of Santa Barbara, and Company D of Los Angeles.

38. "Native California Troops," *Daily Alta California*, March 11, 1863.

39. Prezelski, *Californio Lancers*, 153–88.

40. Company B, based in San Francisco, received orders to aid the Humboldt Militia in their efforts to remove the Hupa and open the land to Anglo-American settlers. Throughout California, the Native Californian Cavalry was an army unit dedicated to Indigenous removal. For Company B actions, see Prezelski, *Californio Lancers*, 79–84.

41. The Mojave Trail is a traditional Indigenous route historically used by the Chumash and Colorado Basin tribes for trade. Initially, Indigenous communities allowed for Anglo-American use of the trail, but an increase in Anglo settlement in the Indigenous world resulted in various Indigenous communities using violence to prevent encroachment on their lands. Colonel Curtis ordered the Cavalry to patrol the Mojave Trail in April 1865, two months after he received settlers' complaints about raiding Chemehuevi groups. Military orders and newspapers reported on the Cavalry and their role in protecting California and the Mojave Trail from the Apache and other "Indians." For example, see *Weekly Butte Record*, April 15, 1865; *Wilmington Journal*, August 19, 1865; Prezelski, *Californio Lancers*, 97.

42. *Wilmington Journal*, July 15, 1865.

43. DeLay, *War of a Thousand Deserts*, 306–9.

44. *Daily Alta California*, November 9, 1864.

45. *Daily Alta California*, November 9, 1864.

46. *Los Angeles Star*, January 3, 1863.

47. *Los Angeles Star*, July 25, 1863, 2.

48. Taylor, et al., *Seeking El Dorado*, 12.

49. Fisher, "History of the Political and Social Development of the Black Community," 60–62.

50. *Elevator*, June 30, 1865.

51. Prior to the creation of *The Elevator* in June 1865, Bell had cofounded the *Pacific Appeal* with Peter Anderson in 1862. Due to political tensions, Bell founded *The Elevator*.

52. Fisher, "A History of the Political and Social Development of the Black Community," 96–100.

53. *Proceedings of the California State Convention, 1865*, 84–86.

54. *Proceedings of the California State Convention, 1865*, 86.

55. *Proceedings of the California State Convention, 1865*, 3.

56. Delegate William Hall from San Francisco even condemned the writers of the California Constitution for establishing a Free State without extending rights to men of African descent. *Proceedings of the California State Convention, 1865*, 8.

57. "The Convention," *Elevator*, November 3, 1865.

58. "Report of the Committee on Industrial Pursuits," in *Proceedings of the California State Convention, 1865*, 20.

59. "Report of the Committee on Industrial Pursuits."

60. "Colored Laborers for the Pacific Coast," *Elevator*, September 22 1865.

61. Davis, *History of Political Conventions in California*, 265.

62. Samuel Brinkeroff to Pablo de la Guerra, July 9, 1865, GFC.

63. State of California, *Journal of the Senate of the State of California*, 534.

64. For example, W. S. Green, a Democrat, presented a resolution that declared freed people "incapable of self-government" and that the enfranchisement of freed people was "unconstitutional and void."

65. "Legislating on the Negro," *Elevator*, December 15, 1865.

66. "Legislating on the Negro."

67. Anti-Catholicism became all the more rampant in California after the Civil War, especially in San Francisco where a large Irish Catholic population lived. The Irish Catholic, much like the Californio Catholic, I would argue, were not considered white or Christian enough. Paddison, "Anti-Catholicism and Race in Post-Civil-War San Francisco."

68. "The Manner in Which We Are Being Reconstructed," *Daily Alta California*, February 3, 1866.

69. This anxiety compelled the US Congress to extend the right to become a citizen only to people of African descent. Lew-Williams, *Chinese Must Go*, 44.

70. Message from Governor Frederick Low, *Journal of the Senate of the State of California*, 49.

71. Berwanger, *West and Reconstruction*, 120.

72. Waite, *West of Slavery*, 220.

73. *Sacramento Daily Union*, June 24, 1867.

74. During the nomination process, the other nominee, Joseph Roberts Jr., withdrew from the race to ensure that Coronel received the nomination. "1867 June 26, Thos. N. Cazneau to Antonio F. Coronel," ACP; "1867 Junio 21, Juan Lugo a Antonio Coronel," ACP.

75. "Henry Haight Speech at California Democratic Convention," *Daily Alta California*, July 10, 1867; "Haight's Record," *Red Bluff Independent*, July 10, 1867; "News of the Morning," *Sacramento Daily Union*, July 10, 1867. See Bottoms, *An Aristocracy of Color*, 55–94; Foner, *Free Soil, Free Labor, Free Men*, 261–301.

76. "A Los Hijos de Pais," ACP.

77. "Coronel Speech," ACP.

78. "Public Speeches of A. F. Coronel," ACP.

79. "J. Janssens to Soledad Coronel," ACP.

80. Axtell, "Alocucion [*sic*] de S. B. Axtell, ESQ," ACP.

81. Axtell.

82. Axtell.

83. Axtell.

84. Caleb Fay, an Independent Republican, received 2,088 votes.

85. "1867 Octubre 9, Juan Luco a Antonio Coronel," ACP.

86. "1867 Septembre 22, J Jenssens a Antonio F. Coronel," ACP; "1867 Septembre 16, Romualdo Pacheco a Antonio F. Coronel," ACP.

87. Thomas N Cazneau to Antonio F. Coronel, June 26, 1867, ACP.

88. "22 Octubre 1867, James Alex Forbes a Don Antonio F. Coronel," ACP.

89. "Keep It Before the People," *Red Bluff Independent*, September 4, 1867.

90. Haight, "Inaugural Address," December 5, 1867.

91. Haight.

92. Haight.

93. Haight, "Message of H. H. Haight," 152.

94. Haight, 149.

95. Haight, 158.

96. "The Election," *Sacramento Daily Union*, October 25, 1869.

97. "Brief Items," *Sacramento Daily Union*, November 24, 1869.

98. "Petaluma Items," *Marin Journal*, December 11, 1869; "District Judges Commissioned," *Sacramento Daily Union*, December 11, 1869.

99. Martin Kimberly, roll M593_87, 467A, Family History Library Film 545586, Ancestry.com.

100. There is little information about Eugene Lies. Born in New York, Lies moved to Santa Barbara in 1850. As a lawyer he argued many cases; in some instances, he even served as a translator. There is little known about the relationship between Lies and de la Guerra, but they had sixteen recorded instances of communication from 1853–69.

101. "Supreme Court," *Marysville Daily Appeal*, June 8, 1870.

102. People ex rel. Kimberly v. De La Guerra, 40 Cal. 311 (1870).

103. *People ex rel. Kimberly*.

104. U.S. Congress. Cong. Globe, 30th Congress, Second Session, vol. 17, (January 4, 1848), p. 49.

105. Cong. Globe.

106. Cong. Globe.

107. Cong. Globe.

108. United States, *A Compendium of the Ninth Census*, 28–29.

109. Colman, "John Ballard," 206.

110. *Los Angeles Star*, April 16, 1870.

111. Colman, "John Ballard," 216.

112. Colman.

113. "Important Decisions on the Fifteenth Amendment," *Los Angeles Star*, May 7, 1870.

114. State of California, *Journal of the Senate of the State of California*.

115. Los Angeles County Great Registers, 1870, SCWR.

116. *Petaluma Weekly Argus*, February 15, 1878; "The Pacific States," *New York Times*, September 9, 1876.

117. *Pacheco v. Beck*, 52 Cal. 3 (1877); Genini and Hitchman, *Romualdo Pacheco*, 149–50.

Chapter Five

1. Cleland, *Cattle on a Thousand Hills*, 117–37.

2. *Los Angeles Star*, January 13, 1864.

3. Cleland, *Cattle on a Thousand Hills*, 131.

4. For example, from 1826 to 1848, the ranchos of Alta California exported over a million hides and sixty-two million pounds of tallow, which generated family fortunes. Rancheros grew their herds and by 1863, there were 1.8 million cattle in the state, a 25 percent increase from 1852. Gates, *California Ranches and Farms*, 5.

5. For perspective, in 1851, fifteen thousand cattle were slaughtered for consumption. In 1853, twenty-five thousand cattle (a 60 percent increase) were slaughtered for consumption. Gates, 18.

6. Homestead Act of 1862, ch. 75, 12 Stat. 392 (1862). For more on the Homestead Act as a legislative goal of free-soil politics, see Suval, *Dangerous Ground*, 83–114, 190–200.

7. Chávez-García, *Negotiating Conquest*, 126.

8. Gates, *California Ranches and Farms*, 14.

9. Camarillo, *Chicanos in a Changing Society*, 35.

10. US Department of Agriculture, *Monthly Report of the Department of Agriculture*, 33.

11. My use of the term "Mexican" here indicates a person with Mexican nationality who migrated to California after the ratification of the Treaty of Guadalupe Hidalgo.

12. In this chapter, I am building on the argument Camarillo makes, that "the multiple effects of a slumping cattle industry and a cycle of floods and droughts led to the economic demise of Mexican ranchos." Camarillo, *Chicanos in a Changing Society*, 35.

13. Phillips, *Vineyards and Vaqueros*, 313–16.

14. Solomon, *Pio Pico*, 141.

15. Cleland, *Cattle on a Thousand Hills*, 319; 1864 Los Angeles Tax Assessment Book, SCWHR.

16. Jensen, James M. "John Forster," 42.

17. Gray, *Forster vs. Pico*, 104.

18. Gray, 118.

19. Solomon, *Pio Pico*, 145–47; Gray, 200.

20. The only potential Californio juror, José Estudillo, was dismissed by Forster's lawyer.

21. Gray, *Forster vs. Pico*, 161–72.

22. Cassidy, "Life and Times of Pablo de la Guerra," 166.

23. Cassidy, "Life and Times of Pablo de la Guerra," 180.

24. "Real Estate Sale," *Ventura Signal*, August 24, 1872; "Notice," *Ventura Signal*, September 7, 1872.

25. Chávez-García, *Negotiating Conquest*, 142.

26. McKain and Miles, "Santa Barbara County Between Two Social Orders," 313.

27. United States. *A Compendium of the Ninth Census*, 28.

28. Haight, "Biannual Message to State Legislature, 1869."

29. Haight.

30. According to Senate records, the body failed to move forward on such legislation because the Committee on Immigration failed to write laws that clearly established the duties and obligations of a government agency in charge of encouraging immigration. During the 1869–70 session, the senate attempted to pass three separate acts: first, an act that would establish a State Immigration Board; second, an act that would encourage Scandinavian immigration; and third, an act to protect the people of California "from the evils of Asiatic immigration." State of California, *Journal of the Senate During the 1869–1870 Session*, 126, 528, 703, 712, 876.

31. In *All About California and the Inducements to Settle There*, the manager of the California Immigrant Union describes the inability of the state legislature to put forth an operational plan as a "regret to all the classes." California Immigrant Union, *All About California*, 1.

32. "California Immigrant Union; Statement of Its Objects, Purpose and Plan of Operations," *Evening Bulletin*, May 13, 1870.

33. The brochure was highly influential and widely circulated. Within five years, the pamphlet was reprinted ten times. Winther, "Colony System of Southern California."

34. California Immigrant Union, *All About California*, 4.

35. California Immigrant Union, 5.

36. California Immigrant Union, 62.

37. "The Lompoc Colony," *Santa Barbara Weekly Press*, January 1, 1872.

38. "Santa Barbara—Lompoc Homesteads," *Morning Press*, August 27, 1874; "Hopeful Scheme," *Santa Barbara Daily Press*, May 1874; "Can It Be Possible?," *Santa Cruz Weekly Sentinel*, September 5, 1874; "A Great Californio Rancho," *Sacramento Daily Union*, September 26, 1874.

39. Lompoc became a city in 1888. It is now a tourist destination known for its flowers and wine.

40. "Certificate of Incorporation," in California Immigrant Union, *Supplement to All About California*.

41. California Immigrant Union.

42. "Centinela Colony," *Pacific Rural Press*, December 19, 1874.

43. Max Strobel was a German immigrant who had been instrumental to founding the agricultural colony that developed into Anaheim.

44. "From San Diego," *Marysville Daily Appeal*, January 18, 1873.

45. "Foster's Immigration Scheme," *Daily Alta California*, January 18, 1873; "Don Juan Foster Has Not Yet Sold His Island," *Daily Alta California*, July 19, 1873.

46. The owners of Rancho Temecula and Pauba engaged in colonization schemes. "Another Colonization Scheme," *San Diego Union*, October 11, 1873.

47. "California Letter," *Los Angeles Daily Star*, December 13, 1874.

48. "Colonization," *San Jose Mercury Weekly*, February 4, 1875.

49. "New Homestead Plan," *Santa Barbara Weekly Press*, May 1, 1875; *Ventura Signal*, June 12, 1875.

50. "Small Farms—Handsome Words for Lompoc," *Santa Barbara Weekly Press*, December 30, 1876; "Advent of the People and the Plow—the Effect," *Santa Barbara Weekly Press*, May 26, 1877.

51. The 1862 Homestead Act only compounded the notion that these lands were public domain. The fact that the US Congress did not ratify the 1851 Indian Treaties had lent credence to this notion a decade before. Agents of the Bureau of Indian Affairs identified this as an outcome of the unratified treaties. See Annual Report of the Commissioner of Indian Affairs for the Year 1870, H.R. Exec. Doc. No. 1, 41st Cong., 3rd Sess. 91 (1870).

52. *Annual Report of the Commissioner of Indian Affairs for the Year 1868*, 128.

53. B. C. Whiting to N. G. Taylor, San Francisco, October 10, 1868 in *Annual Report of the Commissioner of Indian Affairs for the Year 1868*, 125–28.

54. Annual Report of the Commissioner of Indian Affairs for the Year 1870, 92.

55. Annual Report of the Commissioner of Indian Affairs for the Year 1870, 94.

56. Phillips, *Chiefs and Challengers*, 194.

57. Phillips, 205.

58. "The Mission Indians," *San Diego Daily Union*, October 21, 1874.

59. "The Mission Indians," *Los Angeles Herald*, October 29, 1874; "The Mission Indians," *Daily Alta California*, October 26, 1874; "From Los Angeles," *Marysville Daily Appeal*, October 22, 1874; *Sacramento Daily Union*, October 22, 1874.

60. "The Temecula Indians," *San Diego Union*, September 13, 1875; Phillips, *Chiefs and Challengers*, 183.

61. "Indians on War Path," *Los Angeles Herald*, October 3, 1875; "Threatened Indian Trouble in San Diego County," *Daily News*, October 4, 1875; "Trouble from Temecula," *San Diego Union*, October 4, 1875.

62. "The Temecula Indians," *Daily Alta California*, October 3, 1875; "The Mission Indian Question," *San Diego Union*, October 8, 1875.

63. Annual Report of the Commissioner of Indian Affairs for the Year 1886, H.R. Exec. Doc. No. 1, 49th Cong., 2nd Sess. 306 (1886).

64. My analysis of Californio intentions during the 1871 Anti-Chinese Massacre is based on Torres-Rouff, *Before L.A.*, 181–97. As other scholars have argued, the Anti-Chinese Massacre was punishment for the threat Chinese immigrants posed to whiteness and white political power in the city and state during Reconstruction. See Jew, "Anti-Chinese Massacre of 1871 and Its Strange Career"; Zesch, *Chinatown War*.

65. During the Spanish era, residents named the street Calle de Los Negros after its dark-skinned residents. The street has since been renamed Los Angeles Street.

66. Zesch, *Chinatown War*, 111.

67. Torres-Rouff, *Before L.A.*, 193.

68. Torres-Rouff, 194.
69. Torres-Rouff, 183.
70. Zesch, *Chinatown War*, 174.
71. See chapter 4.
72. Zesch, *Chinatown War*, 174.
73. Zesch, 205.
74. Zesch, 164.
75. Zesch, 164.
76. Shelton, *Squatter's Republic*, 1–10.
77. "Our Nominee for Governor," *Mariposa Gazette*, July 10, 1875.
78. Saxton, *Indispensable Enemy*, 72.
79. Kearney borrowed the name from a socialist labor party, the Workingman's Party of the United States, but he did not establish the Workingmen's Party of California upon Socialist ideals. German immigrants founded the Workingman's Party of the United States in the eastern part of the United States as a labor party influenced by Marxist thought. The party campaigned for the eight-hour workday and the nationalization of railroads. Saxton, *Indispensable Enemy*, 113; Kauer, "Workingman's Party of California."
80. Shumsky, *Evolution of Political Protest*, 29.
81. Saxton, *Indispensable Enemy*, 122.
82. "The Chinese Must Go!" was essentially the slogan of the Workingman's Party of California. Saxton, *Indispensable Enemy*, 115–18.
83. Saxton, 117.
84. *Los Angeles Daily Star*, January 5, 1878; *Los Angeles Daily Star*, February 27, 1878.
85. *Los Angeles Daily Star*, January 5, 1878.
86. Gray, *Clamor for Equality*, 264.
87. "Constitutional Convention," *Union Democrat*, October 6, 1877.
88. An Act to provide for a Convention to frame a new Constitution for the State of California Statutes of California, Act of Mar. 30, 1878, ch. 490, 1877–78 Cal. Stat. 759.
89. Vivian and Waldron, *Biographical Sketches*, 14.
90. Willis and Stockton, *Debates and Proceedings*, 3–4.
91. Willis and Stockton, 50.
92. Willis and Stockton.
93. Willis and Stockton.
94. Willis and Stockton.
95. Willis and Stockton, 51.
96. Ooley, "Inventory of the Working Papers of the 1878–1879 Constitutional Convention," 50–56.
97. See chapter 3.
98. As Lozano argues, "Language in this case served as the primary discriminatory indicator, rather than an individual's physical characteristics." Lozano, "Translating California," 353.
99. Willis and Stockton, *Debates and Proceedings*, 801.
100. Willis and Stockton, 801.

101. After the delegates approved the English-only provision, a delegate motioned to add an amendment that required the state to print important information in English and Spanish. A debate emerged in which opponents to Spanish translation declared that they should not offer special treatment to "foreigners." The delegates collapsed the ability to speak Spanish with noncitizenship status. The delegates also characterized immigrants from Mexican states, like Sonora, as a pestilence on society and linked Spanish fluency to racial inferiority and inherent criminality. This racializing language would become prominent in the 1880s and 1890s. For a majority of the delegates present, Spanish-speaking residents were foreigners, if not racial others, and, therefore, not entitled to participate in state politics and governance. Willis and Stockton, 801–3.

102. Cal. Const., art. IV (1879).

103. As one of its first acts of business the delegates assembled a Committee on the Chinese to recommend constitutional amendments that would withstand the scrutiny of the US Supreme Court. Swisher, *Motivation and Political Technique*, 85–91.

104. I use the concept of "alien" as described by Lew-Williams, *Chinese Must Go*.

105. Cal. Const., art. XIX, § 1 (1879).

106. Section 1 of Article XIX used the idea of public health to racialize Chinese inhabitants. This kind of racialization transformed Chinese immigrants into diseased bodies that needed to be excluded. For more on the confluence of public health and the construction of race, see Molina, *Fit to Be Citizens?*

107. Section 3 empowered county and municipal governments to exploit the labor of Chinese persons in a manner that did not threaten free white labor and fueled cities' expansion and economies. Hernández details how municipal and county governments used incarceration to address racial threats and abet the settlement, expansions of settlement, and the growth of urban and rural economies. Hernández, *City of Inmates*, especially 37–39, 63; Cal. Const., art. XIX, § 3 (1879).

108. Cal. Const., art. XIX, § 4 (1879).

109. Cal. Const., art. XVII, § 1 (1879).

110. Cal. Const., art. XVII, § 2 and 3 (1879).

111. Lustig, "Private Rights and Public Purposes," 50.

112. Cal. Const., art. XIII (1879).

113. Sargent, "California Constitutional Convention of 1878–9," 7.

114. In re Tiburcio Parrott, 1 F. 481 (U.S. Cir. Ct., D. Cal. 1880).

115. Saxton, *Indispensable Enemy*, 128.

116. *Daily Alta California*, June 15, 1870.

117. *Los Angeles Daily Star*, June 16, 1870.

118. Andrés Pico died in 1876.

119. "Pio Pico's Death," *San Francisco Call*, September 14, 1894; "Fly, Mexicans, in all Haste," *Los Angeles Herald*, September 30, 1894.

120. Coronel died in 1894. His last known donation to the Democratic Party is dated 1890.

121. Pearson, "'Call me a Californio.'"

122. Carpio, "Zorro Down Under," 113.

123. Williams, *North from Mexico*; Kropp, *California Vieja*; Carpio, "Zorro Down Under."

Epilogue

1. "History." *Union Station Los Angeles*, accessed April 5, 2026, https://www.unionstationla.com/history/.

2. Kropp, *California Vieja*; Carpio, "Zorro Down Under," 111–42; Estrada, *Los Angeles Plaza*.

3. Kropp, *California Vieja*, 209.

4. The effort to memorializes Los Pobladores began in the 1920s, when the city's first Black librarian, Miriam Matthews, began a campaign to memorialize the city's multiracial founders. The city installed a plaque in 1981 during the city's bicentennial celebrations Estrada, *Los Angele Plaza*, 259.

5. "Past Due: Report and Recommendations of the Los Angeles Mayor's Office Civic Memory Working Group," Civic Memory, accessed April 5, 2026, https://civicmemory.la/.

6. Huang, "Here's the Winning Design for LA's Memorial to the 1871 Chinese Massacre," LAist, May 3, 2023, https://laist.com/news/la-history/chinese-massacre-1871-memorial-winning-design.

7. Lupe Tellez, quoted in Mayo, "Dancing Is An Expression of Identity for Aztec Family in LA," *Greater LA*, October 20, 2022, https://www.kcrw.com/news/shows/greater-la/born-razed/aztecs-dance.

8. Licas, "Protesters in L. A. Topple Statue of Junipero Serra, Who Helped Colonize California," *Los Angeles Daily News*, June 21, 2020, https://www.dailynews.com/2020/06/20/protesters-in-l-a-topple-statue-of-junipero-serra-who-helped-colonize-california/.

9. By "racial scripts" I mean the idea, developed by Natalia Molina, of racial projects that affect different groups simultaneously. I use "racial script" here to demonstrate that the idea of the perpetual foreigner has been a powerful tool in the construction of racialized groups, past and present. Molina, *How Race Is Made in America*.

Bibliography

Archival Sources

Berkeley, CA
- Bancroft Library, University of California at Berkeley
  - Antonio Coronel, *Cosas de California*
  - Benjamin Hayes Scrapbooks
  - Documents Pertaining to the Adjudication of Private Land Claims in California
  - Halleck, Peachy, and Billings Records
  - Hubert Howe Bancroft Records
  - Jose Lugo, *Vida de un Ranchero*
  - José Ramon Pico, "Christmas in California Before the Gringos Came"
  - Papers on the Bear Flag Revolt, 1848–1878
  - Pico Family Papers, 1864–1876
  - Salvador Vallejo, *Notas Historicas sobre California, 1874*
  - Vallejo Family Papers
  - William McKendree Gwin Papers

Los Angeles, CA
- Charles E. Young Research Library, UCLA
  - Archibald H. Gillespie Papers, 1812–1878
  - William S. Rosecrans Papers, 1819–1898
- Seaver Center for Western History Research
  - Antonio F. Coronel Papers
  - Articles of Capitulation at Cahuenga
  - Del Valle Collection
  - Great Registers of Los Angeles
  - Tax Assessment Books

Sacramento, CA
- California State Archives and Library
  - 1849 Constitutional Convention Records
  - 1879 Constitutional Convention Records
  - Militia Company Records
  - United States, Bureau of Indian Affairs Records, 1851 Aug. 9–Nov. 19
- California State University, Dominguez Hills Archives
  - Rancho San Pedro Collection

San Marino, CA
- Huntington Library
  - Abel Stearns Papers
  - Bandini-Winston Family Collection

Benjamin Davis Wilson Collection
California Land Cases Collection
Guerra Family Collection
Halleck, Peachy, and Billings Records

Published Government Documents

Congressional Globe

Debates and Proceedings of the Constitutional Convention of the State of California Convened at the City of Sacramento in 1855, 1856, 1865

1849 Constitution of California

1851–1852—Eighteen Unratified Treaties Between California Indians and the United States

1879 Constitution of California

Henry Haight. *First Biennial Message of H. H. Haight, Governor of the State of California, to the Legislature: Eighteen Session, December, 1869*. Sacramento: D. W. Gelwicks, 1869.

Orton, Richard. *Records of California Men in the War of Rebellion*. Sacramento: State Office, 1890.

State of California. *Journal of the Assembly of the State of California, 1849/1850–1879.*

———. *Journal of the Senate of the State of California, 1849/1850–1879.*

———. Appendix to the Journals of the Senate, of the Eleventh Session of the Legislature of the State of California. Sacramento: C. T. Botts, 1860.

United States. Census Office. *Seventh Census of the United States: 1850*. Washington, DC: Robert Armstrong, 1853.

———. *A Compendium of the Ninth Census (June 1, 1870)*. Washington, DC: Census Office, 1872.

United States. Congress. Committee on Indian Affairs. (1924–1925). *Hearings Before a Subcommittee of the Committee on Indian Affairs, in the Sixty-Eighth Congress, first session*, 1924: 2nd sess., 1925. Washington, DC.

United States. Congress. Office of the Historian, Wasniewski, Mathew, et al. [*Hispanic Americans in Congress, 1822–2012*. Washington, DC: US Government Printing Office, 2013.

United States. Congress. Senate. (1852). *Journal of the Executive Proceedings of the Senate of the United States of America, Volume 8*. Washington, DC.

United States. Department of Agriculture. Bureau of Statistics, and United States Department of Agriculture. *Monthly Report of the Department of Agriculture, for the Condition of Crops*. Washington, DC, 1863–1876.

United States. District Court (California: Northern District). *Reports of Land Cases Determined in the United States District Court for the Northern District of California: June Term, 1853, to June Term, 1858, Inclusive*. San Francisco: Sumner Whitney, 1862.

United States. *Journal of the Executive Proceedings of the Senate of the United States of America, 1850–1879.*

United States. Office of Indian Affairs. *Annual Report of the Commissioner of Indian Affairs for the Year, 1868*. Washington, DC, 1868.

United States. War Department et al. *The War of the Rebellion: A Compilation of the Official Records of the Union and Confederate Armies*. Volume 50. Washington, DC: Government Printing Office, 1880–1901.

Newspapers

California Star
Daily Alta California
El Clamor Público
The Elevator
Los Angeles Star
Marysville Daily Appeal
Marysville Daily Herald
Mirror of the Times
Pacific Appeal
Placer Times
Sacramento Daily Union
Sacramento Transcript
San Diego Herald

Published Primary Sources

Aptheker, Herbert. *A Documentary History of the Negro People in the United States*. New York Citadel Press, 1951.
Beasley, Delilah L. *The Negro Trail Blazers of California*. Los Angeles: Times Mirror Printing and Binding House, 1919.
Beebe, Rose Marie, and Robert Senkewicz. *Testimonios: Early California Through the Eyes of Women, 1815–1848*. Norman: University of Oklahoma Press, 2015.
Bennett, Nathaniel. *Reports of Cases Argued and Determined in the Supreme Court of the State of California*. San Francisco: Marvin & Hitchcock, 1851.
Bidwell, John, and Annie E. Kennedy. *What Makes a Man: The Annie E. Kennedy and John Bidwell Letters, 1866–1868*. Edited by Chad L. Hoopes. Fresno, CA: Valley Publishers, 1973.
Brent, Joseph Lancaster. *Memoirs of the War Between the States*. New Orleans: Fontana, 1940.
Brewer, William H. *Up and Down California in 1860–1864: The Journal of William H. Brewer*. New Haven, CT: Yale University Press, 1930.
Browne, John Ross. *Muleback to the Convention: Letters of J. Ross Browne*. San Francisco: Book Club of California, 1950.
———. *Report of the Debates in the Convention of California on the Formation of the State Constitution in September and October, 1849*. Washington, DC: J. T. Towers, 1850.
California Immigrant Union. *All About California and the Inducements to Settle There*. San Francisco: A. L. Bancroft, 1870.
California Immigrant Union. *Supplement to All About California; Referring Particularly to the Centinela Colony, Near the City of Los Angeles*. Los Angeles: Herald Steam Book and Job Printing House, 1874.
Chun-Chuen, Lai. *Remarks of the Chinese Merchants of San Francisco upon Governor Bigler's Message, and Some Common Objections*. San Francisco: Whitton, Towne, 1855.
Crespí, Juan. *A Description of Distant Roads: Original Journals of the First Expedition into California, 1769–1770*. Edited by Alan K. Brown. San Diego: San Diego State University Press, 2001.

Davis, William Heath. *Sixty Years in California*. San Francisco: A. J. Leary, 1889.
Frémont, John Charles. *The Expeditions of John Charles Frémont*. Volume 2. Urbana: University of Illinois Press, 1970.
Garcia, Margaret. *Tree of Califias*. Metro Art, Los Angeles County Metropolitan. https://art.metro.net/artworks/tree-of-califas/.
Gibbs, Mifflin Wistar, and Booker T. Washington. *Shadow and Light: An Autobiography*. New York: Arno Press, 1902.
Hastings, Lansford. *Emigrants' Guide to Oregon and California*. Cincinnati, OH: George Conclin, 1845.
Ide, William B., and Simeon Ide. *Who Conquered California?* Claremont, NH: Simeon Ide, 1880.
Jones, William. "Report on the Subject of Land Titles in California made in Pursuance of Instructions from the Secretary of State and the Secretary of Interior." Washington, DC: Gideon and Co, Printers, 1850.
Lord, Israel Shipman. *At the Extremity of Civilization*. Jefferson, NC: McFarland & Co, 1995.
de Mofras, Eugene Duflot. *Travels on the Pacific Coast*. Translated by Marguerite Knowlton. Santa Ana: Fine Arts Press, 1927.
Newmark, Harris. *Sixty Years in Southern California, 1853–1913, Containing the Reminiscences of Harris Newmark*. New York: Knickerbocker Press, 1916.
Ord, Angustias, Thomas Savage, and Giorgio Sabino Antonio Perissinotto. *The California Recollections of Angustias de la Guerra Ord (Occurrences in Hispanic California)*. Washington, DC: Academy of American Franciscan History, 2004.
Pico, Pío. *Don Pio Pico's Historical Narrative*. Edited by Martin Cole and Henry Welcome. Translated by Arthur P. Botello. Glendale: Arthur H. Clark, 1973.
Pleasants, J. E. *In Pioneer Days: A Visit to Santiago Canyon Sixty Years Ago*. Orange County, CA: n.p., 1931.
Proceedings of the California State Convention of the Colored Citizens, Held in Sacramento on the 25th, 26th, 27th, and 28th of October, 1865. San Francisco: Printed at the office of "The Elevator," 1865.
Proceedings of the First State Convention of the Colored Citizens of the State of California. Held at Sacramento Nov. 20th 21st, and 22d, in the Colored Methodist Chuch [*sic*]. Sacramento: Democratic State Journal Press, 1855.
Traas, Adrian. *From the Golden Gate to Mexico City: The US Army Topographical Engineers in the Mexican War, 1846–1848*. Washington, DC: Office of History, Corp of Engineers, 1993.
Vallejo, Mariano Guadalupe. *Recuerdos: Historical and Personal Remembrances Relating to Alta California, 1769–1849*. Volume 2. Edited by Rose Marie Beebe and Robert M. Senkewicz. Norman: University of Oklahoma Press, 2023.
Wilson, Benjamin. *Benjamin Davis Wilson's Observations on Early Days in California and New Mexico*. Edited by Arthur Woodward. Volume 16. Historical Society of Southern California, 1934.
Wilson, Benjamin, and John Walton Caughey. *The Indians of Southern California in 1852: The B.D. Wilson Report and a Selection of Contemporary Comment*. San Marino, CA: Huntington Library, 1952.

Secondary Sources

Adelman, Jeremy, and Stephen Aron. "From Borderlands to Borders: Empires, Nation-States, and the Peoples in Between in North American History." *American Historical Review* 104, no. 3 (1999): 814–41.

Akins, Damon B., and William J. Bauer Jr. *We Are the Land: A History of Native California*. Berkeley: University of California Press, 2021.

Almaguer, Tomás. "Interpreting Chicano History: The World-System Approach to Nineteenth-Century California." *Review (Fernand Braudel Center)* 4, no. 3 (January 1, 1981): 459–507.

———. *Racial Fault Lines: The Historical Origins of White Supremacy in California*. Berkeley: University of California Press, 1994.

Anderson, Benedict. *Imagined Communities: Reflections on the Origin and Spread of Nationalism*. New York: Verso, 1983.

Anderson, Kate. *Tending the Wild: Native American Knowledge and the Management of California's Natural Resources*. Berkeley: University of California Press, 2005.

Arenson, Adam, and Andrew R. Graybill, eds. *Civil War Wests: Testing the Limits of the United States*. Berkeley: University of California Press, 2015.

Bancroft, Hubert Howe. *History of California*. Volume 5. San Francisco: History, 1884.

Banner, Stuart. *Possessing the Pacific: Land, Settlers, and Indigenous People from Australia to Alaska*. Cambridge, MA: Harvard University Press, 2007.

Bastian, Beverly E. "'I Heartily Regret that I Ever Touched a Title in California': Henry Wager Halleck, the Californios, and the Clash of Legal Cultures." *California History* 72, no. 4 (December 1, 1993): 310–23.

Beavers, Herman. *Geography and the Political Imaginary in the Novels of Toni Morrison*. Cham: Springer International Publishing, 2016.

Berwanger, Eugene H. *The Frontier Against Slavery: Western Anti-Negro Prejudice and the Slavery Extension Controversy*. Urbana: University of Illinois Press, 1967.

———. *The West and Reconstruction*. Urbana: University of Illinois Press, 1981.

Bigelow, John. *Memoir of the Life and Public Services of John Charles Frémont*. New York: Derby and Jackson, 1856.

Blackhawk, Ned. *The Rediscovery of America: Native Peoples and the Unmaking of U.S. History*. New Haven, CT: Yale University Press, 2023.

Bolton, Herbert E. *The Spanish Borderlands: A Chronicle of Old Florida and the Southwest*. New Haven, CT: Yale University Press, 1921.

Bottoms, D. Michael. *An Aristocracy of Color: Race and Reconstruction in California and the West, 1850–1890*. Norman: University of Oklahoma Press, 2013.

Boutelle, R. J. *The Race for America: Black Internationalism in the Age of Manifest Destiny*. Chapel Hill: University of North Carolina Press, 2023.

Bouvier, Virginia Marie. *Women and the Conquest of California, 1542–1840*. Tucson: University of Arizona Press, 2001.

Camarillo, Albert. *Chicanos in a Changing Society: From Mexican Pueblos to American Barrios in Santa Barbara and Southern California, 1848–1930*. Cambridge, MA: Harvard University Press, 1979.

Campbell, Marne L. *Making Black Los Angeles: Class, Gender, and Community, 1850–1917*. Chapel Hill: University of North Carolina Press, 2016.
Carlin, Amanda. "The Courtroom as White Space: Racial Performance as Noncredibility." *UCLA Law Review* 63, no. 2 (2016), 449–84.
Carpio, Geneveive. *Collisions at the Crossroads: How Place and Mobility Make Race*. Oakland: University of California Press, 2019.
———. "Zorro Down Under: Settler Colonial Architecture and Racial Scripts en Route from California to Australia." *Aztlan: Journal of Chicano Studies* 46, no. 1 (2021): 111–42.
Carrico, Richard. "Sociopolitical Aspects of the 1775 Revolt at Mission San Diego de Alcala: An Ethnohistorical Approach." *Journal of San Diego History* 43, no. 3 (1997): 143–57.
———. *Strangers in a Stolen Land*. San Diego, CA: Sunbelt, 1987.
Casas, Maria Raquél. *Married to a Daughter of the Land: Spanish-Mexican Women and Interethnic Marriage in California, 1820–1880*. Reno: University of Nevada Press, 2007.
Castañeda, Antonia I. 1997. "Engendering the History of Alta California, 1769–1848: Gender, Sexuality, and the Family." *California History* 76, no. 2/3 (1997): 230–59. https://doi.org/10.2307/25161668.
Castoriadis, Cornelius. *Imaginary Institution of Society*. Cambridge: MIT Press, 1975.
Chaffin, Tom. *Pathfinder: John Charles Frémont and the Course of American Empire*. New York: Hill and Wang, 2002.
Chávez-García, Miroslava. *Negotiating Conquest: Gender and Power in California, 1770s to 1880s*. Tucson: University of Arizona Press, 2006.
Cleland, Robert Glass. *The Cattle on a Thousand Hills: Southern California 1850–1880*. San Marino: Huntington Library, 1951.
Colman, Patty R. "John Ballard and the African American Community in Los Angeles, 1850–1905." *Southern California Quarterly* 94, no. 2 (2012): 193–229.
Cook, Sherburne Friend. *The Population of the California Indians, 1769–1970*. Berkeley: University of California Press, 1976.
Cooper, Frederick. *Citizenship, Inequality, and Difference: Historical Perspectives*. Cambridge: Cambridge University Press, 2018.
Cronon, William. *Nature's Metropolis: Chicago and the Great West*. New York: W.W. Norton & Company, 1991.
Davis, Winfield J. *History of Political Conventions in California, 1849–1892*. Sacramento: California State Library, 1893.
De Genova, Nicholas. *Racial Transformations: Latinos and Asians Remaking the United States*. Durham, NC: Duke University Press, 2006.
DeLay, Brian. *War of a Thousand Deserts: Indian Raids and the U.S.-Mexican War*. New Haven, CT: Yale University Press, 2009.
Demaratus, DeEtta. *The Force of a Feather: The Search for a Lost Story of Slavery and Freedom*. Salt Lake City: University of Utah Press, 2002.
Deutsch, Sarah. *No Separate Refuge: Culture, Class, and Gender on an Anglo-Hispanic Frontier, 1880–1940*. Oxford: Oxford University Press, 1987.

Deverell, William. *Whitewashed Adobe: The Rise of Los Angeles and the Remaking of Its Mexican Past*. Berkeley: University of California Press, 2004.

Dubin, Michael. *United States Presidential Elections, 1788–1860: The Official Results by County and State*. Jefferson: McFarland Publishing, 2011.

Dubois, Gary P., and Lisa L. Woodward. *The Temecula Massacre: A Forgotten Battlefield Landscape of the Mexican-American War*. Pechanga, CA: Great Oak Press, 2024.

Earle, Rebecca. *Return of the Native: Indians and Myth-Making in Spanish America, 1810–1930*. Raleigh: Duke University Press, 2007.

Edwards, Malcolm. "The War of Complexional Distinction: Blacks in Gold Rush California and British Columbia." *California Historical Quarterly* 56, no. 1 (1977): 34–45.

Ellison, Joseph. "The Struggle for Civil Government in California, 1846–1850." *California Historical Society Quarterly* 10, no. 2 (1931): 129–64.

Ellison, William Henry. *A Self-Governing Dominion: California, 1849–1860*. Berkeley: University of California Press, 1950.

Estrada, William D. *The Los Angeles Plaza: Sacred and Contested Space*. Austin: University of Texas Press, 2008.

Faragher, John Mack. *Eternity Street: Violence and Justice in Frontier Los Angeles*. New York: W. W. Norton, 2016.

Fehrenbacher, Don Edward. *Slavery, Law, and Politics: The Dred Scott Case in Historical Perspective*. Oxford: Oxford University Press, 1981.

Field, Kendra, and Daniel Lynch. "'Master of Ceremonies': The World of Peter Biggs in Civil War–Era Los Angeles." *Western Historical Quarterly* 47, no. 4 (November 1, 2016): 379–406.

Fields, Barbara. "Ideology and Race in American History." In *Region, Race and Reconstruction*, edited by J. Morgan Kousser and James McPherson. Oxford: Oxford University Press, 1982.

Fisher, James A. "The Struggle for Negro Testimony in California, 1851–1863." *Southern California Quarterly* 51, no. 4 (1969): 313–24. https://doi.org/10.2307/41170257.

Foner, Eric. *Free Soil, Free Labor, Free Men: The Ideology of the Republican Party Before the Civil War*. Oxford: Oxford University Press, 1995.

———. *Reconstruction: America's Unfinished Revolution, 1863–1877*. New York: Perennial Classics, 2002.

Foreman, P. Gabrielle, Jim Casey, and Sarah Lynn Patterson, eds. *The Colored Conventions Movement: Black Organizing in the Nineteenth Century*. Chapel Hill: University of North Carolina Press, 2021.

Fox, John. *Macnamara's Irish Colony and the United States Taking of California in 1846*. Jefferson, NC: McFarland, 2000.

Gates, Paul Wallace. "Adjudication of Spanish-Mexican Land Claims in California." *Huntington Library Quarterly* 21, no. 3 (1958): 213–36.

———. *California Ranches and Farms: 1846–1862*. Madison: State Historical Society of Wisconsin, 1967.

———. "The Frémont-Jones Scramble for Lands in California," *Southern California Quarterly*, 56 (Spring 1974), 13–44.

———. *History of Public Land Law Development*. Washington, DC: Government Printing Office, 1968.
———. *Land and Law in California: Essays on Land Policies*. Ames: Iowa State University Press, 1991.
Genini, Ronald, and Richard Hitchman. *Romualdo Pacheco: A Californio in Two Eras*. San Francisco: Book Club of California, 1985.
Gibb, Andrew. *Californios, Anglos, and the Performance of Oligarchy in the U.S. West*. Carbondale: Southern Illinois University Press, 2018.
Gómez, Laura E. *Manifest Destinies: The Making of the Mexican American Race*. New York: New York University Press, 2007.
González, Deena J. *Refusing the Favor: The Spanish-Mexican Women of Santa Fe, 1820–1880*. New York: Oxford University Press, 1999.
González, Michael J. *This Small City Will Be a Mexican Paradise: Exploring the Origins of Mexican Culture in Los Angeles, 1821–1846*. Albuquerque: University of New Mexico Press, 2005.
Gonzales, Rose. "Toward a Critical Race Theory of Evidence." *Minnesota Law Review* 101, no. 6 (June 2017): 2243–312.
Gray, Paul Bryan. *A Clamor for Equality: Emergence and Exile of Californio Activist Francisco P. Ramírez*. Lubbock: Texas Tech University Press, 2012.
———. *Forster vs. Pico: The Struggle for the Rancho Santa Margarita*. Spokane, WA: Arthur H. Clark, 2002.
Greenberg, Amy S. *A Wicked War: Polk, Clay, Lincoln, and the 1846 U.S. Invasion of Mexico*. New York: Vintage, 2013.
Griswold del Castillo, Richard. "The del Valle Family and the Fantasy Heritage." *California History* 59, no. 1 (1980): 2–15.
———. *The Los Angeles Barrio, 1850–1890: A Social History*. Berkeley: University of California Press, 1979.
———. *The Treaty of Guadalupe Hidalgo*. Norman: University of Oklahoma Press, 1992.
Guidotti-Hernández, Nicole Marie. *Unspeakable Violence: Remapping U.S. and Mexican National Imaginaries*. Durham, NC: Duke University Press, 2011.
Gutiérrez, Ramón A. "Hispanic Identities in the Southwestern United States." In *Race and Classification: The Case of Mexican America*, edited by Ilona Katzew and Susan Deans-Smith. Stanford, CA: Stanford University Press, 2009.
———. "Unraveling America's Hispanic Past: Internal Stratification and Class Boundaries." *Aztlán: A Journal of Chicano Studies* 17, no. 1 (1986): 79–101.
———. *When Jesus Came, the Corn Mothers Went Away: Marriage, Sexuality, and Power in New Mexico, 1500–1846*. Stanford, CA: Stanford University Press, 1991.
Gutiérrez, Ramón A., and Richard J. Orsi. *Contested Eden: California Before the Gold Rush*. Berkeley: University of California Press, 1998.
Haas, Lisbeth. *Conquests and Historical Identities in California, 1769–1936*. Berkeley: University of California Press, 1995.
———. *Saints and Citizens: Indigenous Histories of Colonial Missions and Mexican California*. Berkeley: University of California Press, 2014.
———. "War in California, 1846–1848." *California History* 76, no. 2/3: 331–55.

Hackel, Steven W. *Alta California: Peoples in Motion, Identities in Formation, 1769–1850*. Berkeley: University of California Press, 2010.

———. *Children of Coyote, Missionaries of Saint Francis: Indian- Spanish Relations in Colonial California, 1769–1850*. Chapel Hill: University of North Carolina Press, 2005.

Hamilton, Holman. *Prologue to Conflict: The Crisis and Compromise of 1850*. Lexington: University of Kentucky Press, 2005.

Haney-López, Ian. *White by Law: The Legal Construction of Race*. New York: New York University Press, 2006.

Harris, Cheryl I. "Whiteness as Property." *Harvard Law Review* 106, no. 8 (1993): 1707–91.

Heizer, Robert F. *The Destruction of the California Indians: A Collection of Documents from the Period 1847 to 1865*. Santa Barbara, CA: Peregrine Smith, 1974.

———. *The Eighteen Unratified Treaties of 1851–1852 Between the California Indians and the United States Government*. Berkeley: University of California, 1972.

Heizer, Robert, and Alan Almquist. *Other Californians: Prejudice and Discrimination Under Spain, Mexico, and the United States to 1920*. Berkeley: University of California Press, 1971.

Hernández, Kelly Lytle. *City of Inmates: Conquest, Rebellion, and the Rise of Human Caging in Los Angeles, 1771–1965*. Chapel Hill: University of North Carolina Press, 2017.

Hornbeck, David. "The Patenting of California's Private Land Claims, 1851–1885." *Geographical Review* 69, no. 4 (1979): 434–48.

Horsman, Reginald. *Race and Manifest Destiny: Origins of American Racial Anglo-Saxonism*. Cambridge, MA: Harvard University Press, 1981.

Howay, Frederick. "The Negro Immigration into Vancouver Island in 1858." *British Columbia Historical Quarterly* 3, no. 2 (1939).

Hurtado, Albert. *Indian Survival on the California Frontier*. New Haven, CT: Yale University Press, 1988.

———. *Intimate Frontiers Sex, Gender, and Culture in Old California*. Albuquerque: University of New Mexico Press, 1999.

———. *John Sutter: A Life on the North American Frontier*. Norman: University of Oklahoma Press, 2006.

Hutchinson, C. Alan. "An Official List of the Members of the Híjar-Padrés Colony for Mexican California, 1834." *Pacific Historical Review* 42, no. 3 (August 1, 1973): 407–18.

Hyde, Anne Farrar. *Empires, Nations, and Families: A History of the North American West, 1800–1860*. Lincoln: University of Nebraska Press, 2011.

Jacobson, Matthew Frye. *Whiteness of a Different Color: European Immigrants and the Alchemy of Race*. Cambridge, MA: Harvard University Press, 1998.

Jacoby, Karl. *Shadows at Dawn: A Borderlands Massacre and the Violence of History*. New York: Penguin Press, 2008.

Jensen, James M. "John Forster: A California Ranchero." *California Historical Society Quarterly* 48, no. 1 (1969): 37–44.

Jew, Victor. "The Anti-Chinese Massacre of 1871 and its Strange Career." In *A Companion to Los Angeles*, edited by William Deverell and Greg Hise. Malden: Willey-Blackwell, 2010, 113–30.

Johnson, Sheri Lynn. "The Color of Truth: Race and the Assessment of Credibility." *Michigan Journal of Race & Law* 1, no. 2 (Summer 1996): 261–346.

Johnson, Susan Lee. *Roaring Camp: The Social World of the California Gold Rush*. New York: W. W. Norton, 2000.

Jones, Martha S. *Birthright Citizens: A History of Race and Rights in Antebellum America*. Cambridge: Cambridge University Press, 2018.

Jung, Moon-Ho. *Coolies and Cane: Race, Labor, and Sugar in the Age of Emancipation*. Baltimore, MD: Johns Hopkins University Press, 2006.

Katzew, Ilona, ed. *Race and Classification: The Case of Mexican America*. Stanford, CA: Stanford University Press, 2009.

Kauer, Ralph. "The Workingman's Party of California." *Pacific Historical Review* 13, no. 3 (September 1944): 280.

Kelly, Robin D. G. "How the West Was One: On the Uses and Limitations of Diaspora." *Black Scholar* 30, no. 3/4 (2000): 31–33.

Kilian, Crawford. *Go Do Some Great Thing: The Black Pioneers of British Columbia*. Vancouver: Commodore Books, 2008.

Kropp, Phoebe S. *California Vieja: Culture and Memory in a Modern American Place*. Berkeley: University of California Press, 2006.

Lamar, Howard Roberts. *The Far Southwest, 1846–1912: A Territorial History*. Albuquerque: University of New Mexico Press, 2000.

Lapp, Rudolph M. *Blacks in Gold Rush California*. New Haven, CT: Yale University Press, 1977.

———. "Jeremiah B. Sanderson: Early California Negro Leader." *The Journal of Negro History* 53, no. 4 (1968): 321–33.

Lapp, Rudolph M., and Shirley Ann Wilson Moore. *Archy Lee: A California Fugitive Slave Case*. Berkeley, CA: Heyday Books, 1969.

Layne, J. Gregg. "Jose Maria Flores: California's Great Mexican Patriot." *Quarterly Publication (Historical Society of Southern California)* 17, no. 1 (March 1, 1935): 23–25.

Lew-Williams, Beth. *The Chinese Must Go: Violence, Exclusion, and the Making of the Alien in America*. Cambridge, MA: Harvard University Press, 2018.

———. "Chinese Naturalization, Voting, and Other Impossible Acts." *Journal of the Civil War Era* 13, no. 4 (December 2023): 515–36.

Limerick, Patricia. *The Legacy of Conquest: The Unbroken Past of the American West*. New York: W. W. Norton, 1988.

Lindsay, Brendan C. *Murder State: California's Native American Genocide, 1846–1873*. Lincoln: University of Nebraska Press, 2012.

Lozano, Rosina. *An American Language: The History of Spanish in the United States*. Berkeley: University of California Press, 2018.

———. "Translating California: Official Spanish Usage in California's Constitutional Conventions and State Legislature, 1848–1894." *California Legal History* 6 (2011): 321.

Lustig, R. Jefferey "Private Rights and Public Purposes: California's Second Constitution Reconsidered." *California History* 87, no. 3 (2010): 46–70.
Lynch, Daniel. "On the Edge of Empires, Republics, and Identities: De la Guerra's Sword of the War and the California Native Cavalry." In *Empire and Liberty: The Civil War and the West*, edited by Virginia Scharff, 105–21. Berkeley: University of California Press, 2015.
Madley, Benjamin. *An American Genocide: The United States and the California Indian Catastrophe, 1846–1873*. New Haven, CT: Yale University Press, 2017.
Magliari, M. "Free Soil, Unfree Labor: Cave Johnson Couts and the Binding of Indian Workers in California, 1850–1867." *Pacific Historical Review* 73, no. 3 (2004): 349–90.
Maizlish, Stephen. *A Strife of Tongues: The Compromise of 1850 and the Ideological Foundations of the American Civil War*. Charlottesville: University of Virginia Press, 2018.
Marszalek, John F. *Commander of All Lincoln's Armies: A Life of General Henry W. Halleck*. Cambridge, MA: Belknap Press of Harvard University Press, 2004.
Martínez, María Elena. *Genealogical Fictions: Limpieza de Sangre, Religion, and Gender in Colonial Mexico*. Stanford, CA: Stanford University Press, 2008.
Mason, William. *The Census of 1790: A Demographic History of Colonial California*. Menlo Park, CA: Ballena Press, 1998.
Mawn, Geoffrey. "Land Grant-Guarantee: The Treaty of Guadalupe Hidalgo or the Protocol of Querétaro?" *Journal of the West* 14 (October 1975): 47–63.
McCurry, Stephanie. *Women's War: Fighting and Surviving the American Civil War*. Cambridge: The Belknap Press of Harvard University Press, 2019.
McGinty, Brian. *Archy Lee's Struggle for Freedom: The True Story of California Gold, the Nation's Tragic March toward Civil War, and a Young Black Man's Fight for Liberty*. Guilford, CT: Lyons Press, 2020.
McKain, Walter, and Sara Miles. "Santa Barbara County Between Two Social Orders." *California Historical Society Quarterly* 25, no. 4 (1946): 313.
McKinley, Maggie. "Petitioning and the Making of the Administrative State." *The Yale Law Journal* 127, no. 6 (April 26, 2018): 1538–637.
McPherson, James M. *Battle Cry of Freedom: The Civil War Era*. New York: Oxford University Press, 1988.
Menchaca, Martha. *The Mexican American Experience in Texas: Citizenship, Segregation, and the Struggle for Equality*. Austin: University of Texas Press, 2022.
Miranda, Gloria E. "Racial and Cultural Dimensions of 'Gente de Razón' Status in Spanish and Mexican California." *Southern California Quarterly* 70, no. 3 (1988): 265–78.
Molina, Natalia. *Fit to Be Citizens? Public Health and Race in Los Angeles, 1879–1939*. Berkeley: University of California Press, 2006.
———. *How Race Is Made in America: Immigration, Citizenship, and the Historical Power of Racial Scripts*. Berkeley: University of California Press, 2014.
———. *A Place at the Nayarit: How a Mexican Restaurant Nourished a Community*. Oakland: University of California Press, 2022.
Monroy, Douglas. "The Creation and Re-Creation of Californio Society." *California History* 76, no. 2–3 (July 1, 1997): 173–95.

———. *Thrown Among Strangers: The Making of Mexican Culture in Frontier California*. Berkeley: University of California Press, 1990.
Montoya, Maria. *Translating Property: The Maxwell Land Grant and the Conflict over Land in the American West, 1840–1900*. Berkeley: University of California Press, 2002.
Moore, Shirley Ann Wilson. "African-Americans Fight Racism in Early California." *California Supreme Court Historical Society Newsletter*, Spring/Summer (2009): 10–13.
———. "'We Feel the Want of Protection': The Politics of Law and Race in California, 1848–1878." *California History* 81, no. 3/4 (2003): 96–125.
Morton, Michelle, and Marie Salta, with assistance from Dean C. Rowan and Randal Brandt. "Finding Aid to the Documents Pertaining to the Adjudication of Private Land Claims in California, circa 1852–1892." Vol. 2. Bancroft Library, University of California, Berkeley. https://oac.cdlib.org/findaid/ark:/13030/hb109nb422/dsc/?query=%22mission%20san%20 rafael%22;dsc.position=1#hitNum3.
Mueller, Ken. *Senator Benton and the People: Master Race Democracy on the Early American Frontiers*. DeKalb: University of Northern Illinois Press, 2014.
Ngai, Mae. *Impossible Subjects: Illegal Aliens and the Making of Modern America*. Princeton, NJ: Princeton University Press, 2014.
Nieto-Phillips, John. *The Language of Blood: The Making of Spanish-American Identity in New Mexico, 1880s–1930s*. Albuquerque: University of New Mexico Press, 2004.
Omi, Michael. *Racial Formation in the United States: From the 1960s to the 1980s*. New York: Routledge and Kegan Paul, 1986.
Ooley, Pat. "Inventory of the Working Papers of the 1878–1879 Constitutional Convention." Sacramento: California State Archives, Office of the Secretary of State, 2008. https://archives.cdn.sos.ca.gov/collections/1879/archive/1879-finding-aid.pdf.
Ortega Soto, Martha. *Alta California: Una Frontera Olvidada Del Noroeste de México, 1769–1846*. México, DF: Plaza y Valdés Editores, 2001.
Osio, Antonio María. *The History of Alta California: A Memoir of Mexican California*. Madison: University of Wisconsin Press, 1996.
Paddison, Joshua. *American Heathens*. Berkeley: University of California Press, 2012.
———. "Anti-Catholicism and Race in Post-Civil-War San Francisco." *Pacific Historical Review* 78 (Fall 2009): 505–44.
Panich, Lee. *Narratives of Persistence: Indigenous Negotiations of Colonialism in Alta and Baja California*. Tucson: University of Arizona Press, 2020.
Pérez, Erika. *Colonial Intimacies: Interethnic Kinship, Sexuality, and Marriage in Southern California, 1769–1885*. Norman: University of Oklahoma Press, 2018.
Perez Tisserant, Emmanuelle. "Revolts in Mexican California: Between Resistance to the State and Integration of Federal Republicanism (1821–1832)." *Journal of American History* 109, no. 4 (March 2023): 759–81.
———. "'Vivre ensemble dans un village, dans des maisons et non dispersés': Projets, représentations et pratiques des modes d'habiter dans les missions franciscaines de Haute-Californie, 1769–1833." *L'Ordinaire des Amériques* 231 (2023).

Phillips, George Harwood. *Chiefs and Challengers: Indian Resistance and Cooperation in Southern California, 1769–1906*. Norman: Oklahoma University Press, 2014.
———. *Indians and Indian Agents: The Origins of the Reservation System in California, 1849–1852*. Norman: University of Oklahoma Press, 1997.
———. "Indians in Los Angeles, 1781–1875: Economic Integration, Social Disintegration." *Pacific Historical Review* 49, no. 3 (1980): 427–51.
———. *Vineyards and Vaqueros: Indian Labor and the Economic Expansion of Southern California, 1771–1877*. Norman: University of Oklahoma Press, 2010.
Pitt, Leonard. *The Decline of the Californios: A Social History of the Spanish- Speaking Californians, 1846–1890*. Berkeley: University of California Press, 1998.
Potter, David M. *The Impending Crisis, 1848–1861*. New York: Harper Perennial, 2011.
Prezelski, Tom. *Californio Lancers: The 1st Battalion of Native Cavalry in the Far West, 1863–1866*. Norman: Arthur H. Clark, 2015.
Pubols, Louise. "Becoming Californio: Jokes, Broadsides, and a Slap in the Face." In *Alta California: Peoples in Motion, Identities in Formation, 1769–1850*, edited by Steven W. Hackel, 131–55. Berkeley: Huntington-USC Institute on California and the West and University of California Press, 2010.
———. *The Father of All: The de la Guerra Family, Power, and Patriarchy in Mexican California*. Berkeley: University of California Press and Huntington Library, 2009.
Reséndez, Andrés. *Changing National Identities at the Frontier: Texas and New Mexico, 1800–1850*. Cambridge: Cambridge University Press, 2005.
———. *The Other Slavery: The Uncovered Story of Indian Enslavement in America*. Boston and New York: Houghton Mifflin Harcourt, 2016.
Roberts, Alaina. *I've Been Here All the While: Black Freedom on Native Land*. Philadelphia: University of Pennsylvania Press, 2021.
Robinson, John W. *Los Angeles in Civil War Days, 1860–1865*. Norman: University of Oklahoma Press, 2013.
Robinson, W. W. *Land in California: The Story of Mission Lands, Ranchos, Squatters, Mining Claims, Railroad Grants, Land Script and Homesteads*. Berkeley: University of California Press, 1978.
Roediger, David. *The Wages of Whiteness: Race the Making of the American Working Class*. London: Verso Press, 1999.
Rosenus, Alan. *General M. G. Vallejo and the Advent of the Americans: A Biography*. Albuquerque: University of New Mexico Press, 1995.
Ruiz, Vicki. *From Out of the Shadows: Mexican Women in Twentieth-Century America*. New York: Oxford University Press, 1998.
Saavedra, Yvette J. *Pasadena Before the Roses: Race, Identity, and Land Use in Southern California, 1771–1890*. Tucson: University of Arizona Press, 2018.
———. "Speaking for Themselves: Rancheras and Respectability in Mexican California, 1800–1850." *California History* 100, no. 1 (February 2023): 3–26.
Salomon, Carlos Manuel. *Pio Pico: The Last Governor of Mexican California*. Norman: University of Oklahoma Press, 2012.
———. "Secularization in California: Pío Pico at Mission San Luis Rey." *Southern California Quarterly* 89, no. 4 (2007): 349–71.

Sánchez, George. *Becoming Mexican American: Ethnicity, Culture, and Identity in Chicano Los Angeles, 1900–1945*. Oxford University Press, 1995.

Sánchez, Rosaura. *Telling Identities: The Californio Testimonios*. Minneapolis: University of Minnesota Press, 1995.

Sargent, Noel. "The California Constitutional Convention of 1878–9." *California Law Review* 6, no. 1 (1917): 1–22.

Saxton, Alexander. *The Indispensable Enemy: Labor and the Anti-Chinese Movement in California*. University of California Press, 1971.

Secrest, William B. *When the Great Spirit Died: The Destruction of the California Indians 1850–1860*. Sanger, CA: Linden Publishing, 2002.

Shelton, Tamara Venit. *A Squatter's Republic: Land and the Politics of Monopoly in California, 1850–1900*. Berkeley, CA: Huntington Library Press, 2013.

Shrine, Laurel Clark. *The Threshold of Manifest Destiny: Gender and National Expansion in Florida*. Philadelphia: University of Pennsylvania Press, 2016.

Shumsky, Neil. *Evolution of Political Protest and the Workingmen's Party of California*. Columbus: Ohio State University Press, 1991.

Smith, Henry. *Virgin Land: The American West as Symbol and Myth*. New York: Vintage Books, 1950.

Smith, Stacey L. "Beyond North and South: Putting the West in the Civil War and Reconstruction." *Journal of the Civil War Era* 6, no. 4 (November 3, 2016): 566–91.

———. "Dred Scott on the Pacific: African Americans, Citizenship, and Subjecthood in the North American West." *Southern California Quarterly* 100, no. 1 (February 1, 2018): 44–68.

———. *Freedom's Frontier: California and the Struggle over Unfree Labor, Emancipation, and Reconstruction*. Chapel Hill: University of North Carolina Press, 2013.

———. "Remaking Slavery in a Free State: Masters and Slaves in Gold Rush California." *Pacific Historical Review* 80, no. 1 (2011): 28–63.

Smythe, William. *History of San Diego, 1542–1908: An account of the Rise and Progress of the Pioneer Settlement on the Pacific Coast of the United States*. San Diego: The History Company, 1908.

St. John, Rachel. "The Unpredictable America of William Gwin: Expansion, Secession, and the Unstable Borders of Nineteenth-Century North America." *Journal of the Civil War Era* 6, no. 1 (March 12, 2016): 56–84.

Stahler, Michael L. "William Speer: Champion of California's Chinese, 1852–1857." *Journal of Presbyterian History* 48, no. 2 (1970): 113–29.

Starr, Kevin. *California: A History*. New York: Modern Library, 2005.

Stegmaier, Mark. *Texas, New Mexico, and the Compromise of 1850: Boundary Dispute and Sectional Crisis*. Lubbock: Texas Tech Press, 1996.

Suárez, Camille. "Junta Democrática: Californios and Reconstruction in California." *Western History Quarterly* 55, no. 4 (2024): 271–90.

———. "A Legal Confiscation: The 1851 Land Act and the Transformation of Californios into Colonized Colonizers." *Journal of the Civil War Era* 13, no. 1 (2023): 29–55.

Suval, John. *Dangerous Ground: Squatters, Statesmen, and the Antebellum Rupture of American Democracy*. Oxford: Oxford University Press, 2022.

Swisher, Carl. *Motivation and Political Technique* in the California Constitutional Convention, 1878–1879. New York: De Capo Press, 1969.
Taylor, Charles. *Modern Social Imaginaries*. Durham, NC: Duke University Press, 2004.
Taylor, Quintard. *In Search of the Racial Frontier: African Americans in the American West 1528–1990*. New York: W. W. Norton, 1998.
Taylor, Quintard, De Graaf, Lawrence, and Mulroy, Kevin. *Seeking El Dorado: African Americans in California*. Los Angeles, Seattle: Autry Museum of Western Heritage; University of Seattle Press, 2001.
Tennis, George. "California's First State Election, November 13, 1849." *Southern California Quarterly* 50, no. 4 (December 1968): 373.
Torres-Rouff, David Samuel. *Before L.A.: Race, Space, and Municipal Power in Los Angeles, 1781–1894*. New Haven, CT: Yale University Press, 2013.
Trouillot, Michel-Rolph. *Silencing the Past: Power and the Production of History*. Boston: Beacon Press, 1995.
Troutt Powell, Eve. *A Different Shade of Colonialism: Egypt, Great Britain, and the Mastery of the Sudan*. Berkeley: University of California Press, 2003.
Tullos, Allen. *Alabama Getaway: The Political Imaginary and the Heary of Dixie.* Athens: University of Georgia Press, 2011.
Turner, Frederick Jackson. "The Significance of the Frontier in American History." In *The Frontier in American History*, 1–38. New York: H. Holt, 1947.
Veracini, Lorenzo. *Settler Colonialism: A Theoretical Overview*. New York: Palgrave Macmillan, 2010.
Vinson, Ben. *Before Mestizaje: The Frontiers of Race and Caste in Colonial Mexico*. New York: Cambridge University Press, 2018.
Vivian, Thomas, and D. G. Waldron. *Biographical Sketches* of the Delegates to the Convention to Frame a New Constitution for the State of California, 1878. San Francisco: Francis & Valentine, 1878.
Waite, Kevin. *West of Slavery: The Southern Dream of a Transcontinental Empire*. Chapel Hill: UNC Press, 2021.
Walker, Dale L. *Bear Flag Rising: The Conquest of California, 1846*. New York: Forge, 1999.
Wash, Victor. "If Walls Could Speak: San Diego's Historic Casa de Bandini." *California History* 88, no. 4 (2011).
Weber, David J. *The Mexican Frontier, 1821–1846: The American Southwest Under Mexico*. Albuquerque: University of New Mexico Press, 1982.
———. "The Spanish Legacy in North America and the Historical Imagination." *Western Historical Quarterly* 23, no. 1 (February 1992): 5–24.
West, Elliott. "Reconstructing Race." *Western Historical Quarterly* 34, no. 1 (February 1, 2003): 6–26.
White, Richard. *It's Your Misfortune and None of My Own: A New History of the American West*. Norman: University of Oklahoma Press, 1991.
Wiley, James. *Politics and the Concept of the Political: The Political Imagination*. New York: Routledge, 2016.
Williams, Carey. *North from Mexico: The Spanish Speaking People of the United States.* Santa Barbara: Praeger, 2016.

Willis, E. B. and Stockton, P. K. *Debates and Proceedings of the Constitutional Convention of the State of California, Convened at the City of Sacramento, Saturday, September 28, 1878*. Sacramento: State Office, 1880.

Winther, Oscar. "The Colony System of California." *Agricultural History* 27, no. 3 (1953): 94–103.

Wolfe, Patrick. "Land, Labor, and Difference: Elementary Structures of Race." *American Historical Review* 106, no. 3 (2001): 866–905.

———. "Settler Colonialism and the Elimination of the Native." *Journal of Genocide Research* 8, no. 4 (December 1, 2006): 387–409.

Wollenberg, Charles. *All Deliberate Speed: Segregation and Exclusion in California Schools, 1855–1975*. Berkeley: University of California Press, 1976.

Wood, Anthony W. *Black Montana: Settler Colonialism and the Erosion of the Racial Frontier, 1877–1930*. Lincoln: University of Nebraska Press, 2021.

Woolsey, Ronald. "A Capitalist in a Foreign Land: Abel Stearns in Southern California Before the Conquest." *Southern California Quarterly* 75, no. 2 (Summer 1993): 101–18.

Worster, Donald. "Beyond the Agrarian Myth," in Limerick, Patricia, Milner, Clyde, and Rankin, Charles. *Trails: Toward a New Western History*. Lawrence: University of Kansas, 1991.

Wright, Doris. *A Yankee in Mexican California: Abel Stearns, 1798–1848*. Santa Barbara, CA: W. Hebberd, 1977.

Wright, George F. *Reproduction of Thompson and West's History of Sacramento County, California, with Illustrations*. Berkeley, CA: Howell-North, 1960.

Wrobel, David M. "Introduction: 'What on Earth Has Happened to the New Western History?'" *Historian* 66, no. 3 (2004): 437–41.

Zappia, Natale A. *Traders and Raiders: The Indigenous World of the Colorado Basin, 1540–1859*. Chapel Hill: University of North Carolina Press, 2014.

Zesch, Scott. *The Chinatown War: Chinese Los Angeles and the Massacre of 1871*. New York: Oxford University Press, 2012.

Unpublished Dissertations

Carrillo Colato, Maria Y. "A Pacific Republic: Southern Influence in Civil War-Era California." University of California, Riverside, 2024.

Cassidy, Joseph Eugene. "Life and Times of Pablo de la Guerra, 1819–1874." PhD diss., University of California, Santa Barbara, 1977.

Fisher, James. "A History of the Political and Social Development of the Black Community in California, 1850–1950." PhD diss., State University of New York at Stony Brook, 1972.

Lynch, Daniel Brendan. "Southern California Chivalry: The Convergence of Southerners and Californios in the Far Southwest, 1846–1866." PhD diss., UCLA, 2015.

Pearson, Chelsea "'Call me a Californio': Translating Hemispheric Legacies in Helen Hunt Jackson, Don Antonio Coronel, and José Martí." PhD diss., UC Santa Cruz, 2013.

Index

www.ingramcontent.com/pod-product-compliance
Lightning Source LLC
LaVergne TN
LVHW101532071026
849616LV00047B/274
* 9 7 8 1 4 6 9 6 9 8 0 2 1 *